Coal Metropolis
Cardiff 1870–1914

Coal Metropolis
Cardiff 1870-1914

M. J. Daunton

Leicester University Press   1977

The publication of this book has been assisted
by a grant from the Twenty-Seven Foundation

First published in 1977 by Leicester University Press
Distributed in North America by Humanities Press Inc., New Jersey

Designed by Arthur Lockwood

Set in Monotype Garamond
Printed in Great Britain by
Western Printing Services Ltd, Bristol
Bound by G. & J. Kitcat Ltd, London
ISBN 0 7185 1139 5

Contents

List of tables

Figures

List of maps

List of plates

Acknowledgments

Above all, I must thank my parents for their support in many ways during the genesis of this book. It started life as a Ph.D. thesis on 'Aspects of the social and economic structure of Cardiff 1870–1914', which was submitted to the University of Kent in 1974. I was fortunate in having as a supervisor, Professor T. C. Barker, who was always ready with encouragement and, when necessary, criticism. Dr W. A. Armstrong and Dr J. Lovell and the other members of the research seminar at Kent provided comment on parts of the thesis. Professor H. J. Dyos examined the thesis and gave helpful advice on revision for publication. My colleague, Dr Duncan Bythell, exceeded the call of duty by reading both the thesis and the first draft of the book, which resulted in many improvements of style. The remaining infelicities are my responsibility. Mr Ranald Michie read Parts I and II, which initiated a continuing debate on investment in housing. Discussions with Mr Neil Evans from the time we were both research students working in Cardiff were of great help in clarifying my ideas. Mr T. J. Hopkins of the Cardiff Central Library must be given pride of place among the librarians and archivists who supplied the material for this study. He provided a sterling and indulgent service, going to much trouble in locating recondite information. I must also thank Mr G. Dart and the other librarians at the Central Library; Mrs Moore and her staff at the Glamorgan Record Office; Mr Tatham of the rates department at the City Hall, who accommodated an intruder in his busy office; and the librarians at the London School of Economics, Public Record Office, British Museum, House of Lords Record Office and National Library of Wales. Mrs R. Könekamp kindly permitted me to consult and quote from the papers of her father, Professor H. S. Jevons. Preparation of the typescript was made possible by a grant from the University of Durham. Finally, I must acknowledge the forbearance of those students, colleagues, and friends who now know more about Cardiff than they ever thought possible or desirable.

M.J.D.

I Introduction

There is no more interesting study in town growth and development than Cardiff. At the Census of 1851 it was a place of some 20,000 inhabitants with no influence in commerce and with no reputation. Now, it is one of the most thriving cities in the country, a centre of trade and commerce and a great port. In every respect the development has been remarkable. *Report of an Enquiry by the Board of Trade into Working Class Rents, Housing and Retail Prices 1908, 132.*

When the nineteenth century opened, Cardiff had been even more insignificant than it was in 1851, trapped in immobility since it had been established after the Norman invasion of south Wales. Throughout these years, it had been a small community huddled around the castle, supplying the needs of the surrounding rural population, and with many of its inhabitants themselves engaging in agriculture. Cardiff in 1801 had experienced little of the effects of the industrial revolution. Its population then was 1,870; it had been about 2,000 in 1262, and about 1,700 in the sixteenth and seventeenth centuries. After these centuries of stagnation, the nineteenth century was a time of frantic change. When the century closed, the erstwhile village with its purely local significance was being referred to not only as 'the metropolis of Wales', but also more grandly as the 'coal metropolis of the world'.[1]

In 1801, Cardiff and its hinterland had a population of around 40,000, of which about a quarter was in the industrial areas of Merthyr Tydfil and Aberdare. Merthyr, with its developing iron works, had become the largest town in Wales with a population of 7,705, but the area remained predominantly agricultural with the bulk of the population still in the villages of the Vale of Glamorgan and the scattered hill farms of the uplands. The trade of Cardiff reflected the dominance of agriculture in the hinterland. Agricultural produce was exchanged for manufactured goods bought at the Bristol fairs. As William Smyth commented, 'there were then two sloops trading to Bristol on alternate weeks, carrying over wheat, oats, barley, butter, sheep and poultry; and they were found sufficient for the traffic and passengers'. The Town Quay on the Taff could handle vessels of 60 to 80 tons, trading mainly to Bristol but also to the smaller Bristol Channel ports such as Minehead and Bridgwater. The area was, as Professor Minchinton has shown, economically dependent upon Bristol, which provided the market for the agricultural produce of south Wales, the capital for much of the industrial development, and the commercial services for disposing of the produce of the ironworks. Cardiff as yet had made no pretensions to taking over the role of Bristol in its developing hinterland.[2]

The first break in the long pattern of stability came in 1798 when the Glamorganshire Canal, with its sea-lock at Cardiff, linked the town with the expanding iron industry of Merthyr. As the south Wales iron industry rose to dominance in the early nineteenth century, the basis of the economy of the hinterland and of Cardiff underwent a profound change. By 1831, the population of the port and hinterland had risen to 72,000. The iron and coal industries now supported something like 30,000, mainly in Merthyr which by 1831 had a population of 22,083. Of an increase in the population of the port and hinterland of 33,000 since 1801, the rural area had accounted for only 9,000. The trade of Cardiff changed to a predominantly industrial character in line with the transformation of the hinterland. Exports of iron rather than agricultural produce became the mainstay of the port. In 1806 the Canal exported 10,400 tons of iron. This rose to 42,624 tons by 1819, 83,876 by 1829 and 132,781 tons by 1839. But the change in Cardiff must not be exaggerated. As in the pre-industrial period, trade was still essentially short-distance. In 1826, 70 per cent of ships were engaged in the coasting trade, chiefly with Bristol; 20 per cent were in the Irish trade; and 10 per cent were foreign-going. Cardiff was not yet a major port or independent commercial centre. In 1831 the financial and commercial services of the iron trade were still provided by Bristol, London or Liverpool; Cardiff was little more than a loading point for iron.[3]

The rise of Cardiff to rank among the major foreign-going ports of the country, and the development of an independent commercial function, were based upon coal rather than upon iron. In 1806, no coal was shipped at all; between 1816 and 1818, 865 tons were exported; in 1819 34,606 tons; in 1829, 83,729 tons; and in 1839, 211,214 tons. Exports of coal had thus passed exports of iron in the early 1830s.[4] But two points should be stressed: the iron industry, not the sale coal trade, was at this time the dominant sector in the south Wales economy; and Cardiff was behind other ports in the export of coal.

In 1840, as a rough estimate, the south Wales iron industry used 2 to $2\frac{1}{4}$ million tons of coal of a total coal output of around $4\frac{1}{2}$ million tons. By the 1870s this proportion had been reduced from a half to a fifth, which is a good indication of the changing position of the iron industry in the south Wales economy. Further, the Welsh share of total pig iron production fell from 45 per cent in 1830 to 19 per cent in 1865 and 12 per cent in 1880. At a time when the south Wales industry was facing com-

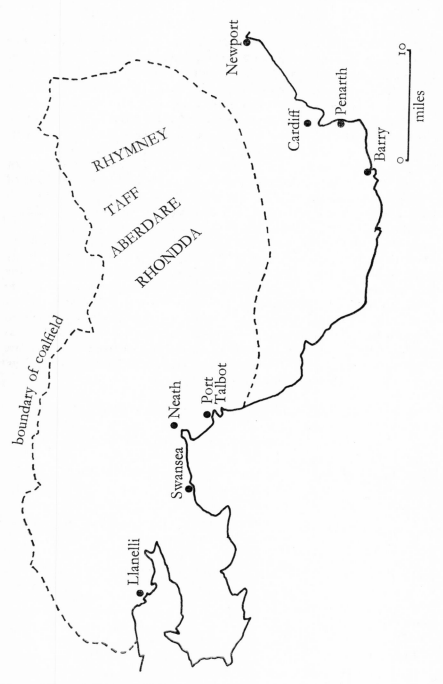

Map 1. The south Wales coalfield area.

petition from areas with low production costs, local supplies of iron ore were being exhausted and south Wales was becoming a high-cost location. The market quotation for Cleveland, west coast and Scottish pig iron was often lower than the cost of production in south Wales. From about 1850, the south Wales economy moved from its age of iron to the era of coal.[5]

Although the tonnage of coal shipped at Cardiff had passed the tonnage of iron in the 1830s, the port was not yet the leader of the sale coal trade. In the 1830s the bulk of the sale coal was provided not as later in the century by the central area of the coalfield forming the hinterland of Cardiff, but rather by the anthracite and dry steam coal area around Swansea and Llanelli, and by the bituminous coals exported through Newport. By 1851 the situation was reversed and the primacy of Cardiff and the central area of the coalfield established. From 4½ million tons in 1840, the output of the south Wales coalfield rose to 8½ million tons in 1854 and 16½ million tons in 1874. The figures of coal exports clearly show that Cardiff was the main beneficiary. And the movement in the leading sector of the sale coal trade from the east and west to the centre of the coalfield was reflected in a shift towards steam coal in the types of coal produced in the central area. Of the 211,214 tons of coal shipped from Cardiff in 1839, the bulk was from the bituminous seams. The expansion of output was to be initially in steam coal from the Aberdare valley and to a lesser extent in bituminous coal from the Rhondda valleys, and then increasingly in steam coal from the latter as well.[6]

Table 1   *Shipments of coal from south Wales ports in 1840 and 1851 (tons)*

	1840		1851	
	coast	foreign	coast	foreign
Cardiff	162,283	3,826	501,002	249,001
Newport	482,398	7,256	451,491	151,668
Swansea	460,201	33,089	352,247	41,502
Llanelli	192,769	19,275	219,460	9,785

Source: J. H. Morris and L. J. Williams, *The South Wales Coal Industry 1841–75* (1958), 32.

Table 2   *Shipments of coal from south Wales ports in 1874 (tons)*

Cardiff	3,780,000
Newport	1,066,000
Swansea	768,000
Neath	275,000
Llanelli	222,000

Source: J. H. Morris and L. J. Williams, *The South Wales Coal Industry 1841–75* (1958), 91.

The first rapid development of the sale coal trade was in the Aberdare valley, in steam coal. The valley was served by a branch of the Glamorganshire Canal from 1811, and of the Taff Vale Railway from 1846. Although the first sale coal colliery opened in 1837, the real impetus to development came in 1840 with the entry of Thomas Powell, the largest owner in Monmouthshire. He systematically took out mineral leases with the intention of dominating the valley, and so laid the basis of the Powell Duffryn Company, one of the largest concerns in the south Wales coal industry. The valley was rapidly apportioned to various producers, so that by the end of the 1860s the increase of output levelled out and the lead passed to the Rhondda valleys. The development of the coal industry had led to an increase in the population of the valley from 6,393 in 1831 to 37,487 in 1861.[7]

Table 3 Coal output in Aberdare Parish (tons)

1844	177,000	1864	2,048,000
1849	434,000	1869	2,142,000
1854	1,009,000	1874	1,963,000
1859	1,633,000	1884	2,285,000

Source: J. H. Morris and L. J. Williams, *The South Wales Coal Industry 1841–75* (1958), 108; E. D. Lewis, *The Rhondda Valleys* (1959).

The Rhondda valleys eventually became the most important single area of steam coal production. But, unlike the Aberdare valley, the steam coals were overlaid by bituminous coals, and it was upon these that the early development of the area depended. There was only one important producer until the 1840s, when other speculators moved in to exploit the bituminous seams. The possibility of mining the steam coal was shown in 1851 when the Bute estate, the major owner of mineral rights, decided to sink a shaft to the steam seams. The Taff Vale Railway extended its line up the valley, production began in 1855, and in December the first Rhondda steam coal was transported to Cardiff. Output of Rhondda steam coal grew significantly from the 1860s when the more easily worked Aberdare steam coal was taken up, and Rhondda output passed Aberdare in the early 1870s. The population of the Rhondda valleys had been 1,636 in 1831, and in 1861 was still well below Aberdare at 11,737. Growth was then rapid, to 127,980 in 1891. By 1911 the population of Rhondda at 152,781 was three times higher than the population of Aberdare at 50,830.[8]

By 1861 the population of the port and hinterland had grown to 208,145. In the period to 1831 the basis of the economy had moved from agriculture to industry. The industrial base had then changed so that in

Table 4   Coal output in the Rhondda valleys (tons)

1856	205,200	1874	2,070,735
1864	520,022	1879	3,697,367
1869	1,238,124	1884	5,553,823

Source: E. D. Lewis, *The Rhondda Valleys* (1959), 66, 76, 84, 132.

1861 there were 29,292 engaged in coal mining to 11,051 in iron manufacture. As the output of coal continued to expand, so the population
of the hinterland rose to 485,000 by 1891 and about 885,000 by the First
World War. Coal mining became increasingly dominant. By 1881, it
accounted for half the industrial population with 44,864 workers, at
which date iron and steel employed only 11,396. The sparsely populated

Table 5   Coal output in the hinterland of Cardiff (million tons)

	1881	1914
Rhondda	4·95	11·80
Merthyr	1·72	4·35
Aberdare	2·35	4·48
Rhymney	1·22	7·33
Other	0·25	6·17
	10·49	34·13

Coal output in the south Wales Coalfield (million tons)

1874	16·5	1894	33·3
1884	25·5	1904	43·7
		1914	53·9

Source: T. M. Hodges, 'The history of the port of Cardiff in relation
to its hinterland with special reference to the years 1830–1914' (M.Sc.
(Econ.) thesis, University of London, 1946); R. Walters, 'Labour
productivity in the south Wales steam-coal industry, 1870–1914',
E.H.R.· 2nd ser., XXVII (1975).

hinterland of Cardiff had become one of the most densely settled areas in
the country, having experienced a 30-fold increase in population between
1801 and 1914. The pastoral valleys of the early nineteenth century now
had a straggling ribbon of terrace housing along their sides, with river,
railway and pits squeezed onto the valley floor, and tips dominating the
mountain tops.[9]

Coal passed iron in the trade of Cardiff in the 1830s; around 1850 coal
passed iron as the main basis of the economy of south Wales; and at the
same time Cardiff became the major coal port. Further, Cardiff ousted

Bristol as the commercial centre for south Wales. The marketing of coal, and the bulk of the commercial work of the colliery companies, were handled in Cardiff. The Cardiff Coal Exchange was the hub of the south Wales export trade, dealing with coal which was not necessarily shipped at Cardiff. So Cardiff dominated the south Wales coal trade, both in terms of the tonnage physically passing through the town and of the much larger tonnage disposed of on paper at the Exchange. And by the 1880s, south Wales dominated the British coal export industry. Cardiff was then indeed the 'coal metropolis of the world'. The two major coal export areas were south Wales and the North-East of England, and it was in 1881 that their relative positions were reversed, with south Wales taking about 40 per cent to the 30 per cent of the North-East. Cardiff's share of exports from the Bristol Channel had been 60 per cent up to the 1880s, but from 1890 was being caught and finally overhauled by the adjacent

Table 6   Proportion of coal exports taken by the Bristol Channel and the North-East

	Bristol Channel	North-East
1850	13·3	63·6
1860	24·4	53·5
1870	31·2	46·9
1880	39·0	39·5
1890	43·6	31·1
1900	41·9	29·7

Source: D. A. Thomas, 'The growth and direction of our foreign trade in coal during the last half century', *J.R.S.S.*, LXVI (1903), 498.

port of Barry. From 1900 Cardiff's share of exports stabilized at about 30 per cent. The reasons why Cardiff's predominance in shipments was whittled away, even if all the commercial work was retained, is discussed in detail in the next chapter. The situation by the 1880s was clear: the town dominated the south Wales coal trade, which in turn dominated the national export trade in coal; it was one of the largest ports in the country, ranking with London and Liverpool in terms of tonnage cleared; and by 1871 it was the largest town in Wales, passing Merthyr Tydfil and emerging to the head of the urban hierarchy of south Wales.[10]

The rise of south Wales to dominance in the coal export trade was based largely upon the demand for coal by steamships. Admiralty trials in the 1840s showed that south Wales steam coal had a higher evaporative power, occupied less space per ton, lit easily, required less attention, and produced less clinker than its competitors. Admiralty orders were diverted to south Wales, and many merchant lines followed suit. The area of

Table 7   Proportion of Bristol Channel coal exports taken by Bute docks

1860	62·4	1890	52·0
1865	56·9	1895	43·9
1870	43·4	1900	35·7
1875	59·3	1904	30·1
1880	59·1	1908	30·2
1885	58·7	1913	30·4

Source: calculated from figures in T. M. Hodges, 'The history of the port of Cardiff in relation to its hinterland with special reference to the years 1830–1914' (M.Sc. (Econ.) thesis, University of London, 1946); D. A. Thomas, 'The growth and direction of our foreign trade in coal during the last half century', *J.R.S.S.*, LXVI (1903); H. S. Jevons, *The British Coal Trade* (1915); and exports of coal from Bute docks in Cardiff Central Library, Bute MSS., XI 56, and Annual Reports of Cardiff Chamber of Commerce.

Table 8   Tonnage entered and cleared from the main ports in 1888 (thousands)

	entered	cleared
London	5,470	7,470
Liverpool	5,370	4,940
Cardiff	2,930	5,150
Newcastle	1,900	3,320
Hull	1,900	1,500

Source: M. Mulhall, *Dictionary of Statistics* (1892).

export is easily calculated – it was predominantly to France and the Mediterranean.

It is unfortunately not possible to calculate the amount used for navigation purposes. D. A. Thomas, a leading coalowner, speculated in 1903 that 'the great bulk of our export is for the use of steamships and it is within the mark to say that over half of our exports are for navigation purposes, and further that more than half the coal exported is for British consumption abroad'. Shipments to locations such as Port Said, Aden, Cape Verde, and the Canaries were practically entirely for bunkering steam vessels, and a large part of shipments to Genoa, Marseilles, Le Havre, Buenos Aires, Monte Video, and Rio de Janeiro were for this purpose. And since British steamers had a greater registered tonnage than those of the rest of the world put together, it followed that most of this coal was bought by British firms.[11]

As the trade of Cardiff grew, so did its population and physical extent. When the nineteenth century opened, Cardiff was much as portrayed by Speed, whose 'map of 1610 may be taken as representative of the whole

Table 9   Destination of south Wales coal exports (%)

	1880	1900
France and the Mediterranean	69	71
Baltic and Black Sea	3	8
Brazil, Uruguay, Argentina	6	8
West Africa	2	3
South Africa	2	2
India	4	–
Middle and Far East	7	4
U.S.A. (Atlantic), W. Indies, central America	4	1
Peru, Chile, U.S.A. (Pacific)	1	1
East Africa	2	2

Source: D. A. Thomas, 'The growth and direction of our foreign trade in coal during the last half century', *J.R.S.S.*, LXVI (1903), 500.

period between 1350 and the late eighteenth century'. The map of 1824 shows the town to be broadly similar to that of 1610. The shape of the town was to be revolutionized about 1840 by the incursion of the railways and the building of the first stage of the dock system to the south of the old settlement between 1834 and 1839. In 1824 the town was confined by the river on the west, looping in to the Town Quay on St Mary Street. In 1849–53 this loop was cut off and the Town Quay left high and dry. The land reclaimed from the river was used by the Great Western Railway, which opened in 1850 and ran east to west across the southern fringe of the old town. This formed a barrier between the area of medieval settlement to the north and the new settlement around the dock to the south. The line of the town wall on the east, reinforced by the canal running alongside, was also clear in 1824. The Taff Vale Railway, which was built between 1836 and 1841, took the same route to the dock, forming a further barrier to the east. The railway lines, the river, and the castle to the north, very clearly delineated the medieval settlement, and continue very clearly to define the central business district within these boundaries. In 1824, the area was still only partly settled. As in 1610, the bulk of the population was in the immediate vicinity of the castle in a tight cluster of streets, while to the south houses straggled along the main street with large open spaces behind. The census of 1801 showed that the northern parish of St John had a population of 1,441, compared with the southern parish of St Mary's 429. In the course of the nineteenth century, the open spaces in the south were intensively developed in a series of courts, and the medieval settlement became an area of overcrowding and bad sanitation which was abandoned by the better-off. Then, gradually up to the

Table 10   The population of Cardiff 1801-1911

	St John	St Mary	Roath	Canton	total pre-1875 boundary	total post-1875 boundary	%increase pre-1875 boundary	%increase post-1875 boundary
1801	1,441	429	n.a.	n.a.	1,870	–	–	–
1811	n.a.	n.a.	n.a.	n.a.	2,457	–	31·4	–
1821	n.a.	n.a.	n.a.	n.a.	3,521	–	43·3	–
1831	n.a.	n.a.	n.a.	n.a.	6,187	–	75·7	–
1841	n.a.	n.a.	n.a.	n.a.	10,077	(11,442)	62·9	–
1851	6,592	11,759	n.a.	n.a.	18,351	(20,258)	82·1	(77·0)
1861	8,666	24,288	n.a.	n.a.	32,954	(41,422)	79·6	(104·5)
1871	11,027	28,509	7,991	9,384	39,536	56,911	20·0	37·4
1881	16,614	28,254	23,096	14,797	–	82,761	–	45·4
1891	27,158	29,295	39,657	32,805	–	128,915	–	55·8
1901	29,652	30,351	61,074	43,256	–	164,333	–	27·5
1911	n.a.	n.a.	n.a.	n.a.	–	182,259	–	10·9

n.a. not available

Source: Census of England and Wales 1801 to 1911; B. Thomas, 'The growth of population', in British Association volume, *The Cardiff Region. A Survey* (1960), 111.

1880s and much more quickly thereafter, there was a further change as slums were replaced by offices, hotels, and stores.[12]

The centre of gravity of population first moved south within the old walled borough; by the 1840s it was moving further south again as the area outside the walls and adjacent to the dock was developed. By the 1870s, the major growth was not just outside the walls of the medieval settlement, but completely outside the boundaries of the borough, in Canton to the west and Roath to the east. These suburbs were brought within the borough in 1875, and by 1891 they far exceeded the population of the old borough of St John and St Mary.

The rate of growth of the population of Cardiff in the years being studied – from 1870 to 1914 – was less than in the earlier nineteenth century. In a sense this is misleading because the low initial population made a small absolute increase seem very large in percentage terms. Cardiff's population grew eleven-fold between 1801 and 1851, but this only took it to 20,000. Between 1851 and 1911, the rate of growth was lower – nine-fold over 60 years – but this took the population to 182,000. Such a rapid rate of growth after 1851 was, indeed, unusual. The only other major town to surpass such growth was Middlesbrough, which grew from 8,000 in 1851 to 120,000 in 1911. More typical was a four-fold increase between 1851 and 1911. Cardiff was in this simply following the pattern of the rest of the county: Glamorgan's population rose by 253 per cent between 1861 and 1911, whereas the population of England and Wales rose by 80 per cent.[13]

In all ways, between 1801 and 1911 there was a huge change in the economy and society of Cardiff: from a small market town with purely local trade to a major port with world-wide ramifications; from a village huddled around the castle to a large city with a radius of two to three miles. The changes this involved were immense. Most obviously, it must be explained how the town achieved its rise to dominance in the coal trade. Also, the very process by which the city was built should be analysed. The physical creation of a city of 182,000 was in itself a major task which the historian must not ignore. And the whole way of life in the large town was different. A community of 2,000 on the banks of a river, with large open spaces within the walls, had few problems of water-supply, sanitation and drainage. The increase in scale by the 1840s meant this was so no longer, as it ceased to be possible simply to pour wastes into the ground and take water out in an uncontrolled manner. New ways had to be devised to provide the basic services and to control the urban environment.

The increase in scale also involved changes in social control, in politics, in land use. In the small town of 1801, the well-to-do were indeed con-centrated on two streets, but they were only a few yards from the poorest

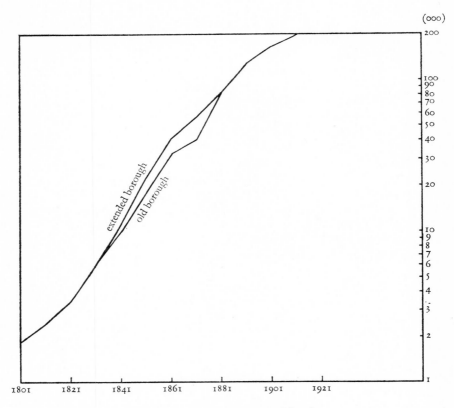

Figure 1. Population of Cardiff, 1801–1911 (source table 11).

inhabitants. Social control was informal and specialization of land use primitive. As the town grew, land use became more specialized, and social control had to be formalized when it was no longer simply a case of knowing other inhabitants and imposing informal constraints. Politically, the town had been a pocket borough of the lords of the castle, both on the municipal and the parliamentary level. In the course of the century independence was established. The social structure was transformed from the relatively simple and cohesive community of craftsmen, small traders and agriculturists, to the much more complex and diverse society of wealthy shipowners and coalowners at one extreme and the casual waterfront workers at the other.[14]

This book deals primarily with the years after the watershed rather than with the actual process of change from the small market town. The development of the docks is considered from the early nineteenth century, because of its crucial importance for everything else, but otherwise the detailed analysis starts at 1870. By then, Cardiff was already the leading coal port and the largest town in Wales. This book is concerned with how the town functioned as 'coal metropolis' rather than with the tensions created as it changed from a market town to a major commercial centre (the process by which this was achieved was fascinating and merits further study). The analysis starts at 1870 and stops at 1914. This forms a well-defined and homogenous period. By 1870, Cardiff's pre-eminence was established and it was already clearly a large town with all that that entailed. After 1914, the coal export trade declined, and Cardiff ceased to be the 'coal metropolis'. Its main function was destroyed, and problems of readjustment arose as the town sought a new role.

It is hoped that the following portrayal of the society which existed at Cardiff from 1870 to 1914 will interest three groups. One is the local inhabitant: an understanding of the economy of these years is relevant to understanding the present predicament of the city, in particular the concern over the absence of industrial employment; also, much of the physical stock which was built in the late nineteenth century is now under threat of redevelopment. In different ways, the analysis should interest Welsh historians. An understanding of the development of the industrial society of south Wales – the transformation of the hinterland of Cardiff which has been briefly sketched – requires a study not only of the iron and coal industries, their communities and labour relations, but also of the commercial centres which catered to their needs. Cardiff became the major port of the south Wales coalfield, and the regional capital of the area. As the largest town in Wales, it is worthy of attention in its own right also. But the main ambition of this book is not to make a contribution specifically to the history of south Wales. It is to analyse in detail a particular example of a general process which transformed

British society in the nineteenth century, the process of urbanization. Cardiff is taken as a case-study of this general society-wide transformation, and must be analysed in terms of what was happening in Leeds or Birmingham or Liverpool and how they adapted to the same process. It is hoped to make a contribution to urban history by testing some general hypotheses and by following some lines of enquiry which have hitherto been neglected.

Part one   Economy

The crucial question, from which everything else follows, is how Cardiff became the leading port and largest town in south Wales. The next chapter provides the answer by analysing the development of the dock undertaking, which was the agent of growth of the local economy. Once it has been shown how the town became the 'coal metropolis', it must be asked how this role was fulfilled, which involves an inspection of the structure of commerce. But there was also a fear that the town was dependent on nothing but coal, which could easily be switched to other ports, and that the prosperity of Cardiff was not securely founded. The fears were justified, for coal was diverted to other ports in the late nineteenth century, whilst the coal trade collapsed after the First World War. The failure to diversify the economy before 1914 was to be of major significance for the future.

2 The docks

The reason for Cardiff's rise to the top of the local urban hierarchy is simple: its harbour facilities were provided earlier and on a larger scale than elsewhere on the coast of south Wales. This was largely the result of the initiative of one man, the second marquis of Bute, whose decision to invest in dock facilities put Cardiff ahead of its rivals, to become the leading shipper of coal and the largest town in the region. In emerging to this position, Cardiff started to provide various services for the mining communities in the hinterland, and on a more specialist level to the whole coalfield, so that the town became the regional capital of the area.

Once the lead had been established, however, things became more complex. For the docks were not a financial success, and became in-adequate for the expanding trade of the hinterland. Competition began to develop, Cardiff's lead as a port came under serious threat, and was indeed surrendered by 1914 in terms of tonnage handled. Neither did the docks encourage the growth of the local economy in quite the manner that was expected, for the multiplier effect of the docks was limited, the linkages with other activities few and slender. So by the late nineteenth century the advantage given by the docks had been whittled away, and the original stimulus to growth had not been strong enough to provide a basis for diversification of trade or for industrial growth. The saving factor was that because the lead had been won and retained for 50 years or so, Cardiff was not surpassed in its role of regional capital, and it was this function which was to become dominant with the decline of the docks, at first relatively, but then absolutely, and in the absence of a large manufacturing base. In this chapter, the reasons why Cardiff gained but then lost its relative advantage as a coal port will be discussed. This amounts to asking two questions. Why at a vital stage did the local land-owner, the marquis of Bute, take the initiative from the other interested parties – the producers and the merchants – in creating harbour facilities for the developing coal export trade? And why in one of the recurring crises as trade outstripped accommodation did these other parties wrest the initiative from a now reluctant marquis of Bute and extend facilities elsewhere on the coast, with serious consequences for the continued growth of the town? In other words, how did Cardiff become the coal metropolis of the world, and why was it then threatened?

I

The Bute estate was one of the largest landowners in south Wales, with
extensive holdings in the coalfield, as well as being the dominant ground
landlord in Cardiff. The role of the estate became important in the 1820s,
when the transport facilities first provided for the *iron* trade in the late
eighteenth century became inadequate for the expanding *coal* trade. The
facilities for the iron trade – both overland transport and the harbour –
had been provided by the producers. The Merthyr Tydfil ironmasters
built the Glamorganshire Canal and its sea-lock at Cardiff to transport
and ship their produce.[1] The sea-lock opened in 1798. By 1806 it was
handling 10,400 tons of iron a year, and by 1839, 132,781 tons, but even
by the 1820s the facilities were proving inadequate and acting as a definite
check upon the exports of coal, which had risen from 865 tons in 1816–18
to 211,214 tons in 1839.[2] The increasing pressure upon accommodation
from the 1820s meant that any initiative by the Bute estate was potentially
important.

In 1828 the second marquis of Bute (1793–1848) commissioned a report
on the state of the harbour at Cardiff. The report concluded that the
sea-lock of the Glamorganshire Canal was inadequate. Its entrance was
$2\frac{1}{4}$ miles from low-water mark, up a winding channel which caused
'great inconvenience and danger'. Larger vessels could enter only for a
few hours each tide, and some vessels could not get in at all, but had
to load from lighters outside the sea-lock. The sea-lock itself shoaled
from 14ft 8in at the sea end to 10ft at the town end, so that ships could
only part-load at the town end, being forced to complete loading from
barges at the sea end. Delay and confusion ensued. Not surprisingly, the
report concluded that the trade of Cardiff was being hindered from
developing to its maximum possible extent:

> and more especially in the article of coal with which the interior of the
> county abounds, and which although now sold with all the existing
> disadvantages of the canal at a lower price than at Newport, little is
> shipped in comparison with that port, the reason of which is generally
> attributed to the detention of vessels in the canal and the intricacy
> of the approaches to it.[3]

The question of the 1820s was who would or could provide the new
facilities which were recommended, that is, a new dock parallel to the
sea-lock, joining the Taff less than a mile from low-water.

Part of the debate on improvement was carried on within the canal
company itself. There were two items of contention among the ironmasters who controlled it: the rates on the canal and the service provided
from Merthyr, and the improvement of harbour facilities at Cardiff. The
'modernizers' in the canal company wished to make improvements to

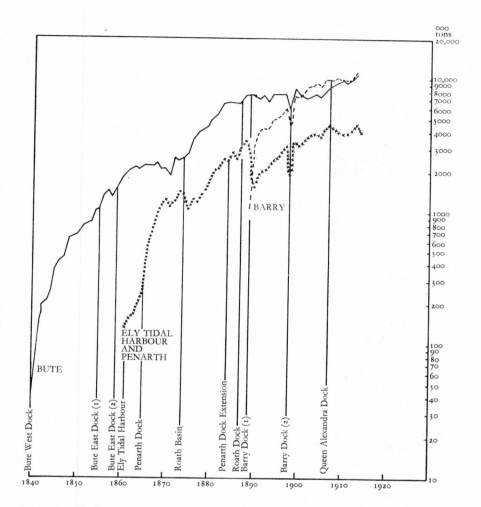

Figure 2. Coal exports from Bute, Penarth, and Barry docks, 1840–1913 (source: C.C.L. Bute V 49, XI 56; Annual Reports, Cardiff Chamber of Commerce).

the existing sea-lock, but were prevented first by the conservatism of William Crawshay, chairman of the canal company, and then by the unco-operativeness of the second marquis of Bute, who owned the land on either side of the sea-lock and so could effectively prevent any improvement of the existing facilities. Such improvement would in any case be of little value. The entrance to the sea-lock was too far from low-water mark, and no amount of widening and deepening could solve this problem. As far as overland transport is concerned, agitation over the cost and efficiency of the canal service from Merthyr had led some of the ironmasters in the 1790s and 1820s to consider building a railway to Cardiff.[4] The threat was made good when the Taff Vale Railway Company (T.V.R.) was inaugurated in 1836. The line was completed to Cardiff in 1841, on the initiative of the producers in the hinterland.

It would be natural to assume that this railway and the dock at Cardiff were planned together from the first, but such was not the case. Bute opted to provide the required dock himself, and actually prevented the producers (at this stage ironmasters rather than coalowners) from supplying their own harbour facilities. In 1830 he obtained powers to build the dock recommended by the report of 1828. Work commenced in 1834, and the Bute Ship Canal (or West Dock as it became) opened in 1839. In this way the control of the Glamorganshire Canal Company over the transport and shipping facilities of Cardiff had been broken at two points, first by the railway built by the leading ironmasters and second by the dock built by the Bute estate. That the two undertakings should have been complementary seems obvious, but a *modus vivendi* was a long time emerging.

The ironmasters backing the T.V.R. had also wanted improved shipping facilities, and planned to construct their own harbour on the River Ely.[5] These ironmasters were, in fact, opponents of Bute for many reasons. The earlier opposition of Bute to improvements at Cardiff rankled, while the very existence of the Dowlais Iron Co. (a major supporter of the T.V.R.) was in danger because of Bute's terms for renewal of leases. As Crawshay saw, opposition to Bute united both the ironmasters loyal to the canal and those sponsoring the T.V.R.[6] The outcome in the 1830s seemed likely to be a harbour on the Ely served by the railway, with Bute's new dock remaining dependent upon the canal. But Bute clearly saw 'that it is important to me to have a Railway from Merthyr to Cardiff, as well as the Glamorganshire Canal'. His policy was to tie the T.V.R. to his dock and to prevent it from proceeding with its own harbour. Agreement was reached in 1846. The proposed line to the Ely was to be abandoned, and the T.V.R. bound itself to ship all goods from the Bute docks as far as possible; in any case, goods not using the Bute dock were to pay wharfage and lockage dues as if they had. The Bute estate leased the east side of the dock to the T.V.R. for 250 years.[7] In 1846, therefore, it seemed that the interests of Bute and the T.V.R. were inextricably bound together.

However, Bute wanted to link other railways to his docks, and the position of the T.V.R. at Cardiff became less favourable than that of subsequent lines, the Great Western Railway and the Rhymney Railway (R.R.). The R.R. was incorporated in 1854 and the line opened in 1858. It reflected Bute policy of extending the hinterland as much as possible. and of forestalling the entry of lines into the hinterland to serve other ports. The aim was to secure a monopoly of the trade of as wide a hinterland as possible. According to the ironmasters, 'the Rhymney was designed by nature for Newport'. The second marquis disagreed and was planning in the early 1840s to secure a monopoly of the Rhymney traffic for Cardiff. His plan was not practicable then, but the R.R. of 1854 was largely a creature of the Bute estate, and was placed in a more favourable position than the T.V.R. The R.R., unlike the T.V.R., was given access to the new dock of 1855, the necessary line being paid for by the estate; the initial capital of the company was raised by the estate and the chairman was a Bute trustee; and a fifth of 1*d.* per ton was remitted to the R.R. to make it more competitive. The T.V.R. saw its relative position deteriorate and accordingly decided to proceed with the Ely Tidal Harbour, which opened in 1859, and to lease the Penarth Dock in 1863. Parliament agreed to this provided that Bute rates were not undercut; in fact, there was no real competition and the Penarth Dock was treated mainly as an overflow. The Bute strategy thus had a mixed success. On the one hand, the Bute docks had lost some trade to Penarth, but on the other hand, the hinterland had been successfully extended to the Rhymney valley. The agreement of 1846 had not therefore created the permanent identity of interest between the Bute docks and the T.V.R. which had been expected. Although the two concerns were obviously complementary, their relationship (at least up to the 1880s when competition to both drove them together) was one of hostility and tension.[8]

Bute had prevented the 'modernizers' within the canal company from improving their shipping facilities at Cardiff, and had then prevented the T.V.R. from providing its own harbour facilities. Why had the second marquis decided to invest on his own behalf in dock facilities? The report of 1828 had come to the conclusion that the new dock would be profitable merely with the coal trade and without any of the iron trade moving from the canal:

> with all the advantages which the new harbour would afford to the shipment of coal . . . this article would become a principal source of revenue independently of the export of iron. . . . The benefits which the

present shippers of coal would derive from the new harbour must ensure their using it in preference to the present canal, but should there prove to be a reluctance on their part to do so, the working of some of your lordship's own extensive fields of coal would amply supply the demands of the market to any extent that could be required.[9]

Here was the rationale of the scheme to build docks at Cardiff. The marquis of Bute would build a dock which would itself be a profitable investment (the expected return was 8 per cent)[10] and it would be linked with the development of the Bute mineral holdings in the coalfield. There was the additional incentive that building development on the Cardiff estate might be encouraged.

The Bute estate owned large areas in the coalfield from which a substantial revenue could be derived. As Bute remarked in 1832:

> as to coals in my own mineral fields nearer to Cardiff and the general exportation of coals from that port; it is admitted that if I lay out a large sum of money to improve that port, the principal source of return to me must be the income which I may directly or indirectly derive from coals.[11]

The export of coal would make the dock a profitable undertaking, and the dock would encourage the development of minerals and so increase the estate's revenue. The mutual dependence of the dock and mineral estate is shown most clearly in the clause in the Bute mineral lease which required all coal to be shipped from the Bute docks. Bute was not, however, willing to enter coal production on his own behalf. On two occasions the Bute estate did sink pits to prove seams, but on both occasions withdrew immediately. The Bute estate did engage directly in coal mining in the North East of England, but the attitude of the second marquis was that the trade there was long-established, and that the output was sold to shipping merchants 'upon a *del credere* commission, which is, the owners pay a higher rate of commission and have no risks of bad debts'. Bute believed this arrangement to be essential, but it could not be effected in south Wales. Without it, 'I am satisfied to submit to the certain loss of letting a colliery at a lower royalty than it is worth, than to be exposed to the unknown amount of loss by bad debts, besides the uncertainty of trade.'[12]

With such motivations, the first Bute dock opened in 1839, at a cost of £222,757 plus materials provided by the estate, later calculated to have been in all about £400,000.[13] The early years were difficult. The financial expectations were not fulfilled, and trade was less than anticipated.[14] The report of 1828 had justified the building of the dock by the coal trade alone, without any of the iron trade moving from the canal. In fact, the iron trade *did* largely stay with the canal. The ironmasters were not only aggrieved by Bute's attitude to the canal, but also felt that the dock charges were too high and that they should be compensated for giving up their wharfs on the canal. Despite the split between the ironmasters on the issue of the railway, it seemed that 'we have one common enemy in the dear shipping port to be made'. The ironmasters' hostility meant that the Bute dock was not altogether successful in the early 1840s, and Bute became obsessed with the existence of a conspiracy to destroy him. He used all means available to coerce freighters to use his dock: pressure could be put on the wharfs around the canal which he let on annual tenancies; he used the mineral leases to secure trade; and he continued to prevent improvements to the sea-lock.[15] Crawshay complained in 1847 about Bute's attitude to the canal:

> The question between us is not whether we are entitled to any specific quantity of land or not. . . . Your lordship knows full well that the real question is – whether you can so cripple us . . . at our shipping port at Cardiff that you can obtain the whole trade of the port through your superior and costly exit to the sea!! . . . My lord, I venture to tell you not only as chairman of the canal company but as an individual freighter of the port of Cardiff – that you cannot succeed in obtaining the whole trade of the port of Cardiff by force.[16]

Bute did succeed eventually, not by force so much as because the growing size of ships meant that the sea-lock became increasingly redundant. Bute was inclined to place more faith in this than in an attempt to win trade by cutting charges,[17] for his policy of preventing the canal company from making improvements gave him a monopoly of facilities capable of dealing with the largest ships.

In the early years of the Bute dock, the vital problem was finding enough trade to fill it. This creation of surplus capacity was crucial for the growth of Cardiff. It is often assumed that the dominance of Cardiff in the coal trade was from the first dictated by the demand for the steam coal located in its natural hinterland, and that the reason why Cardiff's trade came to exceed that of Newport and the western ports was simply the consequence of this factor of location. In fact, the majority of the coal exported from the Bute docks was initially of the same bituminous type as was exported from Newport, and Cardiff's lead was gained in the first place rather by the superiority of its transport and dock facilities.[18] As early as 1828 transport charges were at least a third cheaper to Cardiff than to Newport. It was claimed that the only reason why Cardiff did not already in the 1820s dominate the coal trade was the lack of an adequate shipping place.[19] The provision of the dock of 1839 removed the constraints to trade imposed by the sea-lock. Construction of docks came earlier and on a larger scale at Cardiff than at Newport and Swansea. The Bute dock of 1839 provided 19½ acres of water; the Newport Town dock of 1842 provided a mere 4½ acres and the extension of 1858 only another 7¼ acres; at Swansea the dock of 1852 provided 14 acres.[20] In the 1830s no one but the marquis of Bute had sufficiently wide resources and interests to provide a dock, and the experience of Newport and Swansea emphasizes this. The canal company might have deepened the sea-lock, but however much it was altered it could not be taken any closer to low-water mark. A dock on a different site was needed, and not just ineffective modifications of the existing canal. It is doubtful if the ironmasters could have done this on the scale that Bute did, or would have needed to for their own produce. Indeed, it is virtually certain that nothing on the scale of the Bute dock would have been possible if provision had been left to the producers or merchants. The T.V.R. was merely suggesting staithes on the bank of the Ely, well up-stream. The coalowners were at this time too small to contemplate any such investment, and neither could the few and insignificant Cardiff merchants. Probably it is fair to say that if Bute had not provided the facilities which the report of 1828 found necessary, no one else would have done. The possibility was mooted in 1844 that the three interests at Cardiff – canal, railway and docks – should amalgamate, but the idea collapsed.[21] Hindsight might suggest that if the three concerns could have united, the subsequent history of dock provision at Cardiff might have been more satisfactory. Failing such joint action, the whole of dock provision at Cardiff was to be left to the Bute estate, for 'Lord Bute was the only individual in the vicinity [in 1830] and the Bute estate was the only institution, which could prudently undertake the vast speculation of the docks, or which could by any means obtain the necessary funds'.[22] The importance of the dock of 1839 was that it was provided by the Bute estate where no other agency could do so, creating surplus capacity which meant that trade at Cardiff, unlike that at Newport and Swansea, could expand without obstacle in the 1840s.

The Bute dock of 1839 therefore gave Cardiff a tremendous boost, and the second marquis is justifiably called the 'maker of modern Cardiff'. A. W. Kirkaldy was certainly right when he wrote that 'if Cardiff had waited for municipal enterprise and the working of collectivism to develop a port, it is doubtful whether it would ever become the greatest and most progressive coal port in the world'.[23] But on the other hand, the pattern established by Bute's initiative increasingly acted to check the growth of the town. In virtually every other port in the country, dock facilities were provided either by harbour trusts or by public companies – at Cardiff, their provision was left entirely to the Bute estate. In 1906, D. A. Thomas, one of the most important coalowners, stated that:

so far from the late Lord Bute being creator of Cardiff, the docks in the hands of a private individual have greatly retarded the progress of the port. Marvellous as the growth of Cardiff has been during the last half-century it would have been far greater in other hands, and today we should have Cardiff the capital of Wales with a population of 300,000.[24]

Was Thomas right in his seemingly heretical view that Bute control of the docks held back the development of Cardiff?

II
Bute's policy of waiting for the coal trade to expand and ships to increase in size did pay off in terms of the *volume* of trade. By 1852 the trade of the dock reached a million tons a year, and the surplus capacity had been fully absorbed. By the early 1850s, indeed, the continuation of the trend meant that the dock was too small for the ships and inadequate for the trade, and 'unless additional accommodation be provided the trade will inevitably go elsewhere or will induce parties to undertake a rival plan'.[25] The problem was that while there was an insistent pressure for extension from the shippers, the Bute strategy of a dock both paying in its own right and providing indirect returns to the rest of the estate had failed, so that there was an increasing reluctance to supply the necessary facilities. The docks had succeeded in terms of the volume of trade, but not in financial terms. The provision of docks lagged ever further behind the need for them, and this retarded the growth of Cardiff, as Thomas suggested.

The expectation that the docks would be a profitable investment in themselves was never fulfilled: the intended 8 per cent return was never approached. The indirect returns from ground rents and mineral royalties were not forthcoming, because they were ploughed back to provide yet more docks. The return on the dock investment to the early 1880s was a 'bare three per cent', although one expert thought that a 6 per cent rate of return was required to cover depreciation and interest, and another that the proper rate of return on such investment should be at least 5 per cent.[26] According to the Bute officials, the return to 31 December 1865 was 4·17 per cent; in the 27 years to 1 January 1882, it was 3·07 per cent; in the ten years to 1 January 1882, it was 3·15 per cent. This was without any allowance having been made for depreciation.[27] The situation did improve a little in the 1880s, but thereafter deteriorated seriously. If the largely unremunerative railway investment after 1897 is excluded, the rate of return on the docks alone was £5 12s. 1d. per cent in 1885, falling to £4 0s. 2d. per cent in 1900 and £2 12s. 4d. per cent in 1912.[28] The low rate of return on the dock investment is shown by the experience of the last dock built at Cardiff, the Queen Alexandra Dock which opened in 1907. The average annual profit of the undertaking rose by £17,302 between 1902–7 and 1907–12, which on an investment of £2·25m. in the new dock gave a return of 15s. 4d. per cent.[29] To say the least, the return on the dock investment was unsatisfactory.

The total capital invested in the Bute docks, excluding railway expenditure rose from £609,593 in 1855 to £1,712,429 in 1870, £2,601,727 in 1885, £3,822,106 in 1900 and £5,874,535 in 1912.[30] In addition to the capital investment in the docks, between 1897 and 1912, £704,289 was invested in a new railway.[31] The entire investment was the responsibility of the Bute estate. It was hoped to separate the personal finances of the marquis of Bute from those of the Bute docks by forming the Bute Docks Company in 1886 (to be succeeded by the Cardiff Railway Company in 1897). This intention was never realized. As Dr Davies has well put it, the Bute Docks Company and the Cardiff Railway Company were saved from bankruptcy only by the continued willingness of the marquis of Bute to be exploited. The attempt to make the docks an undertaking separate from the rest of the Bute estate had failed, and there was a share capital of £6·3m. in a company which could not survive independently.[32] Why was this?

One reason was the obsolescence of the older docks. Bute had relied upon the increasing size of ships to fill his dock of 1839 – but the continuation of this trend meant that the dock itself became redundant and unremunerative (without being depreciated because the low rate of return did not permit it) while all the increase in trade was concentrated upon the most recent dock. The average size of ships using the docks increased from 180 tons in 1865 to 627 tons in 1912, the average size of the 20 largest ships from 2,400 tons to 11,900 tons. When the manager of the Bute estates in Glamorgan advocated the construction of a new dock in 1894, he reported that since the opening of the Roath Dock trade had fallen by 10 per cent in the West Dock and 20 per cent in the East Dock, while trade in the Bute docks as a whole had risen by 13 per cent.[33] The effect of the increase in the tonnage of vessels was not just to make the expenditure on the earlier docks increasingly unremunerative, but also to reduce the return on the new docks which were provided. Dues were charged upon registered tonnage, but as ships became larger they carried a greater amount of cargo in relation to their registered tonnage. Between 1853 and 1911 the proportion of tonnage of the ships to the tonnage of coal carried fell from 74·2 per cent to 47·5 per cent. The effect of this was a decline in the tonnage dues on shipping calculated in terms of the tonnage carried from 4·57d. to 3·16d. between 1873 and 1911. Larger ships also required more elaborate shipping appliances – in 1913 they cost six times as much as in 1865, whilst having to be provided twice as intensively.[34] The figures in table 11 show the increasing size and capital cost of each successive dock.

Thus the tonnage rate on shipping was becoming less remunerative. There were, however, two other chief sources of revenue: a charge for the shipment of coal, and wharfage. The wharfage charge on coal was 2*d.* per ton and no specific service was provided for this payment.[35] The charge for shipping coal, 2¼*d.* per ton, became inadequate to cover the cost of the service. The loss in 1877–81 was 1·17*d.* per ton; this was reduced in the 1880s and converted to a small profit, before rising again to a loss of 1·08*d.* per ton by 1912.[36] The reason for this situation was explained in 1879:

> The coal intended to be put on board ship is brought down from the collieries to Cardiff by the public railway companies and placed by those companies upon Lord Bute's sidings to await orders as to the particular tip or staith to which it is to be taken for shipment. The hauling of this coal to the tip . . . is done by Lord Bute without his being entitled to make any charge whatever, which is a peculiarity of the Bute docks. Nor is any charge made for the use of the sidings upon which the train loads of coal are placed.[37]

The charge made for tipping and weighing the coal was less than the cost of providing the so-called 'gratuitous services' in addition. After 1882 the 'gratuitous services' were taken over by the railway companies who were to work the wagons through to the tips before handing over to Bute, but a loss nevertheless reappeared from the early 1890s. So if the tonnage rate for shipping was becoming less remunerative, the charge for the shipment of coal was for most years inadequate to cover the necessary services.

Clearly, it became increasingly difficult to justify continued investment in terms of the direct return. But the initial strategy had suggested indirect returns as well, from ground rents and mineral royalties. Could these justify continued investment? On the whole they could not, and the new investment was of a 'defensive' nature, to prevent the existing capital becoming an absolute loss. This is clear from the memorandum of 1894 recommending the building of a new dock. The justification for suggesting such expenditure with little hope of an adequate return (3 per cent was allowed for but not achieved) was two-fold. Firstly, unless a large modern dock were provided, trade would fall as the existing docks became increasingly obsolete and the investment would become ever less profitable. Refusal to build a new dock would in effect mean writing off a capital which stood at £3·3m. in 1895. Such a course seemed unattractive, but the alternative was scarcely better. This was to say that although a large part of the capital invested in the docks was unremunerative, the

Table 11 The Bute dock system

Dock	Opened	Cost*	Depth of entrance	Area (acres)	Quays (ft)	Lock (ft)	Capital per ft of quay
West Bute	1839	£338,000	s. 28′ 8″ n. 18′ 8½″	19½	9,400	152×36	£35 19s. 1d.
East Bute	1855–9	£401,000	s. 31′ 8½″ n. 21′ 8½″	46¼	10,120	220×55	£39 12s. 6d.
Roath Basin	1874		s. 35′ 9″ n. 25′ 9″	12		350×80	
Dock	1887	£945,565		33	8,620		£109 13s. 10d.
Queen Alexandra	1907	£1,274,348	s. 42′ 0″ n. 32′ 0″	52	6,550	850×90	£194 11s. 0d.

Source: H.L.R.O., Minutes of evidence, H.L., 1913, Cardiff Railway, Capital expenditure for construction of docks, including entrance locks and gates, but excluding embankments, entrance channels and shipping appliances; *Welsh Coal and Shipping Handbook, 1913*.

* including entrance locks and gates, excluding embankments, entrance channel, shipping appliances
s.= spring tide; n.= neap tide.

building of yet another new dock might make just enough profit to ensure that the undertaking as a whole remained profitable. The first justification for building a new dock was therefore defensive, that an additional large investment at a low rate of return was preferable to letting the docks decline and writing the capital off as a loss. As was said when it was decided to proceed with the new dock, 'it is a measure rather of defence and precaution intended to preserve rather than extend the company's business'.[38]

The second justification was based upon the original strategy of development – the benefit to the rest of the Bute estate. But this strategy had failed to a very large extent. The 1894 memorandum remarked 'that it may safely be estimated that your annual income from building ground rents would be considerably increased'. The figures in table 12 were presented to show the benefits derived from dock expenditure.

Table 12   Building ground rents from Bute estate in Cardiff

	Gross ground rents		
	£	s.	d.
1830 Bute Dock Act obtained	214	3	0
1840 West Dock open for a year	258	3	0
1850	621	19	6
1860 East Dock open for five years	5,319	5	5
1870	6,324	1	0
1880 Roath Basin open for five years	11,486	5	7
1890 Roath Dock open for two years	23,411	0	7

Source: C.C.L. Bute XI 20.

Certainly, if the dock expansion was allowed to take place entirely at other points on the coast, the Bute building estate at Cardiff would be less profitable. There is less justification for regarding the return from mineral leases in the hinterland as an indirect benefit of dock investment. Bute had gained from the opening of the coalfield: the mineral income from the Bute estate had risen from £21,435 in 1850–1 to £48,900 in 1880–1, and reached £117,477 in 1919.[39] But this would have happened even if others had supplied the docks. As a Bute official pointed out when asked if the docks had given an impetus to colliery development on the estate:

Yes, there is no doubt that Lord Bute has a share of the indirect advantages but you must always remember this, that there are scores of people who are colliery and royalty owners who have spent nothing upon the docks and they reap a share of the advantages in common with Lord Bute.[40]

Bute had gained no more from the docks so far as the development of the mineral estate was concerned than those who had not invested in any dock facilities.

The significance of the mineral income for the Bute estate was less that it was augmented by the building of the docks than that it gave the Bute estate sufficient resources to provide the docks. The docks were more a parasite than an asset. The insatiable demands of the dock for capital dominated the estate. In 1871, the accounts of the Bute estate in Glamorganshire showed the following position:

Table 13   Finances of the Bute estate in Glamorganshire, 1871

	£	s.	d.
Total receipts from docks	48,947	14	10
Mineral income	40,204	0	5
Agricultural and building land	10,022	2	9
	99,173	18	0
Expenditure at Bute docks	98,071	14	6
Interest on loans	19,881	12	9

Source: C.C.L. Bute X 6.

The cost of providing new docks exceeded the receipts of the Bute estate in Glamorgan and loans had to be raised which were scarcely reduced before the next extension became necessary. Bute had to mortgage the estate, and even in 1922 outstanding loans were nearly £1m.[41] As early as 1853 a trustee of the estate wrote:

> I am confounded by the increasing demands forced upon the trust by the growing trade of Cardiff; another thousand feet insisted upon in the new dock and a confident assurance that, in two years, even that will be insufficient for the trade. The residue of my days will be passed in a perpetual worry at an increasing expenditure and an undiminished debt.[42]

This set the pattern of Bute attitudes towards dock provision at Cardiff, which was confirmed by an exchange in 1882:

> Q.   As a matter of personal feeling I believe I may take it that Lord Bute is not anxious to spend more money?
>
> A.   I should say not. He has looked upon it as a very serious matter both for himself and his family, having such a very large sum of money in a class of investment such as dock property. The sum

which has been expended up to this time is about £2,500,000 and he certainly hesitates about spending any more when he gets a very small return upon that expenditure.[43]

What had in 1839 been described as 'one of the most spirited undertakings of the present age'[44] was being treated as a misfortune. The strategy of the 1820s had failed. There can be little doubt that the Bute estate would have been in a better position financially if it had not itself provided the docks at Cardiff.

This was the main reason why the docks increasingly lagged behind requirements. Another reason was fortuitous – the death of the second marquis in 1848 when his heir was a year old. The second marquis had dedicated himself to estate management and was more of a dynamic entrepreneur than a landed aristocrat. After 1848 the estate was run by trustees who were reluctant to incur large-scale expenditure, whilst Parliament was reluctant to give them powers.[45] The provision of facilities thus lagged ever further behind demand. The situation did not change when the third marquis (1847–1900) came of age. Unlike his father, he took little interest in estate management, and was often unavailable; he preferred the activities of the scholar, builder, and mystic. The trust was accordingly continued. The father had created a modern town at Cardiff; the son spurned it to rebuild the castle as a stage on which to live a life of fantasy in feudal splendour. 'The dominant character of his mind', it has been said, 'to which all his actions were referable, was his devotional temperament and his reverence for ancient institutions'.[46] The running of the estate was left to Sir W. T. Lewis (1837–1914), who was himself a major coalowner and well aware of the requirements of the trade.[47] He was, however, fundamentally constrained by the financial position.

There is another reason for the lack of success. Estate officials realized that if the docks were to be a paying proposition there should be a widening of the base of trade away from coal. Further, it is probably a fair generalization that the profit from docks stems less from shipping charges than from rents of associated industrial areas. Failure to develop an associated industrial area and a more diversified trade – the subject of the next chapter – was another reason why the Bute dock system was not a financial success.

III

The lag of accommodation behind trade increased seriously after the opening of the East Dock in 1855–9. The Roath Basin (which was all Parliament would sanction during the third marquis's minority and which opened in 1874) was not enough. Eventually in 1874 the powers to build the Roath Dock which had been urgently sought as long ago as 1864 were obtained. But in 1876 Bute announced that 'I do not see that it would be advantageous to me to begin at present the active construction of the proposed dock'.[48] His point of view might have been justified, but it was forcing the shippers to look elsewhere:

> it was an important thing for them to have a proper outlet for their commodities. The dock accommodation of Cardiff was not sufficient to meet the demand of the district, and inasmuch as Lord Bute refused to construct more dock accommodation, it had become necessary to find another outlet.[49]

By the 1880s the shortage of dock accommodation was creating a crisis, as the figures in table 14 indicate.

Table 14   Tons of trade per acre of dock

West Dock		West and East docks		West and East docks Roath Basin	
1841	2,361	1861	35,432	1876	56,623
1846	29,022	1866	43,754	1881	84,989
1851	47,094	1871	40,431	1886	102,914

Source: calculated from trade statistics in part II of M. J. Daunton, 'Aspects of the social and economic structure of Cardiff 1870–1914' (Ph.D. thesis, University of Kent, 1974); see also figures in C.C.L. Bute XI 46.

This situation led to an approach in 1880 and 1881 from the Chamber of Commerce and the Corporation to take over the docks, and Bute was initially in favour.[50] However, in 1881 Bute for some reason changed his mind and announced that he would retain control of the docks and provide the required extensions. He proposed not to use the powers of 1874, but to construct something considerably better. The Chamber welcomed this, provided that the dock bill was fair to producers generally, and the present dock charges left undisturbed.[51] But when the Bute Docks Bill of 1882 was published, it was felt that these conditions had not been fulfilled. It was not an extension but a curtailment of the plan of 1874, and there were two objectionable features in it. Bute was unwilling to construct a new dock unless he received 1*d*. a ton for the 'gratuitous services'; it was also proposed that the dock authorities should have sole control of labour at the docks, which was opposed by the coal shippers, who insisted that it was vital that they be responsible for loading their own coal.[52] What must be stressed is the basic change in the situation since 1839. It was not possible for the coalowners and freighters then to consider investing large sums in docks, but by 1882 they were in a position to take action on their own account. So if Bute's conditions were unacceptable (however necessary in terms of his finances) they had the option of providing alternative accommodation. As one coalowner, David Davies, commented:

we want a new dock; but we do not say the marquis of Bute shall make it. We do not say that we are here to demand Lord Bute to make that dock that he had power to make in 1874. . . . [Dock accommodation is] very much wanted and must be made by somebody, but we say this, if the marquis of Bute wants the increased charges on the old docks, there is no pretext for such a thing, and it is an injustice to us. . . . By degrees we have grown strong, and now we find we are as strong as the marquis of Bute, and we want our own docks. Up to now we were entirely dependent.[53]

Bute's increasing reluctance to invest in the docks at Cardiff was paralleled by the rise of coalowners and freighters to a position where they could challenge Bute in wealth and could construct their own docks outside Cardiff. The new situation formed a watershed in the history of the docks and the town.

In 1884, led by David Davies, the coalowners (with support from some shipowners) obtained an Act to build the Barry dock and railway. These opened in 1889. The dock at Barry was to surpass Cardiff in the years before 1914 as the major coal port of south Wales. Why were the traders prepared to sink money in docks when Bute was facing such difficulties? The increasing lag between dock provision and the growth of trade meant that by the 1880s the position of the Bute docks was no less chaotic than that of the sea-lock in 1828. Between 1874 and 1882 trade had risen by three million tons without any extension of facilities, and the docks and railways seemed to be in danger of grinding to a halt. It was felt that the losses caused by congestion were more than the charges which would be incurred in providing a new dock, and it was this consideration which made the decision to demand 1d. a ton for the gratuitous services unacceptable, however justified it might have appeared to Bute.

The loss was incurred in two ways. The first was through delays at the docks disrupting railway traffic. Collieries loaded direct into wagons so that they were frequently forced to stop production by the detention of wagons at the docks, while the increase in the time taken to make a round trip meant that more wagons had to be hired. It was calculated that this led respectively to an increase in production costs of 2d. a ton and an annual additional cost of £41,000. The latter was sufficient to pay the interest charge for new docks both at Cardiff and Barry. But of course whilst the coalowners could consider their investment in a dock as part and parcel of the economics of coal mining, Bute had to consider the return on the dock investment apart from the costs of producing and shipping coal. This meant that what was justifiable to Bute was an imposition to the coalowners. The second source of loss was through delays to shipping. Almost half the ships were kept waiting outside the docks, at a cost estimated conservatively at £50,000 a year – or the interest which could be incurred in providing two docks. Once inside the dock, it could take 16 hours to reach the berth, and pressure on the railways meant delays in the arrival of cargo which further increased the time it took ships to turn around.[54]

The building of the Barry dock had two further justifications. Since there would not be the burden of undepreciated and unremunerative antiquated docks, it could be made to pay. Up to 1897 dividends were 20 per cent per annum, and thereafter between 12 and 19 per cent. It was also hoped to break the monopoly position of the T.V.R. in certain areas of the coalfield, which resulted in higher rates.[55]

The Barry docks and railway which were created as a result of these considerations provided the first real competition to the Bute dock and the T.V.R., for Penarth – the only other rival – had been essentially an overflow. They broke the second marquis's policy of monopolizing and extending the hinterland. After 1890 a large part of the growth of the coal trade was diverted to Barry. The breach would have been worse, if it had not been for the earlier success in extending the hinterland, for as part of the trade of the Rhondda and the T.V.R. was hived off to Barry, the R.R. provided an increasing share of the trade of the Bute docks. While the T.V.R. share of coal carried to the Bute docks fell from 72·4 per cent in 1881 to 49·0 per cent in 1910, that of the R.R. rose from 20·0 per cent to 34·7 per cent.[56] Despite this offsetting feature, the effect on Bute finances was serious. Net revenue in the 1890s fluctuated around the level attained in the early 1880s, although capital expenditure had greatly increased.[57] The rate of return fell from a peak of 5 per cent in 1888 to 3 per cent and less in the early 1890s. What was the attitude of the Bute estate to this new situation?

Bute's resolve to dispose of the docks was strengthened. The Corporation discussed forming a harbour trust, but was too alarmed at the state of the undertaking to go ahead. Various proposals for amalgamation with the T.V.R. and other interests met with parliamentary refusal. The aim of these schemes was to link the docks much more firmly with a railway, to have one concern owning both dock and railway as at Barry. The T.V.R. equally felt that this was a necessity.[58] But Parliament refused to sanction amalgamation, so in 1897 the Bute Dock Company became the Cardiff Railway Company in order to build its own line to the coalfield. The rationale of this was explained to the parliamentary select committee:

the nature of the scheme was to put the Bute undertaking at Cardiff into something like the same position as its fierce competitors were in . . . with regard to the possession of railways which feed their docks. . . . We have . . . exhausted . . . all means of self-preservation and the emancipation from our present alarming position which amalgamation with existing railways would supply us with . . . the only remaining method is to assimilate our position to that of the other great dock undertakings about us by getting railways of our own. These lines . . . are our last resort. This is our only chance of redemption.[59]

This misunderstood the difference between the Bute and Barry docks, which was that the Barry company was not hampered by a weight of undepreciated, obsolete docks. Cardiff's 'only chance of redemption' in fact almost damned the undertaking. By 1912 when the Cardiff Railway opened, £704,289 had been spent on the scheme. But the line only reached the southern limit of the coalfield and scarcely carried any coal. It was a massive white elephant which only served to over-capitalize the undertaking even further. After 1900, the rate of return on the docks alone was running at under 3 per cent; when the expenditure on the railway is included, the return was under 2 per cent. To add to the problems, in 1913 Parliament refused to sanction increased charges, and it was obvious that any further dock provision at Cardiff was out of the question. A crisis similar to that of the 1880s was building up again, and was only to be resolved by the post-war decline in the coal trade.[60]

IV

Thus in the early nineteenth century, monopoly gave way to competition for the trade of the immediate hinterland of Cardiff. And as the base of the economy of the hinterland moved from iron to coal, so the party supplying transport facilities changed. The producers of iron had in the late eighteenth century supplied their own overland transport and harbour facilities. In the infancy of the coal trade in the 1830s, the landowner at Cardiff constructed the new dock which was demanded, but the iron producers constructed the railway which serviced it. By the 1880s, however, the coalowners were in the ascendent and could provide both their own dock and railway to break the monopoly of the Bute docks and the T.V.R. The initiative of the 1830s, both of the T.V.R. and the Bute estate, had enabled Cardiff to move to dominance in the coal trade during the 1840s. The dock of 1839 was a speculation in advance of trade, in the hope that coal exports would expand to fill it, and was built both earlier and on a larger scale than other docks in the area. And Cardiff's lead was confirmed by the earlier provision of a railway. While the T.V.R. was completed in 1841, the lines to Newport and Swansea were not opened until 1850 and 1860 respectively.[61] The railway and dock were not planned together – they were independent concerns with different initiators and motivations. But it was a definite policy of the Bute estate to bind the railways to the docks and to ensure that no lines were built into Cardiff's hinterland to serve other ports. However, as dock provision began to fall increasingly behind the increase in trade, competition developed for the trade of the immediate hinterland of the port. The inadequate return of the docks meant that the delay in the provision of facilities was quite understandable from the point of view of Bute, but it forced the coalowners and freighters to build their own dock and railway which took much of the increase of trade away from Cardiff and made a massive breach in the Bute policy of monopolizing the trade of the hinterland.

This process lies at the basis of the development of Cardiff. The Bute docks were the very *raison d'être* of Cardiff, but also its principal weakness. Cardiff depended upon the continued modernity and growth of its docks; the coal trade demanded efficient and cheap docks, but was not necessarily concerned that they should be at Cardiff; the Bute estate was the sole provider of docks at Cardiff but found it increasingly difficult to supply the facilities required by the coal trade and for the continued prosperity of the city. This was the central weakness of the position of Cardiff before 1914, and was well put by the *South Wales Daily News* in 1880 when it pointed out that the docks were:

> the lungs of the entire framework of this considerable town. Any constriction and congestion in that vital part is fatal to her growth and marks the hour of her certain and premature decline. . . . It is not to be supposed that the coal trade of south Wales would be fatally hindered from attaining its natural stature if Cardiff should come to a dead stop in its progress. . . . It would be hampered and for a short time disorganised, but ultimately a vent for its products would be found at some other ports in the channel.[62]

What must now be asked is why this was so: why did the docks not generate a dynamic industrial sector; why was there so little trade except coal?

3 Economic growth: obstacles and opportunities

You will forgive me for saying so; you have obtained all your prosperity from the superiority of your mineral wealth; and, no doubt, manipulation comes in as well. . . . In the main it is to the superiority of your product that your prosperity is due; but go to the Tyne, go the to Clyde, and there you will find that success is due to the superiority of workmanship, superiority of brain, and I venture to say that it is a prouder thing for the country to boast of. Why should not south Wales and Cardiff develop into one of the greatest manufacturing centres in the whole Empire? *Lloyd George speaking to Cardiff Chamber of Commerce, 1907.*[1]

Why not indeed? Contemporaries were baffled. 'Cardiff is', it was said, 'undoubtedly a unique centre for the enterprise of manufacturers or capitalists.'[2] Economic historians have expressed the same sort of perplexity as Lloyd George. Peter Mathias has remarked on 'the failure of the south Wales economy, developing largely upon a mining and heavy industry base during the nineteenth century, to specialise out into the engineering industries. . . . In some ways this is curious because mining was so dependent upon the supply of engineering skills and equipment. What', asks Mathias, 'explains this failure of spread effects from a mining base into engineering which became the spring-board for so many of the growth industries of the twentieth century?'[3] Indeed, what mining engineering Cardiff had developed went into decline in the face of competition from outside the region.[4] And not only did the town fail to become a manufacturing centre. It also failed to become a well-balanced port with a sizeable import trade and a diversified export trade. It may have been the 'coal metropolis of the world', but it was little else. The vision of Cardiff in 1869 as 'the Liverpool of the South' was never remotely approached by reality.[5] Instead, Bristol recovered from a period of stagnation and became a general import port and an industrial centre while Cardiff failed to do either. The opportunity was there but the obstacles were too great.

Here is a problem central to the economic development not only of Cardiff, but of south Wales generally. South Wales was a major producer of pig iron (later steel) and coal; but these were exported in a semi-finished or unprocessed state. They were not used within south Wales as the basis of manufacturing. Merthyr Tydfil was the major centre of the iron industry in the country up to 1850, but the metal trades were completely absent. As A. H. John has observed, 'from its beginnings, industry on the south Wales coalfield specialised in the production of capital goods and . . . attempts to establish secondary industries were unsuccessful'.[6] Lloyd George's plaint of 1907 was merely an echo of the same complaint in Merthyr 70 years earlier:

> would that we could induce our own ironmasters or stranger speculators to manufacture our iron into various useful things in our domestic economy . . . we surely ought to find the skill, the capital and enterprise for so desirable a consummation. Are we to go on in the same old-fashioned way subject to the ebb and flow of a very uncertain trade . . . a large encampment sent merely to exhaust the mine and coal and then to fall into ruin and decay. Or are we to have . . . new manufactures, a greater division of labour, fresh competition, and a boundless field for ingenuity and welfare of future generations.[7]

The answer was depressingly negative. And if Merthyr was at a disadvantage in the early nineteenth century, Cardiff in the late nineteenth century was at an even greater disadvantage simply because Merthyr *had* failed.

South Wales lacked any industrial tradition in the eighteenth century. As John has said,

> the position of south Wales contrasted sharply with that of Lancashire, for example, or the Midlands. There was nothing comparable to the long established textile industry in the neighbourhood of Manchester, Blackburn, Bolton and Rochdale or the many small metallurgical industries centred in Birmingham, Wednesbury and Dudley. The numerous small masters already in existence in these areas provided much of the enterprise for the subsequent development of their respective regions. . . . In south Wales there was no such industrial tradition.[8]

If this was so of the eighteenth century, places like Merthyr failed to do much about it in the early nineteenth, specializing as they did in goods characterized by bulk rather than craftsmanship. Further, development was dominated by highly integrated firms – Dowlais, Cyfarthfa and the like – which possibly limited the growth of other and more diversified activities.[9] While areas such as Tyneside and the Midlands could go on in the nineteenth century developing the industrial tradition and firmly establishing an industrial structure based upon the mid-Victorian transformation in the heavy industries, south Wales was left behind. Cardiff in the late nineteenth century could not break with the past of the region. This has, of course, raised a whole range of questions about the regional economy, and it is time that the analysis of John was carried into the late nineteenth century. While this cannot be done here, it is believed that an answer in terms of Cardiff is also largely an answer for the region. When the need to import ores led the Merthyr ironmasters to build a new plant at Cardiff in the 1880s, it was expected that the town could become a shipbuilding centre.[10] It did not, and as at Merthyr the products of the plant were sent elsewhere for manufacturing into finished products. An explanation of this failure is also in large part an explanation of why south Wales was unable to follow Tyneside, Teesside, or Clydeside, and become the centre of engineering and shipbuilding and the metal trades. This is the central issue to resolve.

I

The trade of the port was always narrowly based. In 1939, E. L. Chappell could look back over the years of the depression and rue the fact that 'few seaports have been developed in so lop-sided a fashion'.[11] What was the nature of this over-commitment, and what was the explanation?

Total trade was overwhelmingly dominated by coal exports. Coal accounted for a minimum of 70·1 per cent of trade in 1871, and from 1875 to 1914 remained above three-quarters of total trade, touching a peak of 82·3 per cent in 1885. Total imports accounted for a maximum of 21·6 per cent of trade in 1902. During the late nineteenth century there had been a slight upward trend in the share of imports, from around 15 per cent in the mid-70s to around 20 per cent after 1900. However, the character of Cardiff's trade remained essentially unchanged, as an export port which exported little but coal. Table 15 shows the distribution of trade at a number of dates. There were two major categories of imports – iron ore, and timber and pitwood – whilst the only other large export, after the decline in the iron industry, was coal in another form, as patent fuel. Exports of general merchandise were negligible. The over-commitment of Cardiff's trade to one sector is indubitable.

On the face of it, Cardiff was missing an opportunity. Most ships were entering Cardiff in ballast, having unloaded elsewhere, as the figures in table 16 show. Typically a ship unloaded at Bristol or London or Liverpool or Amsterdam and then moved to Cardiff in ballast and with a skeleton crew to take on a cargo of coal. The availability of coal as an outward cargo was a factor of some importance for the operation of the British shipping industry. What chagrined contemporaries was that Cardiff itself derived little benefit.

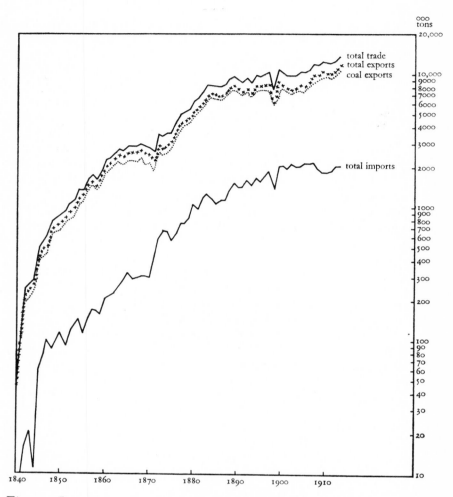

Figure 3. Imports, exports, and total trade, Bute docks, 1840–1913 (source: C.C.L. Bute XI 56; Annual Reports, Cardiff Chamber of Commerce).

Table 15   Percentage distribution of the trade of Bute docks

	Total imports	Iron ore	Iron	Timber	Pitwood	Grain, flour	General merchandise
1850	12·9	7·2	0·4	1·9	1·1	–	2·3
1860	9·3	5·1	0·3	0·9	1·3	–	1·7
1870	10·7	4·2	0·4	1·4	2·6	–	2·0
1880	16·6	8·3	0·4	1·5	3·1	1·2	2·1
1890	15·5	6·2	0·2	1·4	4·3	1·9	1·3
1900	20·3	7·3	0·3	1·7	5·4	2·2	3·3
1910	15·2	5·4	0·6	1·3	2·5	2·9	2·5

	Total exports	Coal	Patent fuel	Iron	General merchandise
1850	87·1	75·7	–	10·7	0·7
1860	90·7	80·6	0·4	9·2	0·5
1870	89·3	75·0	2·8	10·8	0·7
1880	83·4	77·0	2·6	3·2	0·7
1890	84·5	80·5	2·5	0·8	0·7
1900	79·7	73·3	4·1	1·2	1·2
1910	84·8	78·0	4·1	1·1	1·5

Source: Based upon data in C.C.L. Bute XI 56 and Annual Reports of Cardiff Chamber of Commerce.

Table 16   Tonnage of shipping entering port of Cardiff with cargo and in ballast

	1887	1897	1907
With cargo	1,032,818	1,655,504	1,593,015
In ballast	4,321,608	7,081,308	9,070,713

Note: the Port, to which official figures refer, included Penarth and Barry.

Source: Annual Reports, Cardiff Chamber of Commerce.

In 1913 coal employed five million tons of tramp shipping, of which three million tons were British. This amounted to 25 per cent of all British shipping or about 40 per cent of British tramp shipping. The coal trade provided outward cargoes for tramps bringing home bulky commodities, giving a competitive advantage to British tramps and leading to lower freight rates.[12] As D. A. Thomas explained,

more than four-fifths of the weight of our exports consists of coal; without it the great bulk of the shipping bringing corn, cotton, wood, wool, sugar etc. to our shores would be compelled perforce to clear without cargo and in ballast. No outward freights would be earned in the majority of instances, and, consequently, in order to earn profit, or, for the matter of that to make both ends meet, a very much heavier freight would have to be charged on articles of import, which would thereby be heavily increased in price to the consumer. Indeed, it is hardly conceivable that our foreign trade could have reached its present dimensions had it not been for the outward freight provided by coal.

The rise of coal exports had changed the relationship between the tonnage of imports and exports. Other British exports had a high value in relation to their weight, whereas imports were generally bulky in relation to their value. In the early nineteenth century, ships had entered with a cargo and departed light, so that in 1840 for every 100 tons of shipping leaving with a cargo, 124 tons entered. By the late nineteenth century this had been reversed. In 1900, for every 100 tons of shipping leaving with a cargo, 83 tons entered. This change was due to the rise of coal exports.[13]

Many expected that Cardiff would benefit greatly as a result, becoming a leading import and general export port. They certainly had a point, for Cardiff seemed to have a considerable advantage over, say, Bristol or Southampton, due to 'the fact that coal offers a bulky outward cargo which is considered part of the voyage, the result being that cereals, timber and other commodities which this country lacks is brought home at an exceptionally cheap rate'. It was claimed in 1883 that if goods were imported through Cardiff rather than taken elsewhere and obliging the ship to move to south Wales to load, there could be a saving of 20 per cent on freight. Also, there was the attraction that a ship bound for, say, the East Indies with a general cargo would require 1,000 tons of bunker coal and it would be a benefit if both the cargo and the bunkers could be loaded at one port. What could not be understood was why in practice the imports were more often than not taken to Bristol or London or Liverpool rather than to Cardiff.[14] Most tramps, whether Cardiff-owned or not, did not return directly to Cardiff. Having unloaded the coal, they had to find a return bulk cargo and take it where the charterer wished. Around the turn of the century, perhaps two-thirds of south Wales coal went to the Mediterranean, and about half of the tonnage involved relied upon Russian grain for the return cargo. D. A. Thomas pointed out that whole fleets of steamers were engaged in taking coal from south Wales on a round voyage, part of which was made in ballast. Coal was taken to the Mediterranean, and grain from the Black Sea to, say, Hamburg or London, from whence the ship returned for another cargo of coal. Or coal was taken to the Mediterranean, and a light voyage made to the U.S.A. or South America for grain for Europe.[15] Clearly, Cardiff could not have taken the whole of the return cargoes of grain and other produce. What *is* surprising is that it took so little, not supplying even the needs of the hinterland.[16]

The complaints of the timber trade are a good illustration of some of the problems arising from the congestion of the docks which were encountered by import merchants. In 1874, William Alexander, one of the largest timber importers, outlined his method of working. Timber was unloaded by throwing it out of the ship into the dock, where it was made into rafts which were, after three to six days in the water, towed to the Glamorganshire Canal where Alexander had his yard. The timber was then lifted and stored. The timber trade was severely handicapped by the lack of wharfage and timber ponds. No merchants had wharfs on the dock side, which was restricted to the coal trade. The cost of moving timber, either by water or truck, to a distant yard added 10s. a standard to costs. Further, it took three to four weeks to unload a ship at Cardiff compared with six days at Gloucester or Bristol. But in view of the declining profitability of the docks and the constant demand for new investment for the coal trade, it was unlikely that the timber merchants would get their wish – a completely separate dock for timber, with a large timber pond.[17] As one timber merchant remarked in 1883, Sir W. T. Lewis's attitude to the timber trade was unsympathetic but understandable:

> I gathered from him that the difficulty was in a great measure that the timber ships occupied the docks much longer than the ships that came in to load coal, and that as they did not pay as well as coal ships, it was hardly competent for them in their endeavour to do the best they could with Lord Bute's property, to provide us accommodation for floating timber in the docks, which was wanted still more for the coal trade of Cardiff.[18]

Merchants in other trades were in general agreement that the benefits of a ready outward cargo were rendered void by the congestion of the docks. It took three weeks to load a steamer for Bombay at Cardiff, compared with three days at London or Liverpool, which outweighed any advantage to be gained in loading bunkers at Cardiff. It was felt that the warehouses built by Bute were quite marginal to the problem: they needed quay space provided with open sheds. As it was, goods had to be left out in the rain, mud and coal dust. However, it was impossible for quay space to be withdrawn from the coal trade. The feeling was

> that greater accommodation ought to be given to the import trade and by and by we shall require a new import dock altogether. It is impossible to carry on the import trade at Cardiff, jumbling up imports with coal. The rush is so great in the coal docks that it is no use persons importing or attempting to import stuff into Cardiff.[19]

It was not that the Bute estate was hostile to a more diversified trade.

Quite the contrary. In 1872 the Bute estate sponsored the South Wales Atlantic Steamship Company which had five ships by 1874.

> From the other side of the Atlantic we may expect to receive large quantities of breadstuffs, and as import docks and warehouses commensurate with the demand likely to arise from consignees and others, will doubtless be brought into existence, an era of unparalleled commercial success may justly be predicated for this portion of the principality.

But in 1875 the company collapsed in acrimony.[20] The estate certainly saw the dangers of being so reliant upon only one item of trade. It was for this reason that £60,000 was given to save the Cardiff Milling Company; that cattle lairs were built in 1907, and £50,000 spent on refrigeration in 1913, to encourage the meat trade; that Sir W. T. Lewis had a vision of integrated steelmaking and shipbuilding; that warehouses were built in 1861, a pier in 1868, and improved passenger facilities in the 1890s. The downturn of trade in the 1870s and then the development of Barry impelled the Bute estate to consider how to widen trade.[21] While there is no doubting the desire to encourage non-coal trade, the attitudes of the merchants show quite clearly that Bute initiatives were marginal, and that effective action was impossible. Merchants were quite clear what would be effective, 'that the export and import trades of the port should be done in separate docks', which would end delays and provide adequate facilities.[22] The financial position of the undertaking made this quite unacceptable. A merchant put the position well in 1891:

> the export of coal on a given surface of dock area brought in a larger amount of money than the importation of goods for the same area. That was a fact which they had to admit, and it was pressed upon them that, as a commercial transaction, the docks had to be worked so as to earn the greatest amount of money. . . . While the money earned by an import dock would not be anything like that earned by exporting coal, the number of men employed in the import trade would be ten or twenty times as many as in the export. They would therefore have to face the fact that an import dock was absolutely necessary and that such a dock would not be made by a dock owner as a matter of investment simply.[23]

The dilemma noted in 1891 was crucial. Cardiff needed an import dock, but it was not in the interest of the only investor in docks in Cardiff – the Bute estate – to provide it. The Bute estate was increasingly reluctant to invest in new docks, and in consequence the existing docks (or rather the more modern docks) were perpetually crowded, leading to delay and added expense for shipowners and merchants. If the Bute estate wanted a large import trade, this would increase the time a ship spent in dock discharging, so increasing the pressure on accommodation and requiring a new dock that much sooner. This was the paradox. Imports might be desired to help pay for the unremunerative docks, but would in themselves require a further increase in dock investments which was not welcomed. Further, the provision of warehouses such as at Bristol might cost as much as a dock. The Bute aim of increasing imports was thus fundamentally limited. The flaw in the local economy was that the outlook of Bute and of the town did not coincide – the one concerned for the return on the dock investment, the other with the effects upon the town's economy. The provision of docks by an individual was an obvious weakness. He could not consider the economics of the docks for the producers (as the Barry promoters did) nor the benefits for the town (as the local traders conceivably would have done if there had been a harbour trust). Unlike Bristol, say, or Liverpool, the agency providing the docks did not need to consider the general interests of the town. Bute interest might be to encourage general trade, but the desire for a rapid turn-around of shipping meant that imports were not altogether welcomed, the pressure of the coal trade made it impossible to withdraw quay space, and the financial position made a separate import dock out of the question. The benefit of a readily available outward cargo was nullified.

The Bute estate could thus only take action short of what might have been effective in permitting Cardiff to break into the established trading pattern. And even if it had been possible to make the Bute docks as efficient as its rivals, was the ready availability of coal as an outward cargo in itself a large enough incentive to induce traders to abandon Bristol or Liverpool in order to obtain cheaper freights at Cardiff? There is room for doubt, for it could be argued that parity alone would not have been enough when other ports already had the specialist facilities. The mercantile structure had already been firmly established – Bristol had the expertise to deal with sugar and tobacco, Liverpool with cotton – and it was no easy task for Cardiff to insert itself within an already long-established pattern. Against this it could be argued that if Southampton could succeed then so could Cardiff. As it was, the question was never given a chance to arise and it remains in the realms of speculation – the congestion of the docks and Bute's reluctance to alleviate it always more than offset the advantages of ready outward cargoes, making it cheaper to unload elsewhere and move to Cardiff in ballast.

The only potentially effective action, which might have removed the question from the realms of speculation to fact, would have been to form a harbour trust. The corporation discussed this very thoroughly on a number of occasions, with the definite intention of using it to widen the trade of the docks, to replace coal by commodities which would have a greater impact upon investment and employment in the town. However, the expense meant that on each occasion the scheme was abandoned.[24] In the absence of such an initiative, there was little that the Cardiff Importers, Exporters and Manufacturers Association of 1894, the Import Section of the Chamber of Commerce of 1897, and the corporation's Development Committee of 1908, could do.[25] No fundamental breakthrough was made. It was Bristol, not Cardiff, which eventually found the impetus to provide the necessary import docks at Avonmouth and Portishead. Cardiff's hope of becoming the 'Liverpool of the South' was not realized. It was unfortunately true that 'the Cardiff docks do . . . a very small trade for the city of Cardiff. The Cardiff docks are the group of docks for the valleys of Glamorgan . . . [but] the actual trade done by the docks for Cardiff is nothing compared with the interest of the Glamorganshire valleys in the port.'[26]

II

The docks had a limited multiplier effect. The industrial base remained narrow, it failed to become self-generating, and declined in the inter-war period. It is this limited and narrow linkage between the docks and the local economy which must now be analysed.

Of course, linkages were not wholly absent. Obviously, railway rolling stock had to be built and repaired. In 1896 it was calculated that 3,000 men were employed in this activity in Cardiff and district, most of them actually in Cardiff. Again, firms developed to make ropes and cables for shipping and mines, and foundries were established to make marine and constructional castings. The Tharsis Company opened a plant in 1873 at the docks, to extract copper and other ores from Spanish pyrites. Another dock-based industry, utilizing imports, was flour-milling. The most important firm was Spillers, which up to 1854 had been a Somersetshire concern with three water-mills and a small steam-mill. In 1854 it was decided to establish a steam-mill at Cardiff docks, and eventually three mills were built, capable of supplying a population of 600,000. Subsequently, two bakeries were established to make sea, dog, and fancy biscuits. The only industry directly related to the coal trade was the manufacture of patent fuel by mixing pitch and coal. This was first attempted in the 1850s, but really became efficient in the 1860s. By 1882 there were four works grouped together in north Cardiff along the canal which was used to transport the product to the docks. Patent fuel provided from 3 per cent of exports in the 1870s to 5 per cent after 1900.[27] In addition to these industries, there were two of far greater importance – steel production and ship repair. Many contemporaries thought that they could and should combine to form a shipbuilding industry. This, however, never happened and a self-sufficient independent industrial base never emerged. Generally, the industries declined with the coal trade and never became an alternative economic base.

It became increasingly obvious that the iron industry on the northern outcrop of the coalfield was in an impossibly high-cost location in the second half of the nineteenth century. Local ore deposits were becoming inadequate by the 1820s, and ore had to be imported from the Forest of Dean, Cornwall and Cumberland. By 1872, the Dowlais Iron Company's annual import was 82,619 tons of Spanish, 34,909 of Cumberland, and 71,306 of Northamptonshire ore. Then in 1873 the D.I.C. took a quarter share in the Orconera Iron Company, which started to supply Spanish ore in 1876. By 1881 the D.I.C.'s annual import was 228,751 tons of Spanish, 11,266 tons of Cumberland, and 9,760 tons of Northampton-shire ore. This need to import ore had considerable repercussions upon the competitive position of the south Wales industry. In 1877 it was cal-culated that the transport of iron ore contributed 13s. 6d. a ton to the cost of south Wales iron, compared with 2s. 9d. in Staffordshire. A move to the coast would at least save freight on iron ore between the port and Merthyr and the return journey by the manufactured iron, which in 1877 amounted to 2s. 3·45d. and 2s. 9·2d. per ton respectively. On the other hand, coal had to be brought to the coast, and wages would be higher. On balance the D.I.C. decided to build a plant at Cardiff, and construction started in 1888. Production of iron commenced in 1891, and in 1895 open-hearth steel was added.[28]

This was the only major industry to be developed at Cardiff, and even then its multiplier effect was weak, for the iron and steel produced was not used in manufactures within the town. The plant became part of the Guest, Keen and Nettlefold conglomerate in 1901–2, and the actual manufacturing sectors were retained in the Midlands. It was only in the 1930s that some manufacture of tubes, screws, and nails was introduced. Until then, all the basic pig iron and steel was sent elsewhere. The plant was in any case a great disappointment even though it was one of the most up-to-date in the country. For the first 15 years or so, costs were actually *higher* at Cardiff than at Dowlais, with its old plant and high-cost location. In 1904 the cost of producing a ton of pig at Dowlais was £2 5s. 9d. against £2 7s. 2d. at Cardiff, while steel f.o.b. at the docks cost £4 2s. 2d. if sent from Dowlais, compared with £4 4s. 7d. from the Cardiff plant on the dock side. This raises the vexed question of the performance of the British iron and steel industry before 1914. There are certainly grounds on which to criticize D.I.C. management. The problem was that the general management remained at Dowlais which hampered the Cardiff managers who found, for example, that Dowlais always had prior claim on ore. Neither did the Cardiff officials know how to get the best out of the plant. Eventually an American manager was appointed in 1902 and by 1908 with efficient use of the plant costs fell markedly below those at Dowlais. However, the available records cover little but managerial performance and do not deal with a number of other potentially relevant factors such as the costs of transporting coal to Cardiff relative to transporting ore to Dowlais; the possible under-utilization of capacity due to inadequate demand; the level of wages; and any differences in technology.[29]

One of the motivations for the Cardiff steel plant was the expected development of a shipbuilding industry, on the lines, say, of Middlesbrough. This had seemed a possibility in the 1870s. In 1872 one local company launched a steamship, and another company followed in 1873. The feeling was that 'it will be a remarkable thing if ere long . . . [Cardiff] does not rank amongst the great shipbuilding ports'. These ambitions were periodically revived in the 1880s, and both the D.I.C. and the Bute estate were prepared to give the matter serious consideration. In fact, the highest tonnage launched in any year was 1,893 in 1890, and up to 1913 only on seven occasions did launchings top 100 tons, and never again 1,000 tons. This was something which perplexed contemporaries such as Lloyd George, who could not understand why Belfast with imported steel and coal, could become a shipbuilding centre, while Cardiff with readily available supplies, could not.[30]

Cardiff *was* a major ship-repairing centre, probably the most important in the country. Ships arriving at Cardiff in ballast could conveniently enter dry dock for repairs before obtaining a cargo, which would be readily available when repairs were completed. Also, local shipowners had a large interest in ship repair firms. The industry was transformed in the 1880s, when the need to enlarge the dry docks led to joint stock companies taking over from existing firms, with completely new concerns also emerging. This largely occurred between 1881 and 1884, with local shipowners in the forefront. In addition to the firms owning dry docks, there were a number of concerns which had only engineering shops and who used either the public dry docks or made some arrangement with one of the dry dock companies in order to carry out bottom repairs. There was often tension between the two sets of firms, with the less capital-intensive 'outside' firms undercutting the dry dock owners. The

Table 17   Trade of the Cardiff dry docks

	Ships	Gross register tons
1907	1,057	2,855,039
1910	1,035	2,718,913
1912	1,037	2,896,706

Source: *C.J.C.*, 26 January 1909, 1 February 1911, 1 January 1913.

capital of the dry dock companies was quite large. Of the firms floated
in 1881–4, the original capital ranged from £60,000 to £200,000. The
original capital of the outside firms was less, usually between £15,000 and
£20,000. The total trade handled by the dry docks was considerable, as is
shown in table 17. The value of this work was put at £1m. in 1907.
There is no denying the scale and importance of the ship repair trade.[31]

It is, however, wrong to argue that the ship repair trade was a 'supplement to the coal trade' so that Cardiff was no longer dependent upon one
staple.[32] Such a claim was misguided. As the experience of the 1920s and
1930s was to show, ship repairing fell off in step with coal. Without coal
to provide the attractive cargo, there was little incentive for ships to use
the Cardiff dry docks. Independently of the coal trade, the ship repair
industry could not provide a dynamic sector for the economy of Cardiff,
nor could such activities as wagon repair. Neither did the steel works
provide a genuine alternative base. The iron and steel was, as in the case
of Merthyr, sent elsewhere.

The manufacturing base of Cardiff was virtually non-existent. It is a
valid question to ask why this was so. The development of an industrial
sector was not so unlikely as to make the question absurd. For example,
when the Windsor estate developed Grangetown after 1857 it was intended to be an industrial suburb of Cardiff, and plenty of land was made
available. An abortive attempt was made to establish an ironworks, one
of a series of futile attempts made to start metal trades in the town.
Again, at one time Cammell Laird was considering a shipbuilding plant
at Cardiff to employ 6,000.[33] The *Cardiff Journal of Commerce* thought 'it
has always been a matter of great wonder that the manufacturing interests
of the country have not taken advantage of the opportunity of establishing their works' at Cardiff. There should be not just imports but a broadly-
based manufacturing sector. 'Why cannot we have sugar refineries as well
as Bristol, or copper works as at Swansea, or cotton manufactories as in
the neighbourhood of Liverpool?'[34] Why, for example, could Cardiff
not follow the same path of development as the previous major export
coalfield, that of the north east? Why could the area of the Taff not develop
in the late nineteenth century as Tyneside had in the early nineteenth
century?

III

This raises the whole question of the nature of the urban growth process. Some current models portray growth as a circular and cumulative
process.[35] The introduction of an industry into a town leads to the
growth of linked activities, to the expansion of public utilities and transport, to new construction activity, and to various tertiary activities.
There are also enhanced possibilities for the formation of new industries,

especially as the local population and the market increase in size. This sort of self-contained process can fit some examples of nineteenth-century British urban growth. Nottingham is one.[36] Lace and hosiery were introduced into the town. This had a multiplier effect, leading to construction, to textile machinery firms, and to the development of tertiary activities to serve the local population, including such large concerns as Boots. Innovation occurred and new industries emerged, in particular Raleigh in cycles and Players in tobacco. The model appears to fit Nottingham, forming a continuous and self-contained process. But what of, say, Merthyr Tydfil? Iron furnaces were introduced to exploit the local charcoal and iron ore, and these grew so that the town became the largest iron producer in the country. But the multiplier was very weak from the iron industry to the rest of the urban economy. There was no linked industry, no diversification, no broadly-based manufacturing. The cumulative and circular process was aborted, although in theory it should have been very strong.

The weakness of such theories is in the failure to consider the supply side, and in particular the attraction of factors from outside, for 'factor flows are at the heart of the growth process in open economies such as the city'.[37] The supply side is certainly important. In the case of labour, the historical pattern of development of industry is important for the character of the local labour force. At Coventry, skills developed in the ribbon and watch industries provided the basis for cycles and the motor industry.[38] On the other hand, skills developed in heavy industries might not be suitable for new, light industries, or wages might be too high. Merthyr had no industrial tradition before the advent of the iron industry which trained its own men. This was worthwhile because of the great advantages of the location for the iron industry, but for any other industry the effort of getting men at Merthyr and training them would be too great, and the industrial skills which the iron industry had created were not of much use. As far as capital is concerned, local supplies must be available for small or new firms. This in part depends upon how the local wealthy react and upon what local agencies exist. For the development of the iron industry in Merthyr, capital had to be brought in from outside by men with contacts in Bristol and London. No local financial agencies developed, and the ironmasters on the whole took their capital out of the town, and did not seek to encourage the development of other industries.[39] This links closely with the third factor of production, enterprise. The social structure might be more or less conducive to the development of entrepreneurs. In the case of Merthyr, the relative absence of social groupings between the ironworkers and four or five capitalist families was a constraining influence, even if capital had been available. Finally there is land: the wealth of the hinterland, the cost of sites and services.

Merthyr, with a thinly populated and poor hinterland and geographically isolated, was in a weak position for the development of a large service sector and general manufacturing industry.

If this factor endowment approach can explain why the initial growth stimulus at Merthyr proved to be so weak, can the same sort of analysis be applied to Cardiff? Contemporaries certainly pointed to disadvantages in respect of each factor of production to explain the absence of ship-building specifically and of manufacturing generally. The Liberals stressed the non-availability of land, blaming the policy of the Bute estate of short leases for industrial land. It is true that Bute industrial leases were generally for 63 years, but the estate was willing – as in the case of the D.I.C. – to extend the period to 99 years and to give reasonable terms. It does not seem likely that Cammell Laird were driven from Cardiff by the terms of the lease offered, as was claimed by the Liberals. In any case, the policy of the Windsor estate was to encourage 'local industrial establishments . . . giving employment to numbers of men and without them Cardiff and more especially the Grange estate cannot become permanently prosperous'.[40] And the hinterland of the town was populous and prosperous so that market thresholds were being passed for local industries. The land argument does not appear to be an adequate explanation.

It was easy to blame labour and the unions. The dry dock owners put the onus on high wages and union obstructiveness for the failure of shipbuilding to develop. Wage rates in ship repairing were certainly higher than in shipbuilding, by perhaps a third, and with strong craft unions this would certainly have caused problems.[41] However, the argument about the lack of existing industrial skills applies less to Cardiff than to Merthyr earlier in the nineteenth century. Engineering skills *were* present, having been developed in ship repair, in the railway and wagon workshops. Again, this is not an adequate explanation.

Another popular complaint was the lack of capital and of entrepreneurs: 'the real want is capital. . . . Capitalists are wanted to build cotton mills, sugar refineries, general hardware factories, woollen and linen looms, and large warehouses for the storing of imported produce.'[42] Unlike Merthyr in the early nineteenth century, Cardiff did not have a social structure grossly unfavourable for the provision of capital and capitalists. It was rather the uses to which both were put. There was not the simple social structure of Merthyr, making it difficult to obtain capital and making the emergence of entrepreneurs difficult. Men did emerge – it was the avenues they chose which was the problem: 'The local man has given his attention to the local staple, and may not be seduced into a consideration of anything else. As a point of fact he came here intent on coal and coal only. For the matter of that, he is making a sufficiently good thing of it.'[43] This is certainly true. Men moved to Cardiff to engage in the coal trade and shipping. Often they left once they had made their fortune. Usually, they had no ties with the locality or town. They had not grown out of a previous industrial tradition in the area, able to develop shipbuilding from this existing structure and their involvement in it as on the Tyne. The coal and shipping trades did attract men from outside, and gave opportunities for those in the town. But there was no existing small-scale industrial base from which men could emerge and which they could expand and adapt.

The argument therefore returns to the industrial tradition of south Wales, stressing that rather than the *absence* of capital and entrepreneurs, or even of a skilled and adaptable workforce. It was this consideration which made Cardiff an unsuitable site for shipbuilding and other industrial developments. The nature of the shipbuilding industry must be understood as it had developed by the end of the nineteenth century:

> the construction of ships had become an intricate business, a combination of many industrial processes, not all of which were carried on in the shipyard, which is generally regarded as constituting the industry. Many industries, distinct in ownership and even remote in their location, were concerned with the production of ships. . . the tendency for the shipbuilder to concentrate on producing the hull, and for the yards to become the assembly point for component parts of machinery and equipment provided by sub-contractors outside the industry became more and more pronounced.[44]

The development of shipbuilding was much more than building a yard and slipway at Cardiff. The whole range of industries required to assemble a ship had also to be developed. It was this industrial base which south Wales as a whole lacked, and which Clydeside and Tyneside and Teesside had. The south Wales economy consisted of mining coal, making steel or tinplates, but not in using the basic products in manufacturing. This was essentially the reason why a steel works and a ship repairing industry in Cardiff could not lead to a shipbuilding industry. In many ways Cardiff was better placed than Merthyr had been in the supply of resources – but its development in the late nineteenth century was fundamentally constrained by the earlier failure of Merthyr to break with the established pattern.

By the late nineteenth century it was really too late for Cardiff to break with a pattern by then even more firmly established, and develop a diversified trade and widely based manufacturing sector. It is noticeable that urban growth in the second half of the nineteenth century was not in industrial towns but suburbs. The urban pattern established during the industrial revolution, based upon the technology of steam and iron and steel, broadly survived until the old staples declined, a new technology developed, and there was a switch of population from the areas reliant upon the old staples to the Midlands and South-East. The growth of Cardiff was too late to break into the industrial pattern existing at the time of its growth, with a more or less fully developed technology. It is true that Nottingham could in the late nineteenth century develop a cycle industry, but this could grow out of the textile machine manufacture for the long-established lace and hosiery trades. As the industrial pattern and the urban pattern dependent on this became established in the nineteenth century, it became difficult for a newcomer to break into the stream of development and adaptation. There had first of all to be fundamental technological discontinuity. This is to return to an argument presented when explaining the lopsided trade of the port, that once the specialist merchants and their institutions had been established in one port, it was not easy for another port to take its place. Cardiff might have developed earlier than other ports on the coast; for a large and self-sufficient industrial structure it was not early enough, as the different experience of Sunderland and Newcastle indicated.

IV

What has so far been left out of the analysis of the economy of Cardiff is the sector which became dominant during and since the interwar period – the service sector associated with Cardiff's role as a regional capital. The way in which Cardiff stole a march on the other members of the urban hierarchy around 1840 did lead to the development of an alternative function for the town: it became the regional capital of south Wales. The docks might have lost their initial advantage and might have been inadequate to support diversified trade and manufacture, but the lead had been held for long enough for Cardiff to become the 'mother city' of the area and to maintain that function as the docks declined first relatively and then absolutely. Cardiff's rivals as ports never seriously challenged for the role of regional capital.

Cardiff, by the time the rivalry started around 1890, had become the commercial centre of a very large part of the coalfield, and even when the actual coal was shipped at Barry, the commercial work was still done at Cardiff and none of the merchants and shipowners moved their offices. The Cardiff Exchange which opened in 1886 became and remained the centre of the south Wales coal trade, with the commercial offices concentrated around it. Increasingly, not just the marketing but the whole business of production and sale was run from offices at Cardiff. In addition, the headquarters of bodies such as the South Wales Miners Federation and the Monmouthshire and South Wales Coal Owners Association were located in Cardiff, and the town provided many professional services to the region as a whole.

Cardiff was also a retailing and wholesaling centre for a wider area. As in most towns in this period, large stores developed and a specialist retail area was created. There were two major department stores, those of James Howell and David Morgan. Howell set up business in 1865, Morgan in 1879, and both gradually extended their shops to cover whole blocks, transforming their businesses into department stores serving the region.[45] Other more specialist stores also developed, and the central business district underwent transformation particularly from the mid-1880s as large hotels and office and shop blocks replaced the old housing and the courts of the mid-nineteenth-century city. A mixed residential area gave way to specialized commercial use. One interesting feature of this was the building of shopping arcades to increase the frontage available, possibly exploiting the long, narrow, medieval burgage plots. The first of importance opened in 1858, and was followed by four in the mid-1880s, and others in 1896–9 and 1901. These arcades provided – and still do – small units with low rents and rateable value for small, specialist shops which might not otherwise survive in the town centre. At the same time the main streets were being rebuilt on a larger scale, and these increasingly became the preserve of large units or of multiples. A contrast was created between the arcades and the streets which is still marked. On the fringes of the retail centre, wholesale firms were set up to supply Cardiff and the valleys. The best example of this was the warehouse of the Co-operative Wholesale Society which opened in 1915 and which catered for the whole coalfield.[46]

It was Cardiff's role as a regional commercial and service centre which became increasingly important as the port declined.[47] The initiative of the marquis of Bute and the T.V.R. in the 1830s had enabled Cardiff to achieve leadership in the local urban hierarchy, and while it failed to diversify in trade or industry, and the docks failed to meet the demands put upon them, Cardiff was able to retain its position at the head of the urban hierarchy and make that its prime function. Ironically, Cardiff's failure before 1914 meant it was less committed than Sunderland or Newcastle to the old technology and was less affected by the depression of the inter-war period, when the failure to develop shipbuilding seemed less a cause for regret.

4 Commerce:
coal merchants and shipowners

So far attention has concentrated upon why the process of growth should have been restricted, how Cardiff could become 'coal metropolis' but nothing else. It is now necessary to turn from what might have been to the sectors which *did* dominate the town's development. How did the 'coal metropolis' go about its business? Obviously it is vital to analyse the operation of the coal trade. And if the existence of coal as a ready outward freight did not encourage the development of a general import trade as many expected, what it did encourage was the ownership of tramp shipping. Coal and shipping are the key to understanding both the economy and society of Cardiff.

I

On the whole, the businesses of coal and shipping were distinct. An analysis of the commercial directories gives the pattern shown in table 18. Shipowners would, not surprisingly, also function as ship brokers,

Table 18   Mercantile structure of Cardiff, 1882, 1889, and 1900

	1882	1889	1900
One function			
ship broker	29	43	50
coal factor	28	29	76
timber importer	17	15	19
shipowner	12	22	43
Two functions			
shipowner, broker	24	26	18
ship broker, coal factor	14	25	76
timber importer, shipowner	2	1	—
timber importer, ship broker	2	3	3
coal factor, timber importer	2	1	8
coal factor, shipowner	—	2	—
Three functions			
ship owner, broker, coal factor	19	13	14
timber importer, shipowner, coal factor	1	—	—
timber importer, ship broker, coal factor	1	3	10
Four functions	1	2	1

Source: *Cardiff Tide Tables and Almanac*, 1883, 1890, 1901.

for the expertise involved was the same – 24 per cent did so in 1900. There was also a growing link between the two middleman functions of ship broker and coal factor. In 1900, 41 per cent of all coal factors acted as ship brokers, and 44 per cent of ship brokers as coal factors. But the connexion between coal factors and ship*owners* was minimal or non-existent. This is confirmed by comparing the list of ownership of shipping with the tonnage of coal and coke exported by merchants and coal owners as given by the Bute authorities. The conclusion to emerge from table 19 is that not many firms appeared in both guises, and, if they did, they were either important in one and marginal in the other, or small to middling in both. Essentially, shipowning and coal exporting and owning did

Table 19   *Shipowners and coal shippers, 1882, 1886, and 1889*

1882	shipowners		coal shippers
Number	50		46
Median (tons)	2,172		59,168
Mean (tons)	2,731		107,294
Common cases (tons)	1,137	and	3,177
	469	and	581,702
	2,292	and	4,323
1886			
Number	56		64
Median (tons)	2,204		34,573
Mean (tons)	3,069		98,629
Common cases (tons)	5,378	and	10,197
	6,281	and	47,850
	2,723	and	9,595
	2,291	and	15,752
	620	and	776,815
1889			
Number	66		69
Median (tons)	2,940		54,776
Mean (tons)	5,531		110,960
Common cases (tons)	23,252	and	21,969
	7,433	and	90,123
	2,393	and	30,022
	6,112	and	39,682
	1,420	and	25,809
	2,940	and	733,875
	570	and	80,122

Source: *Cardiff Tide Tables and Almanac*, 1883, 1887, 1890; C.C.L. Bute XI 56.

not form an interconnected, unified élite. The commercial élite was divided internally, although, as will appear in a later chapter, it was also as a whole set apart from the town, which was of great significance for the political structure.

What was the internal structure of the two segments of the economy, how concentrated or fragmented, open or closed? The Bute authorities' listing of tonnages of coal exported by coal owners and shippers gives the distribution shown in table 20. The coal trade was certainly highly concentrated by the 1880s, and as table 21 shows this was also true of the shipping industry where there was a very marked increase in the degree of concentration by 1905.

Table 20   Percentage of coal exported by largest shippers

	1882	1889	1908	1911
Largest 5	38·5	35·4	35·2	34·5
Next largest 5	16·2	16·3	17·8	20·7
Next largest 5	11·6	11·6	9·3	10·4
Largest 15	66·4	63·4	62·4	65·7

Source: C.C.L. Bute XI 56, IV 12(b).

Table 21   Percentage of tonnage owned by largest shipowners

	1881	1885	1890	1895	1900	1905
Largest 5	34·3	36·3	38·2	41·9	53·6	55·4
Next largest 5	21·2	16·5	20·7	17·7	13·8	17·5
Next largest 5	14·1	10·7	10·9	10·5	8·8	10·0
Largest 15	69·6	63·5	69·8	70·2	76·2	82·9

Source: *Cardiff Tide Tables and Almanac*, 1882–1906.

Both were highly concentrated, and this will be of importance when the social structure of the town is analysed. It is important, however, to probe beneath the façade of the statistics to appreciate the tensions and changes they mask. This will be attempted in the next two sections, taking first coal and then shipping.

II

The list of coal exports given by the Bute authorities covered both coal *owners* and *shippers*, that is, both producers and middlemen. The changing relationship between the two is the crux of any analysis of the coal trade. Essentially, the trend was a drawing together of the two functions of producing and merchanting. This operated in two ways: a movement from merchanting back into production, particularly in the initial development of the coalfield; and a movement forward from production to complete control of marketing, particularly in the latter part of the period.

In the years up to about 1870, it was possible for coal exporters to move back from their middleman function to own and produce coal on their own behalf. Two examples may be given. In 1828, George Insole had opened a shipping office at Cardiff, specializing in coal. The pressure of demand forced him to obtain an assured supply, and he decided to produce his own coal. He took his first mineral lease in 1832, but the crucial development was the decision to enter the Rhondda in 1844.[1] The same sort of process occurred in the case of Cory Brothers, which was to be one of the dominant coal-owning companies. The concern was started by Captain Richard Cory who, after trading in small vessels between Cardiff and the West Country, decided to set up business at the sea-lock, supplying ships' stores. In 1844 his sons entered the firm as Richard Cory and Sons, shipbrokers and coal exporters, acting as agents to one of the pioneer coal producers. The father retired in 1859 and the firm was reconstituted as Cory Brothers. The two brothers – Richard and John – developed the concern in two ways. In 1869 they acquired a colliery in the Rhondda, and thereafter their colliery interests were greatly extended. Also about this time the idea developed of opening coaling stations throughout the world. By 1908 they had 118 agencies and depots, supplying coal on all the major shipping routes.[2] On the whole, this movement from merchanting to producing was confined to the pioneering stage of development, and it ceased around 1870.

In the years before 1914, the trend was in the opposite direction, from producing to marketing. Colliery companies established sales divisions at Cardiff which very often handled the whole process of distribution without involving middlemen. The D.I.C. is a good example of the trend. The company had started selling coal in 1860, and in the early years sold to merchants rather than direct to consumers. The Cardiff agent of the company remarked that 'we never know who the purchaser of the coal in our wagons will be until it is on board ship'. This situation was to alter – the trend generally as well as specifically for the D.I.C. was for the producer to take a much more direct role in marketing. An attempt was made to secure orders direct from consumers. The aim was to obtain a 'regular connection' to keep the collieries going full time, when demand was not at its peak. On 1 January 1891 it was estimated that there would be 565,000 tons for sale over the year; by then 320,667 tons had already been sold on contract. The problem was that output varied – in six weeks in 1891 from a minimum of 7,566 to a maximum of 14,474 tons – and so did the regularity of customers' demands:

It very often happens that we have a minimum demand from our customers just when we are receiving maximum quantities from the
collieries. When the trade is strong we can almost always fill up vacancies by new sales but it is not always possible in a weak state of the
market. In a weak and falling state of the market buyers always get
into arrear with the contracts.

The work of the Cardiff agency was in the first place to cover as large a
part as possible of the output by contracts. As the agent said in 1891, 'the
bulk of the steam coal trade is done by contracts and any large colliery
with few contracts when supply exceeds the demand is in a very helpless
condition'. These contracts were direct to consumers – to railway companies and shipping lines – but also to merchants of a particular type.
When it is said that the majority of coal was sold by the producer on
contract, this by no means cuts out the middleman in every case, for what
were known as 'legitimate' middlemen also took contracts in their own
right. The D.I.C. agent, having covered as much of his output as possible
by contracts, then had a second task – to cover the remaining output
as completely as possible, taking account both of the fluctuations in output and of variations in the speed at which contracts were taken up. The
only coal which could be stock-piled was that placed in the railway
wagons, so it was a finely balanced exercise. The aim had to be to keep
the pits going full-time if at all possible, in order to keep the overhead
costs per ton at the minimum. To achieve this, odd cargoes were sold at
short notice, and it was here that 'speculative' middlemen had a role.[3]

The pattern, as far as the D.I.C. was concerned, was a sale of the bulk
of output by contract, direct to consumers or to 'legitimate' middlemen,
and the covering of output as far as possible by short-term sales to 'speculative' middlemen. This would appear to have been the general pattern,
for in 1915 Jevons wrote that: 'in south Wales . . . the proportion sold
on contract ranges from 60 to 75 per cent, and at times even 85 per cent
of the total output. The margin of coal not sold under contract is disposed
of in lots of 200 or 300 tons up to 4,000 or 5,000 tons for prompt delivery
to meet current requirements.' The extent of change may be exaggerated,
for Morris and Williams suggest that already in the period 1841 to 1875,
'the greater part of the Welsh coal output was probably sold without
the intervention of middlemen'. The position was nevertheless changing
in the late nineteenth century in three respects.[4]

The first change was in the structure of the coal industry. It was not
just that producers were squeezing merchants: the producers were becoming highly concentrated, a closed group. By the 1870s the pioneer
days of the coal trade were over. Earlier, entry was relatively easy. The
industry was fragmented, the units were small-scale, and men with a

little capital could enter the industry without too much trouble. The coal industry was much more open than the iron, and men of quite small means from within the coalfield itself could enter the industry: David Davies of the Ocean Co. was a sawyer, Samuel Thomas of the Cambrian Co. a grocer at Merthyr, David Davis of the Ferndale Co. a draper, also at Merthyr, whilst others rose from the ranks of working colliers, often via positions as managers or engineers. Up to the 1870s, there was some increase in the size of units, but 'as much of the extra production was obtained by the multiplication of new units rather than by the extension of older undertakings'. But by the mid-1870s the larger companies were starting to dominate in the steam coal trade and as increasingly large amounts of capital were required to sink pits the industry moved towards a 'concentration of capital in large public companies' which ended the relative ease of access. In 1890 the Rhondda Fach had 12 pits operated by six companies; by 1914 the number of pits had risen by a third to 16, while the number of companies had fallen by half to three. At the turn of the century, 80 per cent of all steam coal was produced by 20 companies. So it was not just that producers were taking a more positive role in merchanting, but that the structure of producers had also changed. Morris and Williams might be right in saying that producers even before 1870 marketed the majority of coal; however, after 1870 not only did this proportion rise, but the scale of producers also increased, making the mercantile structure at Cardiff much more closed than it had been.[5]

In the second place, there was a move beyond the D.I.C. pattern, for producers not just to sell on contract to 'legitimate' middlemen, but actually to buy them out. Coal production had become concentrated and closed; now the producers were squeezing the 'legitimate' middlemen and further reducing openings. The changed structure of the coal industry meant that middlemen could no longer themselves move back into production. The trend was now in the opposite direction. In 1908, the Ocean Coal Co. amalgamated with the depot-owning firm of Wilson Sons. According to D. J. Williams, 'the motive for the amalgamation of these two concerns was to bring under one control the entire process of production and distribution: in this way the middleman was eliminated and the profits which he could claim for his services are realised by the company which owns the collieries.' The other example of this process was D. A. Thomas and the Cambrian Combine. The Cambrian concern had been an amalgamation between a coalowner (Samuel Thomas) and Cardiff merchants (J. O. and O. H. Riches). Samuel's son, D. A. Thomas (1865–1918), took over the Cardiff sales agency on the death of the Riches, and operated in the same manner as the D.I.C. In the years after 1907 he went a stage further. On the one hand he bought out other producers so that by 1916 he controlled two-thirds of the output of the

Rhondda. On the other hand he created merchanting concerns. In 1907 Amaral Sutherland was formed to deal with South America, and in 1908 Lysberg Ltd as pitwood merchants, shipbrokers and coal merchants. In 1908 Thomas bought L. Gueret Ltd, a leading coal merchant with large interests in coaling stations and depots, and the Anglo-Spanish Coaling Co. was formed to market coal in Spain, France, and Morocco. Thomas's stated intention was 'the standardisation, so to speak, of policy, management and administration': 'the effect of a combination of this kind will be to eliminate the speculative middleman but not to interfere with the bona fide merchant, to whose enterprise in the development of foreign markets . . . colliery owners owe so much.'[6]

This leads to the third change, the changing roles of the 'speculative' and 'legitimate' middlemen. The development of the sales agency and then the amalgamation of producers with merchants was circumscribing the role of the latter, but it did still survive. There were relatively few of these firms, they had a large capital, and were in most cases also coalowners. The 'speculative' middlemen continued to make a precarious living selling the job lots left over after contracts had been supplied, and had become increasingly peripheral, differentiated from the larger and more highly capitalized 'legitimate' middlemen.

Why did the 'legitimate' middlemen have a continuing role despite the formation of sales agencies? Why did the sales agencies bother to sell on contract to the middlemen who were themselves simply selling on contract? Basically, it was because the coalowners sold f.o.b. and the middlemen c.i.f. It was necessary to have a knowledge of the freight market to sell c.i.f. and this involved risks. Further, the merchants provided a large amount of working capital. They paid the colliery in seven days, and insurance and a third of freight were paid on loading. But the merchant was not paid for three to six months. The firm of Pyman, Watson claimed to have had £100,000–150,000 tied up in this way at any one time before 1914. Also, the merchants had to buy coal from a number of different collieries and mix it to the requirement of the purchaser. Offices, correspondents, and agents had to be established in foreign markets, and very often coal depots were set up. The merchants therefore urged that they were not parasites taking profits away from the producer but that they had an altogether different class of business requiring a different training and a large amount of capital. Very few concerns were able to fulfil these functions, and there were in 1914 perhaps a dozen 'legitimate' middlemen. A few did emerge in the late nineteenth century, but entry was becoming increasingly difficult. The 'legitimate' middlemen were facing declining opportunities, and large sums of capital were required. As with coal production, it was no longer so easy to secure a place in the marketing structure. Many, indeed, were coalowners themselves. Cory

Brothers was one good example. Another is the firm of the Frenchman Louis Gueret (1844–1908), who was a major coal producer, patent fuel owner, and investor in French shipping and pitwood, with branch offices in France and Italy. Many of the firms were like Gueret's in being national and international rather than simply based upon Cardiff. Lambert Brothers, William Cory, and Watts, Watts and Co., for example, were engaged in trade in London, Newcastle, and other ports as much as in Cardiff. The firm of Moxey, Savon and Co. was based upon Cardiff, London, and Marseilles with coal depots throughout the Mediterranean. Even if the firm was Cardiff-based, the spread had to be world-wide, covering the major trade routes to cater for the demand for steam coal. The list of Cory Brothers depots illustrates the ramifications of the trade: Aden, Cape Verde Islands, Barbados, Rio de Janeiro, Pernambuco, Buenos Aires, Bahia Blanca, Port Said, Algiers, Marseilles, Las Palmas. Cardiff merchants had established a world-wide network reaching along the major steamship routes.[7]

There were, it is true, the more numerous 'speculative' middlemen in a small and precarious way of business. According to Jevons, the 'legitimate' middlemen usually had guaranteed sales and took a moderate profit. The speculative middlemen took larger risks, buying low and selling high:

> These speculators generally have a world-wide knowledge of the state of the markets, and base their operations on reports received from correspondents in various parts of the world. If a big demand is anticipated later, they seek by some artificial means, such as withholding orders, to depress the prices; and when low-water mark is reached they buy in order to sell again at a considerable profit. . . . As a rule these men taboo the markets when prices of odd parcels are high as is the case when an unusually large volume of the output has been covered by long contracts, and during such periods content themselves with buying and selling small quantities only at current prices on day-to-day risks. Their big operations are reserved for periods of slump, when they sell forward and short, calculating on buying later at a lower price.

Such activities were possible because of the manner in which the coal market operated.[8]

The coal industry was particularly liable to extreme variations in price, and to long periods of depression following short periods of high prices. The character of the coal trade was dictated by a number of factors. Any deficiency in supply could not be met immediately and new pits were only put into production in time to add to the depression. Coal had a low elasticity of demand, so a small deficiency led to a large increase in prices. By the time new pits were opened and trade had slackened, they would create a small excess and cause a heavy fall in prices. According to D. A. Thomas, this excess supply would be kept in production by

> the continuous effort on the part of nearly every individual company to reduce the cost of production per ton, by increasing the number of tons over which the fixed charges have to be divided. . . . What mainly influences him in adding to the already excessive supply is the desire to keep down and reduce the cost per ton in his own particular case, and so lessen his loss, or increase the meagre profit he may happen to be making. . . . Unfortunately for his calculations, every one of his neighbours is influenced by the same motives and is making the same efforts to increase the output, and the reduced cost of a few pence per ton is immediately swallowed up in a reduced selling price of perhaps a shilling or more.

Thomas's analysis of how this fall occurred on the Cardiff coal market accords exactly with the mode of operation of the D.I.C. The Cardiff agents were approached for a tender; each then speculated what his neighbours were doing and undercut them in order to keep the colliery going at the insistence of the owner; the purchaser could then use this as a lever to force prices down further. Prices spiralled downwards not because of competition with other areas – south Wales had a virtual monopoly of the best steam coal – but because of competition within the area. It was this which gave the 'speculative' middlemen their role. [9]

The coal trade, then, was made up of a number of different types of concern. There were the colliery companies' sales agencies disposing of their coal direct to consumers on contract, but also the 'legitimate' middlemen. The colliery companies were becoming more concentrated; they were increasing the proportion of coal marketed by their sales agencies; and they were buying out 'legitimate' middlemen. In these ways, opportunities were becoming restricted. The 'speculative' middlemen were small, fringe merchants, increasingly differentiated from the 'legitimate' concerns. The coal-based élite of Cardiff was drawn from the 'legitimate' middlemen and the sales directors of the colliery companies, the 'speculative' middlemen forming a suspect and despised periphery. By the period 1870–1914 the mercantile structure was already firmly established, any change being toward concentration of control in the hands of a few large concerns.

III

The shipping industry at Cardiff was based almost entirely upon tramp ships, that is, ships which did not serve a particular route but which went wherever the charterer wished. Tramp shipping accounted for 60 per cent of British tonnage in 1913. At that date, coal employed 40 per cent of British tramps or about 3 million tons. The coal-carrying capacity of Cardiff-registered ships was about 1·3 million tons in 1907, which immediately places in perspective Cardiff's position as a centre for tramp shipping.[10]

There were two periods of rapid growth. The first was up to 1884; the second was 1897 to 1910. The number of ships owned rose from 138 in 1870 to 331 in 1884, the tonnage from 26,029 to 171,759. In the second period of growth, the number of ships did not change greatly, being 278 in 1897 and 367 in 1910, while the tonnage rose from 187,176 to 451,567.[11] The two periods of growth created two generations of shipowners. The figures showing the degree of concentration hide the fact that the group which dominated at the end of the period was not the same as dominated at the beginning. In the late nineteenth century, when entry to the coal trade was becoming closed, a new group of shipowners emerged to dominance. Whilst there is this important difference from the coal trade, there is also the similarity that it was possible for some shipowners (like the 'speculative' middlemen in coal) to gain entry relatively easily in a marginal and somewhat disruptive capacity. The pattern is to be explained by two features: the nature of shipping finance and technical development.

It was a relatively easy matter to set up as a shipowner. The methods used, indeed, gave Cardiff shipowning a bad reputation. Ships were bought on mortgage. The capital was raised by shares in single-ship companies, which were partly bought by tradesmen who would expect orders in return, but were otherwise largely sold outside south Wales. The person who really profited was the manager of the company, the person who had floated it. He took a commission on gross earnings rather than profits, so that provided he was getting a freight he was not concerned with the profitability of the company. 'The net result', it was said, 'is that we have too much ship mongering and too little shipowning.' Complaints came from all quarters – the seamen's union, the commercial press and shipowners themselves – of the existence of the 'rash and unscrupulous speculator', of 'the ease with which any gambler may write himself down as "shipowner".' But leaving aside possible abuses, the system of single-ship companies did permit newcomers (scrupulous and unscrupulous) to enter the industry. The system could permit rapid growth and high dividends and not merely exploit the shareholders. Many remained at the periphery like speculative middlemen in coal, but a few did emerge as the new leaders of the industry.[12]

This emergence of a new second generation of owners was associated with technical developments in shipping. Existing companies were able to adapt, but the development first of steamships generally and then of specialized vessels for the coal trade did give newcomers a chance to

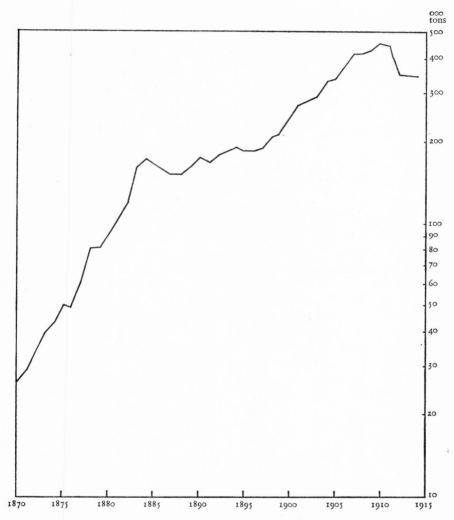

Figure 4. Cardiff-registered ships, 1870–1914 (source: Annual Statement of the Navigation and Shipping of the United Kingdom, in Accounts and Papers annually).

exploit the developments without having to write off old capital, and very rapid growth was possible. During the second period of rapid growth after 1897 the development of new types of ships and the relative ease of raising capital permitted a second generation of shipowners to emerge to dominance.

In the early 1880s the biggest shipowners were Morel Brothers and John Cory and Sons. The Morel brothers, Philip (1841–1908) and Thomas (1847–1903), were from Jersey, moving to Cardiff in 1857 and 1862 respectively to join relatives who had started business as ship brokers in 1856. By the early 1870s they had taken over the concern, which was already quite substantial. They part-owned over 100 sailing ships trading to France and Spain, taking out iron and coal and returning with pitwood and potatoes. To these imports were added Spanish ore, which Morel Brothers were among the first to develop. They were chartering up to 120 vessels a month in addition to those they owned. In 1876 they acquired their first steamship, and others followed built specially for the Bilbao iron ore trade which formed the main interest of the concern. They not only shipped the ore but also invested in Spanish mines. A unique feature was that in 1884 the usual shareholder system and single-ship companies were dropped, and from then all ships were bought entirely with their own money and run for their personal account. When the firm became a limited company in 1887 the capital was £500,000.[13]

John Cory (1823–91) was a farmer's son from Cornwall who had gone to sea, becoming the captain of a small vessel, and setting up business in 1854 as owner of a number of small sailing ships. In 1872 he decided to transfer the business to Cardiff. At that time he was operating two sailing ships of 199 and 514 tons; by 1876 he had ten ships, and by 1884, 19. The fleet was built up using single-ship companies, and the shipping business was in 1898 worth £325,000. John Cory's two sons had entered the firm in 1885, taking over completely in 1891. Their policy was one of consolidation rather than expansion, replacing old ships but not increasing the fleet. As with Morel Brothers, the firm had large interests in the ore trade, importing into south Wales, the Clyde and Middlesbrough.[14]

The interesting point about these owners is that they did not simply charter their vessels, but were also engaging in trade on their own behalf, especially in the ore trade to Spain. This was an option not open to the second generation of leaders, for Cardiff had failed to develop imports on a large scale, and they simply chartered their vessels without engaging in trade themselves. While the first generation of leaders did not decline absolutely, it did relatively and in the second phase of growth was surpassed by newcomers such as W. J. Tatem, Edward Nicholl, William Reardon Smith and Evan Thomas, Radcliffe. These firms experienced quite remarkable growth in the late 1890s.

Edward Nicholl was born in 1862 in Cornwall. He served an engineering apprenticeship with a railway company, and then in 1882 moved to the North as engineer on a steamship. In this capacity he moved to Cardiff in 1884, rising to become marine superintendent and consulting engineer to a local shipping concern. In 1903 he decided to become a shipowner in his own right. His employers agreed that he could continue to work for them, with time to set up his own business. They also agreed to invest £1,000 in each ship and to do his clerical work free of charge. From this favourable position, Nicholl set up business in the manner of which many had complained, ordering ships on long credit and forming single-ship companies. The abuses to which the system often led were avoided. Nicholl was himself the largest shareholder, and regular dividends of 10 per cent were paid.[15]

The success of Nicholl was surpassed by that of W. J. Tatem. Tatem was born in Devon in 1868. After two years at sea he took a clerical position with a Cardiff shipowner, and about 1899 started his own business, pioneering the new type of steamer of the largest available size. As with Nicholl, his companies were all initially single-ship, but in 1909 he decided to amalgamate the 15 existing single-ship companies into one, the Tatem Steam Navigation Co., with a capital of £350,000. By 1906 he could claim to be the largest individual shipowner in Cardiff, having built up a fleet of 150,000 tons d.w. in seven years.[16]

As an epilogue, the remarkable events of the post-war shipping boom should be mentioned, when a third generation of owners emerged. At the end of the war, there was an artificial shortage of shipping, largely due to the dislocation of the ports, which led to a huge rise in freight rates and a feverish speculation at Cardiff as fleets were built up by newcomers or previously small owners. By the end of 1920 there were 122 steamship companies owning 1·5m. tons, which 'raised Cardiff to the status of the greatest tramp steamship owning centre in the world.' Some of these owners, it was claimed with some justice, 'did not know the stem from the stern of a vessel.' The boom had been 'accompanied, on a fairly extensive scale, by the decline or disappearance of old-established firms which had been predominantly associated with the rise of Cardiff as a shipping centre, and by the displacement of these old-established concerns by new companies under the management of young and untried men'. As an indication of this, only six of the 52 shipping companies existing in 1888 survived to 1921. The post-war boom was an experience from which local shipowning did not recover. Reserves had been dissipated, and when the boom broke many companies were forced into bankruptcy by the inability to pay for ships acquired at inflated prices, or had to concentrate upon writing down the value of their ships with little chance of paying a dividend or building up a reserve to modernize the fleet. The experience of the coal industry after the war was no happier, as export markets disappeared. But where the shipping industry experienced a large turnover in personnel, the coal industry rapidly moved towards an even more concentrated structure. The work of D. A. Thomas was continued by D. R. Llewellyn and H. H. Merrett, and the role of the middleman was ever more circumscribed. The post-war experience of the two industries therefore emphasized the difference which had existed before 1914: a changed situation in the shipping industry was exploited by a new generation of owners, whilst the coal trade became even more closed.[17]

IV

The coal and shipping interests were distinct, and the élite of the town was divided. Both were highly concentrated. In coal, entry was virtually closed throughout the period 1870–1914. When the industry had first developed, it had given openings to men of small means who had no chance to enter the capital-intensive iron industry. The shift in the base of the economy around 1850 from iron to coal had thus created a more open situation in which local capital and enterprise played a larger role than had been the case in the iron industry, even if Welsh resources still had to be supplemented from outside. There was certainly a very clear contrast between the structure of the iron and coal industries around 1850 – the one concentrated and the other fragmented – but by 1914 the coal industry had gone the way of its precursor. The change in production was reflected in marketing, for the producers were themselves responsible for large sales and were squeezing the middlemen. The chances of becoming a legitimate middleman were slight; to be a speculative middleman was possible but marginal and precarious.[18]

The shipping industry appears to have been more open, with one generation of owners emerging in the period of rapid growth to 1884, and a second generation in the rapid growth from 1897. But the degree to which shipowning was open must be kept in perspective. After all, only three or four firms rose to the top of the shipowning hierarchy; the process did not involve a large part of the population of the town. Entry to shipping was not analogous to, say, entry to small master status in the Sheffield cutlery trade. Manual workers were obviously excluded completely, and a very specialist knowledge was required, even if it was relatively easy to raise the money. Those who succeeded had spent many years in shipping offices learning the trade. And however open access might have been, the number of shipowners was strictly limited, a small portion of the total population. Very many of the shipowners were in fact men who had been in business in other ports and transferred to Cardiff. These points are illustrated by the examples already cited. John

Cory had been a shipowner in Padstow, W. J. Tatem had worked as a shipping clerk for 17 years, Nicholl had been a marine superintendent. A very large number were migrants from other shipowning areas where they had acquired experience. Philip Turnbull (1849–1925), for example, was born in Whitby, where his father was a shipowner. He went to sea in 1866, and became superintendent of his father's fleet. In 1877 he started his own business at Cardiff. R. O. Sanderson (d. 1930) was born in Hartlepool, and worked for London and Cardiff shipowners before setting up in 1894 as agent for a number of northern owners and subsequently becoming an owner himself. Openness there might have been, but it was not an integral part of the economy as at Sheffield where the manual workers in each unit could aspire to become in time master of a similar unit. Neither was it like the situation earlier in the nineteenth century in towns with a role analogous to Cardiff, such as South Shields and Llanelli, where ownership of small wooden sailing ships was widely diffused. By the late nineteenth century the situation was much more closed, even if there was some flexibility compared with coal and compared with ports such as Liverpool, based not upon tramps but liners organized in 'conferences' and quasi-monopolies excluding outsiders.[19]

Even granted the existence of the peripheral speculative middlemen and shipmongers, and granted that there was a division of functions, the local élite was based upon an economic structure which was concentrated, not diffused, which was absolutely closed even if one part was open relative to the other. The nature of this narrow commercial élite and its relationship with the wider local urban society are of crucial importance to an understanding of Cardiff politics and society. How did the mercantile interests see their role in the town; what was the effect of this élite structure upon the social relations in the community? These are problems to be considered in more depth in Part Three.

Part two   Building a city

The exact content of urban history has been a matter of debate since the subject became a separate branch of historical study. The next four chapters follow one suggested approach, adopting 'a definition of urban history as the process of city building over time. This implies a focus upon the city as a physical entity . . ., an artifact whose forms and structure are greatly determined by decisions which affect land use.'* Quite simply, how was the city built, what determined its physical form, and how did the spatial patterns relate to the social structure?

* R. Lubove, 'The urbanization process: an approach to historical research', *Journal of the American Institute of Planners*, XXXIII (1967), 33–9.

5   Landowners and developers

The first steps in building had, of course, to be taken by the landowner. As Dr Kellett has said, 'in many ways landowners were the most important single agents of change'.[1] The landowner had a number of choices over the way in which he disposed of his land, and how it was turned from fields into streets. He could sell it outright so that the builders could do as they pleased depending upon their assessment of the market. He could retain the freehold and develop it himself along lines dictated in part by the market, but also perhaps by his social aspirations. He could lease it for a shorter or a longer term, keeping a tighter or a looser hold over the character of development. Some owners used the lease very laxly and allowed the developers to set the character of the area, which sometimes meant that the land could 'experience the full declension of meadow to slum in a single generation'. Or the owner could set very strict terms, telling the builder what to erect, and ensuring that the subsequent inhabitants kept the property as near the original state as possible.[2] Admittedly, with the other forces of change at work in the nineteenth-century city, this ideal could never be achieved, but even if the estate owners could not hold change at bay, their decision had established the physical form which was to undergo subsequent transformation. And it has been suggested 'as a working hypothesis . . . that if an estate exceeds a certain size, and the greater part of the financial gain for its owner is pushed far enough into the future, its policies and practices come to resemble those of a public administrative body'.[3]

To a large extent, Cardiff fits this last case, for the bulk of the land was owned by three estates which met such a criterion. However, it is also fair to say that the landowners were operating within narrow constraints, for they could only modify a particular market situation. Their importance was that they were able to prevent housing standards from falling to the minimum levels the market would bear. Obviously, they would not pass the maximum the market would comfortably bear, for houses would simply be unsaleable. At Cardiff, the importance of the dominance of the large estates was that the bulk of housing was kept above the minimum standards – and before 1914 it is a moot point whether the housing being provided was not indeed passing the limits of what the market would bear.

I

The pattern of land ownership around 1850 can be constructed from the tithe plans. This may be set against the plans showing the development of Cardiff at various dates. The starting point must be the period immediately before the first dock was constructed, when the town was still largely confined to its medieval limits, with the castle to the north, the river on its old course to the west, the canal to the east, and a desolate marshy area to the south. The initial growth of the town came by a more intensive development of the area of medieval settlement.

The central area of Cardiff was divided into burgage plots which had frontages of about 30 ft onto the main streets, and a considerable depth. Further, ownership was spread amongst a large number of small owners. The outcome of these two features was a development based upon long leases, of up to 999 years, with very little control by the landowner, largely through a use of courts opening off the main streets. The fact that the plots were long in relation to their width meant that the most profitable use of the land was obtained by building along the sides of the plot. The plates (between pp. 100 and 101) illustrate this. As Bute complained of one of these owners, the 'system of building is most ruinous to the town . . . he lets his land to anyone without reference to any plan of building or of streets'.[4] Most of the increase in population up to about 1841 was housed in this old-established area of settlement, by an increase in the density of development.[5] It was a pattern not followed elsewhere in the town, with the exception of a small area in the north of Grangetown where there was also fragmented ownership and a low standard of development. Otherwise, with one case of freehold development in Canton, the pattern followed was that of the next area to be built – to the south of the old town and alongside the new dock of 1839 – namely, of controlled development using 99-year leases.

The Bute dock was to be the creator of a Butetown. The initial strategy of the Bute estate was that the new dock would lead to an increase in the value of land at Cardiff, and the estate accordingly planned a town alongside the dock, largely separate from the old settlement. It was to be a balanced community housing the merchants as well as the dockers and seamen. This did work for a time, with merchants living in the two squares and the workers in the terraces around. But in time the merchants left, keeping their offices at Butetown whilst living elsewhere. Butetown became largely synonymous with Tiger Bay, the red light area providing for the needs of the seamen. In its initial development in the 1840s and 1850s, the procedures which were to be followed in the construction of most of the town were laid down, even if it proved impossible to preserve the character of the area in the face of forces of change much stronger than the wishes of the Bute estate.

When deciding to develop his land alongside the dock, the second marquis of Bute refused either to sell outright to builders or to build or own houses on his own account. The policy resolved upon was to lease land for short terms. The second marquis wanted a term of 63 years, but in fact 99 years became the normal length. The lease took a standard form. The builder was within a year to erect 'with good and substantial materials . . . substantial dwelling houses according to the plan of an elevation annexed hereto in such manner and with such materials as have been or shall be approved in writing'. The lease would only be assigned when the house had been completed to the satisfaction of the estate agent and certified by him. The lease required the owner of the house to keep the building in good repair, to paint the outside every third year and the inside every seventh year, and to insure the premises at full value. There were also strict provisions about the use of the house. A minimum size plot was fixed of 15 ft by 60 ft, but most were slightly larger.[6] Butetown was marked by greater spaciousness and order than the area of medieval settlements to the north.

Largely as a result of the development of Butetown, the revenue received by Bute from Cardiff ground rents rose from £258 in 1840 to £622 in 1850 and £5,319 in 1860. This was not all clear profit. The increase in income had involved considerable expenditure in providing roads and sewers. In the late 1840s between £1,000 and £3,000 was spent each year, and between August 1851 and July 1859, £16,300 was spent on development. In the 1860s, the Bute income from ground rents rose by only £1,000, both because it was a period of depression in house building and because development was moving to other estates, to the west of the river and eastwards along Newport Road.[7] The major growth was to the east, in Roath, and in particular on the Tredegar estate. Along Newport Road the Tredegar estate developed a high-status residential area – Tredegarville – and it was here that many of the merchants moved from Butetown. To the south of Newport Road, the estate developed a large working-class area. Unfortunately, the Tredegar records give no information on the processes at work. All that is known is that development was based upon 99-year leases, used in a controlled and orderly fashion under the supervision of estate officials. The best insight into the details of development comes from the west of the river, on the Windsor estate at Grangetown. This may be taken to illustrate the typical pattern. Bute, Tredegar, and Windsor were the three large landowners, with extensive estates not just in Cardiff but throughout south Wales. Professor H. S. Jevons, writing just before the First World War, put these estates together as having very largely the same policy: 99-year leases, a refusal to sell land for building, and a strict control of the character of the development. Each was large enough to have a body of officials able to

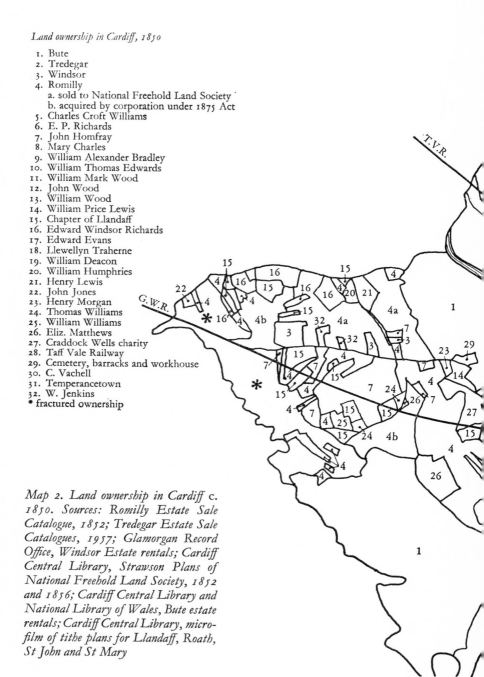

Land ownership in Cardiff, 1850

1. Bute
2. Tredegar
3. Windsor
4. Romilly
   a. sold to National Freehold Land Society
   b. acquired by corporation under 1875 Act
5. Charles Croft Williams
6. E. P. Richards
7. John Homfray
8. Mary Charles
9. William Alexander Bradley
10. William Thomas Edwards
11. William Mark Wood
12. John Wood
13. William Wood
14. William Price Lewis
15. Chapter of Llandaff
16. Edward Windsor Richards
17. Edward Evans
18. Llewellyn Traherne
19. William Deacon
20. William Humphries
21. Henry Lewis
22. John Jones
23. Henry Morgan
24. Thomas Williams
25. William Williams
26. Eliz. Matthews
27. Craddock Wells charity
28. Taff Vale Railway
29. Cemetery, barracks and workhouse
30. C. Vachell
31. Temperancetown
32. W. Jenkins
* fractured ownership

Map 2. Land ownership in Cardiff c.
*1850. Sources: Romilly Estate Sale
Catalogue, 1852; Tredegar Estate Sale
Catalogues, 1957; Glamorgan Record
Office, Windsor Estate rentals; Cardiff
Central Library, Strawson Plans of
National Freehold Land Society, 1852
and 1856; Cardiff Central Library and
National Library of Wales, Bute estate
rentals; Cardiff Central Library, micro-
film of tithe plans for Llandaff, Roath,
St John and St Mary*

scale: 2.9 ins = 1 mile

keep a firm control over the developments, acting in a way as a putative town planning department.[8] This emerges very clearly from the example of Grangetown, which was being developed by the Windsor estate from the late 1850s.

In the 1850s, Lady Windsor was making hopeful references to 'the new town we may now expect to see spring up on the Grange', and between 1858 and 1867, £36,017 was raised by mortgages upon farms in the surrounding area, to develop both Grangetown and further to the west the separate community of Penarth. By 1873, £18,000 had been spent by the Windsor estate upon the provision of roads and drainage at Grangetown. The aim was a 17 per cent return. The achieved gross return did not approach such a level: in 1865 the gross return on expenditure incurred to 1860 was 2·7 per cent; in 1869 the gross return on expenditure incurred to 1865 was 3·3 per cent; and in 1875 the gross return on expenditure incurred to 1873 was 4·7 per cent. Up to 1875 the gross return was about sufficient to cover the cost of the mortgages and maintenance. The failure to do more than break even can in part be explained by the fact that the development which was planned in the peak years of 1856–7 had to contend with a downturn in the building cycle. Further, the development was planned as an industrial suburb and not as a dormitory suburb, but the Grangetown Ironworks upon which hopes were in particular placed was not a success. It was some time before Grangetown came within the accepted limits for travelling to work. Also, before 1875 the estate was outside the Canton and Cardiff Local Boards of Health. In the early stages of development, this was seen as an advantage. The estate could have absolute control over the whole development and could provide all the necessary services to a higher standard than was the case with the areas under the Canton Board of Health. However, the expense of building a complete sewage system and road network meant that profits were squeezed and attitudes changed. When Grangetown was incorporated into the extended borough, the estate was able to sell its sewage system to the corporation to drain the whole area west of the Taff, and was able to pass the cost of road maintenance to the rates. Only after 1875 could the development of Grangetown become profitable.

Throughout the construction of Grangetown the estate was vitally concerned about the nature of the development. The process was similar to that at Butetown. Leases were, with a single exception, for 99 years, and the estate assigned leases to a large number of speculative builders. The activities of these builders were controlled by an inspection of their work, upon which depended the confirmation of the lease. For example, Robert Matthews entered into an agreement to build a house 'with good and substantial materials'. He was repeatedly warned that he was not doing so, and that the consequence would be the forfeiture of the lease, for 'if such premises were allowed to remain they would inevitably become a den of thieves and of the worst characters for no decent person would occupy them'. The many builders were therefore controlled as to the quality of houses built; there was also an overall strategy of development. Land facing the sea was earmarked for 'first-class houses' and anything to upset this plan was vetoed. The site for the church was chosen in 1869 with some thought, for Lady Windsor saw that it 'commercially would benefit the place'. The site eventually chosen was central to the area then being laid out but 'sufficiently removed from the cottages to ensure a better description of buildings in the immediate neighbourhood of the church'. The outcome was not the extremely high standard of planning obtained by the estate at the same time in its development of the high-status residential area of Penarth, but it had been concerned to maintain standards without any local authority supervision.[9]

The Bute estate re-emerged in the later nineteenth century as the major provider of building land. By then most of the smaller estates had been developed, and the Bute estate could largely dictate the subsequent character of development. Perhaps because Butetown had not proved a long-term success in that its social character had declined disastrously, the Bute estate thereafter set much higher standards of development. The plainest working-class housing with a building line directly onto the street was avoided. Where possible, development was for the well-to-do middle class with a high standard of planning; for lower-middle-class or artisan housing, the standard on the Bute estate was always somewhat higher than usual. In south Roath, where the Tredegar estate laid out a grid of working-class streets, the Bute estate laid out a square surrounded by higher-class houses. Bute land in the southern part of Cathays also formed an enclave of large houses laid out with street gardens. The Bute–Windsor boundary in Grangetown is immediately apparent, the Bute area marked by street gardens, houses with bay windows and front gardens; exactly the same point applies to the southern part of Canton. The most interesting example of Bute development was in north Roath, the area to which development was shifting in the years up to 1914; having spread to the south, and then to the east and west, Cardiff was now growing largely to the north.

The 1875 Improvement Act gave the corporation power to provide 'public pleasure grounds'. The first intention was to purchase part of the Plasnewydd estate from the Mackintosh of Mackintosh, but this was dropped when building site value was demanded. The next approach in 1882 was to Lord Tredegar, and by the end of 1886 he had agreed to sell 39 acres to the corporation for £18,541. It seemed as if the council would accept the offer, but the situation was completely changed by a communication from the Bute estate which led to its rejection. The Bute estate had a large area near the Roath brook ripe for development. The brook ran through marshy land involving considerable costs of drainage and preparation for building. By giving the land adjoining the brook to the corporation, the Bute estate could have this useless land laid out as a park, to the great benefit of the surrounding estate. The initial offer was that the Bute estate would give the corporation about 80 acres; the corporation was to lay out $41\frac{1}{4}$ acres of this as a recreation ground, make two lakes of 31 acres and 16 acres, and provide roads of at least 40 feet for $3\frac{1}{4}$ miles around the perimeter. The council in April 1887 accepted Bute's 'valuable and munificent gift'. In its final form, the agreement was that Bute would give 103 acres and other owners 17 acres, the corporation being required to spend at least £30,000 within seven years on the necessary works.[10]

The Bute policy in Roath had been foreshadowed west of the Taff. In 1858 the estate had opened to the public the Sophia Gardens adjoining the river. Partly this was done to compensate for the closure of the castle grounds which had previously been open to the residents of the town. But it was not wholly coincidental that at the same time it was planned that the 'west will be skirted by a long line of beautiful villa residences which are to be erected between the gardens and a new road intended to be formed and called "the Cathedral road".' Each villa was provided with a private entrance into Sophia Gardens. Bute policy here and at Roath Park was followed by Tredegar for areas further down the Roath brook: Waterloo Gardens and Roath Brook Gardens were presented to the corporation in 1897 and 1906, the corporation laying out the land as public parks. Some councillors had been none too happy about the way in which the area was developed. They maintained that the Roath parks had been provided well away from the old-established districts, and were surrounded by fields ready for building rather than by a dense population. The feeling was that the corporation was incurring an expenditure 'upon bog land and improving that land for the sake of some landowners'. There was also the argument of the 'economists' that the rates were too high and parks an unnecessary luxury. The critics did not, however, succeed. Even though £55,000 was eventually spent and it did benefit the landowners, it still seemed a more sensible plan than paying Tredegar for less land.[11]

The other landlords in Cardiff (with one exception, on the former Romilly estate in Canton) adopted 99-year leases as the basis of development. A particularly interesting case of leasehold development was on the Mackintosh estate at Plasnewydd. The attempt to sell the central portion of the estate to the corporation as a park had failed, but the owner decided to provide facilities for recreation on his own account. In 1890 the Mackintosh of Mackintosh presented the old house of Plasnewydd and two acres of land for the use of the inhabitants of the new houses built in its grounds. Billiards rooms, a reading room, a gymnasium, skittle alley and tennis courts were provided. This was unique in Cardiff, a landlord who felt that he should have an interest not only in the reversionary value of the houses, but also an interest in the lives of the people who were in a very indirect sense his tenants. As Mackintosh said, 'of course, the tenants were not directly their tenants, but still they felt that there should be a mutual interest'.[12] No other landlords went so far as Mackintosh, but few permitted an uncontrolled development of their land.

The only estate which was disinclined to develop by 99-year leases and which elected to accept the immediate gains of outright sale was the Romilly estate in Canton, and this area became the only freehold building ground in the town. The estate was put up for auction in 1852, partly as farm land, but in Canton as 'good sites for building', particularly for 'country villas' for merchants.[13] The two main lots in Canton were purchased by the National Freehold Land Society, a total of 110 acres for £14,100. Not only had the owners elected to sell the land rather than develop it by lease – an unusual course in Cardiff – but the purchase by the N.F.L.S. would lead to even more differences in the character of the development. The N.F.L.S. in Cardiff was essentially a Liberal organization. It appealed in two ways to Liberals. On the one hand, the Society extended the franchise by creating 40*s.* freeholders; on the other hand, it gave independence from the strict short-term building lease, which was one of the main *bêtes noires* of Liberalism in Cardiff. The fact that the Bute estate was the mainstay of the local Conservatives and the main user of short leases gave the N.F.L.S. a dual appeal. It is not surprising that the secretary of the Liberal Association lived in the area. But the Society does not only symbolize the social and political conflicts of the mid-nineteenth century; it also had a continuing impact upon the physical structure of the town. The Society issued £30 shares. Members would either pay this up fully or enter a lottery by which a number of shares were drawn weekly, the holder being advanced the amount of the share's value, which he was to repay at 5*s.* per share per month. The share gave the right to choose lots of land to the value of the shares, in the order in which the shares became due. The estate was divided into lots ten feet wide. A shareholder could take any two or more of these lots, depending on the value of the shares held. There was thus considerable flexibility in the size of the plots, from 20 feet upwards, contrasting with the uniformity to be found on leasehold estates. A number of regulations were made: the building line was fixed at 15 feet from the road, and no house was to be worth less than £150. This still left considerable diversity in the size and character of the houses erected, contrasting with the uniformity of development encountered a few streets away on Bute land.[14]

While the effect of estate policies upon the *physical* shape of Cardiff cannot be denied, the effect upon the housing market over time is more contentious. With the exception of the freehold development on the land sold by the Romilly estate, and the long leases of the medieval centre, development was almost without exception by a controlled use of short-term leases. The character of development was set by the three large estates (Bute, Tredegar, and Windsor) and the middling estates (Homfray of Penllyn castle, Croft Williams of Roath Court, Mackintosh of Mackintosh, for example) followed the same procedures. If anything, the importance of the large estates increased before 1914. By then, the available land of the small owners had been used, and development was concentrating on Bute and Tredegar land to the north and east, both inside and outside the city boundary. Probably less than 5 per cent of building development was on freehold land, and the Bute estate accounted for a third of the building land of Cardiff. Essentially, as C. F. Sanders of the Principality Building Society pointed out, 'all the housing of Cardiff has been directed by the ground landlords'.[15] The issue to consider is what effect this had not just upon the physical shape of the town but also upon the structure of the housing market.

II

The problem with contemporary views of estate policies and their impact upon the housing market is that it is difficult to decide which are objective statements of the actual situation and which are ideologically dictated explanations of a situation which existed for some other reason. If the existence of a housing problem was admitted, the blame was usually laid with the ground landlords rather than with a failure of market mechanisms to provide houses. It was possible for Campbell-Bannerman to ask the rhetorical question, 'What is the Housing Question but one phase of the Land Question?' Radicals and progressives in the 1880s put the abolition of leaseholds in the same category as slum clearance and workmen's trains as a solution to the problem of working-class housing. The attack upon the leasehold system of estate development was an urban reflection of the anti-landlordism of the rural areas which was well developed in Wales and an important element in Liberalism. By stressing the injustices of landowners in using the short-term building lease and by maintaining that this was the real cause of the housing problem, a link was effected between the concerns of the two elements in Welsh politics and society: the 'remote and impoverished countryside' and the 'industrial and commercial society of the coalfield'. Urban leaseholds were thus a politically useful gambit for Liberals trying to hold together a coalition of rural and urban interests, and an attempt to reduce rents by removing the element of ground rent was more attractive than the possibility of subsidizing rents to bring them within tolerable limits. Urban leases and estate development policies were central to the Liberal approach to housing in Cardiff. The point to consider is whether it was also central to the housing problem considered objectively rather than ideologically.[16]

In part the attack was upon what was seen as an anomalous incidence of local taxation. This point was put in the Liberal municipal programme of 1897. The growth of the community led to an increase in ground values, but the landlord paid nothing in rates: 'the people create all the additional value; the landowner pockets it all, then leaves them to pay the rates levied to pay the cost of drainage etc. without which the value would not exist'. The remedy to high rates, it was said, lay in the readjustment of the burden of local taxation so that the ground landlord would make a contribution. Pointing to the untaxed income of £250,000–400,000 *per annum* from ground rents and urging that this should be taxed was one response to the demands for municipal economy, for by taxing the landlord it was argued that rates could be reduced without affecting municipal schemes. The remedy, said Councillor Fox, to the demand for economy and reduction of rates, lay not in 'any cheese-paring policy or thimble-rigging of corporation finances':

> the remedy to high rates must be looked for in the Readjustment of Local Taxation, so that the burden will be placed not upon the shoulders of the occupiers but on those who are best able and ought to bear it, the ground landlords; and so we must work in the direction of securing the taxation of ground rents and land values.

A policy of taxation of land values appealed both to Liberal sentiment in its attack upon the landowners, and also to the strong 'economy' sentiment. The demand for taxation of land values and ground rents thus appeared in each Liberal municipal programme, and on two occasions the town council resolved to petition parliament to introduce taxation of ground rents 'in justice to those who are already heavily burdened'.[17]

In addition to a demand for taxation of land values and ground rents, there was a demand for 'leasehold enfranchisement'. The object of this was to enable householders to purchase freeholds at a fair valuation or to fix a perpetual rent. This would remove the grievance that after 99 years the land *and* the house would revert to the ground landlord without compensation. To this end, in 1897 the Cardiff and South Wales Leaseholders Enfranchisement Association was formed.[18] Both of these points – taxation of land values and leasehold enfranchisement – were concerned with very real grievances, but their advocates also saw in the measures the solution to the housing problem.

Cardiff's housing problem, said the Young Liberals in 1914, was a land question. Many argued that by taxing land values and enfranchising leaseholds the land question and therefore the housing problem would be solved. When in 1910 a Welsh committee was formed to promote the taxation of land values, one speaker averred that 'it would solve the problem of unemployment, lead to the abolition of slums, the raising of wages and do away with the present system [of rates], so unfair in its incidence'. It was widely accepted that 'the land question is the first question and should be solved first'. Quite clearly, these views of the housing problem are a gross simplification of a complex problem. The more generally accepted view is that leases encouraged building rather than deterred it. A firm of Cardiff solicitors informed the Select Committee on Town Holdings of 1886–92 'that if the tenure was altered it would put an end to a great portion of the speculative building'. If land had been sold outright, the builder would have to find the money to pay for the plot; building leases, which gave a year free of charge to erect a house and to sell it, meant that the builder was not forced to raise capital to buy the freehold.[19] But if the leasehold system did not deter builders, the way it was used in Cardiff did indeed go some way towards dictating the character and rent of the houses erected.

It is not accepted that the housing problem *was* in essence a land question. The problem was rather that wages were not high enough for many to pay a rent adequate to provide a profitable return upon housing. It was not so much that ground rents took house rents out of the reach of the working class; it was that the structure of the nineteenth-century economy meant that wages were too low to pay a rent which would provide a good house at a profitable rent. It was politically convenient to equate the housing problem with the land question and it was certainly more comforting to Liberals to criticize aristocratic landlords than to criticize nineteenth-century capitalism. The problem was, of course, far bigger than the land question. The eventual solution was to recognize that wages were not high enough to pay the market rent for decent housing, and to provide subsidized local authority housing. But having made these points, it must be accepted that estate development policies in Cardiff *did* act to make house prices and rents higher than might have been the case. The land question did not *create* the housing problem, but it did *intensify* that problem.

III

Rents were evidently higher in Cardiff than in the mining valleys. A striking feature is the absence of low-value rented property in Cardiff. The figures in table 22 were calculated by E. L. Chappell of the South Wales Garden Cities and Town Planning Association.

Part of the explanation of the higher rent level in Cardiff was that rent was essentially a gross return before the owner paid ground rent and rates. Ground rent in the valleys was considerably lower than in Cardiff.

Table 22   *Percentage of working-class houses in Cardiff, Pontypridd, and Rhondda at various rents c. 1914*

Rent	Cardiff	Pontypridd	Rhondda
6s. and under	7·5	39·5	47·5
6s. to 7s. 6d.	18·2	40·6	42·8
7s. 6d. to 9s.	21·7	5·3	2·2
9s. to 10s. 6d.	11·8	2·6	1·2
10s. 6d. to 13s.	24·5	} 12·0	} 6·3
13s. 6d. to 16s.	9·5		
16s. to 18s.	6·8		

Source: E. L. Chappell, *Report on Welsh Housing Schemes* (1915), and *S.W.D.N.*, 18 July 1913.

The most useful figures for comparison are the charges per square yard. In the valleys, ground rent ranged from $\frac{1}{2}d.$ to $2\frac{1}{2}d.$ a square yard. In Cardiff, charges had been $1\frac{1}{2}d.$ a square yard on the Homfray estate in the 1850s, but this was exceptionally low. The Bute estate charges at that time in Butetown were $2\frac{3}{4}d.$ a square yard in the back streets and 6d. in main streets. For lower middle-class houses at Gabalfa around 1910, the Bute estate was charging 6d. a square yard if the estate provided the roads or 5d. if the builder was responsible. Overall, Jevons calculated that charges had risen from 4d. to $4\frac{1}{2}d.$ at 1900 to 6d. by the war.[20] There was a similar difference in rates between the two areas. After allowing for the higher ground rents and rates in Cardiff the *net* return on a house of the same cost in the two areas was probably similar, although in gross terms the rent appeared to be at a higher level in Cardiff. To give some examples:[21]

Cost of house	Rent per week	
	Cardiff	Mining valley
£180	9s.	6s. 6d.
£200	10s.	7s. 6d.
£250	11s.	8s. 0d.

But this does not wholly explain the difference shown in table 22. While the higher gross return including ground rent and rates explains part of the contrast in the distribution of rent levels, a more important explanation is that there were simply more cheap houses in the mining valleys than in Cardiff. The major importance of the 'land question' is its ability to explain the higher unit-cost of housing in Cardiff, but this does not mean that a solution of the land question would totally resolve the problem of housing, for that was essentially a matter of the relationship between wages and house prices.

All commentators on housing – Chappell, Jevons, the Medical Officer

of Health, the Cardiff Master Builders Association, C. F. Sanders of the
Principality Building Society – were agreed that Cardiff rentals were
excessive because the conditions and charges imposed by the estate owners
were unjust and exorbitant, making it impossible for builders to erect
cheaper houses. Two reasons why this should have been so were proposed. One was through the independent investment decisions of builders.
The M.O.H. and Sanders both suggested that the high ground rents in
themselves caused builders to erect larger houses. The builder would
treat the ground rent as a charge upon capital, a deduction from his gross
income or rent. As the value of the house increased, the proportion of
gross income taken by the ground rent fell (see table 23). Since rates and
repair charges would remain more or less constant proportionate to rent,
the builder might be attracted by a larger unit cost to mitigate the impact
of ground rent.[22]

Table 23   Relationship between rent and ground rent in Cardiff, 1913

Rent per week	Average ground rent p.a.	Ground rent as % rent
5s. to 7s. 6d.	£2 10s.	14 to 18
7s. 6d. to 10s.	£3	10 to 16
10s. to 15s.	£3 15s.	9 to 12

Source: E. L. Chappell, *Cardiff's Housing Problem* (1913), 13.

More probably the connexion between high ground rent and larger
houses lay not in the independent investment decisions of builders and
owners but in the requirements imposed upon the builder by the ground
landlord which gave him no room for manoeuvre. When the corporation
was considering a council housing scheme in 1913, the Cardiff Master
Builders Association admitted a shortage of low-rented property, but
argued that the reasons for this lay outside the control of the builders in
circumstances which made it impossible for them to erect cottages:

> At present the landlord rented out portions of land; he formed roads,
> made sewers, and when the whole thing was practically ready for
> bricks and mortar the builders came on the scene. Builders had con-
> ditions set before them which were absolutely unalterable, containing
> a term of lease, the ground rent, estate charges and the minimum value
> of the house to be erected on the site. Even with all these conditions
> it might be possible for them to build a few cottages but the landowners
> were not submitting sites for the building of cottages so that they were
> helpless.

The Master Builders Association urged that if only the corporation could obtain land and make it available to the builders, they would willingly erect cottages. A scheme was proposed whereby the corporation would acquire land compulsorily under the Housing and Town Planning Act, would lay it out and let it to builders to provide cottages, which would then be purchased by the occupiers under the terms of the Small Dwellings Acquisition Act: 'The time has not arrived for the corporation of Cardiff to embark on a building scheme . . . as there is sufficient enterprise in the building trade in this city to provide workmen's dwellings if land can be offered to the building trade or provided for that body by the city corporation.' The analysis of the situation by the builders contained a large measure of self-interest, leading as it did to the conclusion that the private building industry could provide cheap working-class housing as readily as the corporation and that municipal housing was unnecessary.

Nevertheless, advocates of municipal housing concurred with the builders' analysis of the situation. In part this was an outcome of the ideological considerations already mentioned, but there was also an element of truth: the builders were working under considerable constraints. At a conference on Cardiff housing in 1914, E. L. Chappell stated that the Master Builders had summed up the position accurately when they said that they would build working-class cottages if only they were permitted to, but that estate owners would only sanction dwellings of a particular type with a rent from 9*s.* to 14*s.* a week. Estate owners drew up plans for the speculators which were almost invariably for houses of £250 or more. Although he also noted the role of strict bye-laws and heavy rates, he felt that the one thing which more than any explained the housing problem was the leasehold system and the power it gave the landlord to dictate the class of house erected. Before the corporation could solve the housing problem it would have to deal with the land problem. Cheap land would help reduce rents, but more essential was to break down the artificial barrier erected by landowners against small dwellings. His solution was only slightly different from that of the Master Builders Association. The corporation should acquire an extensive area of agricultural land and develop it economically on garden city lines. Plots could then be leased to building agencies and also to private builders, with low ground rents and without a barrier against cheap houses. Chappell differed from the builders in considering municipal activity to be superior to private enterprise, and urged that the council should act to meet the immediate deficiency. But he accepted that public bodies were neither willing nor able to provide all the needs, so that his policy became in practice like that of the Master Builders Association, to 'endeavour to assist builders by removing, as far as possible, the conditions which handicap their activities'. This emphasis upon 'artificial barriers' erected by the landowners against cheaper housing is also found in the analysis of H. S.

Jevons. In his words, the effect of estate development policies was 'the building of pretentious small houses rather than cottages'. Both Chappell and Jevons – like the M.O.H. – did also accept that 'probably the high ground rents asked would have the same effect'. Their point was, however, that the builders were not free agents able to make the choice of what size of house to erect given the financial and economic constraints, for it was dictated to them.[23]

Of course, it cannot be assumed that builders would indeed have done as they claimed and erected cheaper houses if they had not faced high ground rents and 'artificial barriers' erected by landowners. There is at least a suspicion that they would not, for all the claims to the contrary. A lot would depend upon whether investors would be prepared to buy small cottages. The fact remains that neither builders nor investors were permitted to make the choice, and, as Jevons said, 'the cost of the houses in new areas is practically determined by the estate architect whose plans speculators are required to take [and which] . . . require greater expenditure than is necessary to enable cottages to be rented at fairly low rates'. Certainly, it cannot be denied that the typical 'dwelling erected by the speculative builders to whom Cardiff owes almost entirely its structural existence has been of a large and expensive type', a fact of some importance to the housing market of the town.[24] While the views of contemporaries about the effect of ground rents were clearly based upon ideological considerations as much as upon an objective analysis of the situation, it is nevertheless necessary to stress the influence of the landowner upon the character of urban development.

6 Builders and the housing supply

The landlords might initiate development, but their lead had to be taken up by the builders. In the nineteenth century these were pre-eminently speculative builders, and although there was – at least in London – a trend to increased concentration, the industry was above all composed of small-scale units. The builders must be seen as the *agents* of the city building process, but with very little responsibility for the *character* of that process. On the one hand they were constrained by the policies of the landowners who were active in shaping development, telling the builder the value of the house and often providing the plans. But much more important, on the other hand, were the constraints set by a particular socio-economic structure. If the speculative builder erected houses for middle-class suburbanites, it was because the distribution of income was so unequal that the working class could not afford decent housing, and it simply did not pay the builders to do anything else. The builder was simply a pawn in a much larger game, responding flexibly to a given situation but not really shaping it. As Professor Dyos has said, 'his must be regarded simply as the last tittle of responsibility for the way in which his generation was making use of suburban land'.[1]

I

Some economists would go even further and make builders pawns in an international process of factor flows determining the level of activity in the housing industry at any time. This view is particularly associated with Brinley Thomas.[2] He makes the amount of capital available to the building industry in Britain dependent upon a cycle of interaction between the British and the American economies. Building in the two economies was, he argues, inversely related. When economic activity was high in the U.S.A., emigration and the export of capital from Britain were high as well. This reduced both the supply of capital for the construction of houses, and the demand for housing as migrants went to the U.S.A. rather than into the towns within Britain. When activity was at a low level in the U.S.A., however, migration was internal to Britain, from the country to the towns, and there was also a ready supply of capital for use at home. House building thus revived with the availability of both demand and finance. The city building process is thus to be seen as part of the flow of factors within an Atlantic economy.

In Wales, however, this pattern did not apply. The cycles of migration and building were inverse to those in England and Scotland, and hence building in Wales was positively related to building in America. Thomas is able, however, to fit the Welsh experience into his model of the Atlantic economy.

> The interpretation of this inverse relation lies in the fact that Welsh industry was geared almost entirely to the export trade in coal. When we divide Britain into two sectors, home investment and export, the coalmining areas of Wales fall wholly within the export sector. . . . Since the Welsh economy was entirely export-orientated, its upswings coincided with upswings in the English export sector; the latter were accompanied by downswings in the home construction sector of England. During such phases . . . Welsh economic growth was strong enough to retain nearly the whole of the country's natural increase or even to attract an appreciable net inflow from the rest of the United Kingdom, whereas in England the relatively slow rate of growth of the home construction sector caused a large part of the rural surplus . . . to emigrate overseas. Thus, low emigration from (or immigration into) Wales coincided with high emigration from England. On the other hand, when the Welsh economy was in a downswing relative to trend, the English home construction sector was simultaneously experiencing a rapid upswing, with the export sector declining relative to trend. In this phase the workers displaced from the land in Wales, facing a weak demand for labour in the urban areas of their own country, migrated over the border to England where there was a brisk demand for labour in the flourishing home investment sector.[3]

The growth of towns in south Wales is thus integrated into the flow of factors in the Atlantic economy. So far as Cardiff is concerned, J. Hamish Richards has tried to apply the theory by demonstrating that 'there is a marked relationship between the main turning points of the Cardiff housing series and the series showing the value of the total imports and exports of merchandise at the port of Cardiff. The turning points in the latter series precede those in housing by between one and three years'.[4]

Obviously, the whole south Wales economy was dependent upon the export trade in coal, and this was certainly true of Cardiff. The export demand for coal was the main factor behind the growth of output and the growth of population and hence the demand for housing. But the Thomas model is far too neat and sensitive. Certainly Richards' analysis of the Cardiff case does not bear close inspection, for both of his series are inaccurate. The housing series is calculated from an incorrect population, while the trade series should be for the Bute docks and not the port, which also included the shipments at Barry and Penarth. Using the correct series, the relationship discerned by Richards disappeared. His trough of trade in 1875–6 is in fact almost a million tons above his peak of 1873–4, which upsets his explanation of the trough of 1876 and the peak of 1875 in housing. Again, his peak of trade in 1891 'explaining' the peak of house building in 1893 becomes a trough when Barry is excluded. It becomes difficult to accept that the building cycle was immediately sensitive to changes in total trade at the docks as Richards suggested. Obviously, the amount of trade at the docks set long-term limits to the population of Cardiff and the demand for housing. But the relationship was indirect, being transmitted via a series of processes. It was not simply that an extra so many tons of coal required an extra inhabitant or house. The whole multiplier effect has to be considered. The multiplier was not constant. At what point was another shop assistant, or lawyer, or shipping clerk called for? When did the town attain the status of a regional capital and with what effects? The relationship between trade and the building cycle was mediated by the timing of dock extension and was not direct and sensitive. And if this is generally true, the connexion with the U.S.A. in particular is even more dubious, for the U.S.A. was not an important market for south Wales coal. In the Thomas argument, high activity in the U.S.A. meant high emigration and export of capital from the U.K., which reduced the demand for houses and the supply of capital for their production. South Wales is, however, set apart from this because high activity in the U.S.A. meant high demand for south Wales coal and hence high building activity in south Wales at the same time as in the U.S.A.[5] The fact that in 1900 the U.S.A. was taking under 2 per cent of Welsh coal exports casts some doubt on such an analysis. The main market was in Europe, where activity was positively related to cycles in the U.K. and which accordingly cannot explain why the south Wales building cycle was out of phase with the rest of the country.[6] The most likely answer to the problem is that the whole approach is misguided, and that there was a whole series of regional building cycles determined by local factors.

The argument in any case suggests too ideal a mobility of factors of production. A peak in activity in the U.S.A. is immediately translated into a rise in production in south Wales, which is immediately translated into house building and population movement. This surely misunderstands both the nature of investment in the coal industry and in the building industry. The coal industry did not in peak years suddenly require new pits, new labour and so new housing. The process of opening a pit was a lengthy one, so that new pits tended to open after the peak activity, leaving an excess capacity to be utilized in the next peak. It was also speculative. A boom year would encourage speculative investment which would result in a period of over-production.[7] The same points apply to investment in housing.

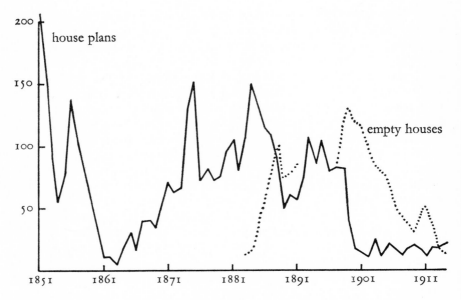

Figure 5. House plans passed and empty houses per 10,000 population, Cardiff 1851–1914 (source: Annual Reports of Medical Officer of Health).

House building was a very speculative activity, the market very imperfect and the industry very fragmented. Activity went in bursts, with a tendency to over-building leading to a surplus of houses which the increase in population had to absorb over time. External considerations were marginal. Investment in housing was largely determined by causes special to the domestic housing market and was not a residual activity undertaken when opportunities for investment elsewhere were poor. Thomas implies that there was one capital market, with money mobile within it, between foreign and home investment, housing and other outlets. But it is more likely that the capital market was to some extent compartmentalized, with house building attracting a particular type of capital which was not freely mobile between all outlets. This point is taken up in the next chapter, but essentially investment in housing was local, an outlet for small amounts of capital by those who wanted to keep an eye on their assets, who were not prepared to put their money into shares or send it abroad. They were not interested in small variations in rates of interest between home and abroad, between housing and other sectors. They wanted something local and safe. This suggests that slight changes in the cost of borrowing were unimportant in determining flows of capital into housing, and there is no sign that building was ever checked by an absence of capital. There was an underlying block of capital peculiar to housing; this is not to deny, of course, that other more fluid capital might not switch to housing in the downturn of the trade cycle when alternative outlets were less attractive. There were no shortages of capital – but there might at times be a glut.

Neither did fluctuations in building result from fine calculations of demand for housing depending upon emigration to U.S.A. Thomas has made the building industry appear very sensitive to small changes in market conditions. It was in fact very insensitive. The loss by emigration was after all a very small part of total demand and could hardly have been a major determinant of building activity. The peak loss by emigration was 601,000 in the 1880s, when the net increase in population was 3·03m. The industry was very insensitive to marginal changes in market conditions – it was imperfect and speculative. A building boom usually came to an end as a result of internal considerations, an overshooting of demand leading to a rise in vacant property and a fall in rents. What determined activity more than any other factor was a local index, the level of empty houses, and the building industry was not very sensitive even to this, for once the process was under way it was difficult to stop. Nevertheless, it was this index more than the trade of the docks immediately which determined the building cycle. Obviously, demand for coal – for which the U.S.A. was a minor market – set parameters to the growth of south Wales and Cardiff. But also of importance were the investment decisions of the Bute estate which mediated between the increasing demand for coal from south Wales and the share of Cardiff in that trade, and the internal structure of both the coal and building industries. Saul makes a valid point when he says that rather than attempting to construct complex interactions between the British and the American economies, for which evidence is very slender, there is a need for a greater understanding of the internal structure of the building industry to appreciate exactly how it operated and responded to changing market conditions.[8] What then, was the structure of the building industry in Cardiff?

II

When a house plan was passed by the Public Works Committee, the name of the person obtaining permission and the number of houses involved were printed in the council minutes.[9] In using this information to analyse the structure of the building industry there are two sources of error: not all plans would be proceeded with; and not all the persons submitting plans were necessarily builders. But having said this, the vast majority of plans *were* obtained by builders and *were* proceeded with, so for all practical purposes an analysis of house plans obtained can be taken as a measure of firms engaged in house building. Four five-year periods were studied. The general pattern is clear from table 24.

Table 24 House plans passed, 1879–1914

House plans obtained	1879–84 firms %	houses %	1889–94 firms %	houses %	1899–1904 firms %	houses %	1909–14 firms %	houses %
1–6	51·4	10·4	46·5	10·8	40·0	10·5	38·6	6·9
7–12	19·9	11·6	21·0	13·0	26·3	19·1	15·7	8·0
13–18	8·7	8·0	7·3	7·4	13·8	15·8	10·0	7·4
19–24	6·5	8·4	7·3	10·7	2·5	3·9	8·6	9·1
25–30	2·2	3·6	4·9	9·0	3·7	7·1	7·1	10·4
31–36	1·4	2·9	3·6	8·4	3·7	9·5	2·8	4·8
37–42	1·8	4·3	2·4	6·6	3·7	11·1	4·3	8·8
43–48	1·8	5·0	1·2	3·7	3·7	12·0	1·4	3·3
49–54	1·1	3·4	1·8	6·5	nil	nil	2·8	7·6
55–60	1·1	3·7	0·9	3·4	2·5	10·9	4·3	12·8
over 60	4·0	38·6	3·0	20·3	nil	nil	4·3	20·9

The small firms, obtaining 12 plans or less over 5 years, formed a decreasing proportion of all firms, falling from about 70 per cent to somewhat over a half. The proportion of house plans obtained by these small firms rose somewhat, from 22 to 30 per cent, but then fell by half to 15 per cent in the years 1909–14. Medium firms (13 to 24 plans in 5 years) increased from 15 to 19 per cent of all firms, and accounted for between 16 and 20 per cent of the plans. Large firms – over 25 plans in 5 years – doubled from 13 to 27 per cent, and were responsible for between 51 and 69 per cent of the houses. These firms were, however, large only by comparison with other builders. The mean size of firm is shown in table 25. By no definition was the building industry concentrated.

Table 25   Mean size of builders in Cardiff

	house plans obtained over 5-year period	annual average
1879–84	16·4	3·28
1889–94	14·7	2·94
1899–1904	13·6	2·72
1909–14	19·5	3·90

Any attempt to go beyond this point comes up against the almost un-relieved anonymity of the builders. The situation can at least be discussed in a negative manner. There were few of the building companies or syndicates which built many houses in Barry from the late 1880s. An example from Barry was the Kingsland Crescent Building Co., which was formed in 1890 with a capital of £7,000 in £5 shares to erect 48 houses. One or two companies of this sort appear in Cardiff, but they were of peripheral importance. Of more significance was the activity in the 1870s and early 1880s of the cottage companies which used money borrowed from the Public Works Loan Commissioners at 4 per cent to build low-rent pro-perty. There were four such companies. The first – the Cardiff Work-men's Cottage Co. – was formed in 1869 and by 1884 reached its peak of 348 houses. The Glamorgan Workmen's Cottage Co. was formed in 1881, and in all built 222 houses. The other two companies were small, and altogether the cottage companies accounted for 3 per cent of the housing stock of 1891. In the early 1880s the activity of the companies was seen as 'the most practical way of dealing with the mooted artisan dwelling house question', and as 'singularly well-adapted to the wants of the work-ing-classes', while at the same time the companies were 'a sound invest-ment for capitalists'. Certainly, the Cardiff Cottage Co. paid dividends of $7\frac{1}{2}$ to 8 per cent at least up to the early 1880s. And the cheap money from the Public Works Loan Board, with the unusually low ground rents of as little as 8s.–£1 on the Windsor estate, allowed cottages to be let at 5s. a week which, in the opinion of the Medical Officer of Health, provided excellent accommodation for one family. The snag was that only about 650 of these cottages were built, or 5 per cent of the houses erected between 1871 and 1891.[10]

If building companies and cottage companies made only a minor contribution to the housing stock, the activities of employers providing houses for their workers was even less. This was in contrast with the mining areas of south Wales where, in the early stages of development and again after 1910, the coal companies were forced to provide housing for their workers in the absence of other agencies. In Cardiff, the employers were not obliged to provide housing by the failure of anyone else to do so, but rather by a desire to maintain control over the workforce. The only significant example was the Dowlais Iron Co. Otherwise, employers provided under 100 houses. When the D.I.C. transferred its main steel plant to Cardiff, ten acres were taken adjacent to the works and 222 cottages erected. Tenants were D.I.C. employees, and dismissal from work seems to have implied eviction. Not only had the works been transferred to Cardiff, but also the attitudes formed in Dowlais as an industrial community had been created in the early nineteenth century.[11]

The final negative point to be made is that whereas in Swansea, the eastern valleys of Glamorgan and in Monmouthshire, building clubs provided a large part of housing, in Cardiff there is no evidence of such activity. Unlike other areas of south Wales, builders were not usually engaged by building companies or clubs, or by employers – at least 90 per cent of houses were built as a speculation, by builders in a small way of business.[12] Around 1880 they were responsible for a capital investment of the order of £200,000 a year.[13] The only other capital investment in Cardiff which could rival this was the investment in the docks. But despite the importance of the topic, there is a dearth of information on the financing of the builders. Clearly, they must have been building on credit, and hoping for a quick sale to pay off their debts. Exactly where the credit came from is uncertain – some came from building societies but more than that cannot be discovered. An informant of H. S. Jevons suggested that there was a change in the nature of finance after the late 1890s, because mortgages given by solicitors became unpopular as a means of investment. When the building boom ended in 1898 more houses had been built than were required and mortgagees lost money. Until then, Cardiff had been regarded as a good investment for mortgages; after 1898, confidence was never regained.[14]

The exact nature of financing of builders is not clear, but is unlikely to have been very different from the general pattern of building societies, insurance companies and solicitors providing the necessary finance.[15] What can be shown is to whom the builders disposed of the houses and so who eventually invested in housing, rather than who provided short-term loans to builders This is an even more neglected topic than the structure of the building industry, and will be discussed in detail in the next chapter. But first of all it should be asked: how successful was this process of city building in meeting the demand for housing? And how did contemporaries aim to overcome any shortcomings?

If Olsen is to be believed, the question to be asked is not 'why were Victorian cities so badly built', but 'how it was they were built as well as they were'. He even claims that the working class got housing which was adequate and at a price which it could afford. Building land was cheap and plentiful; there was a host of builders ready to risk everything; and an abundance of investors 'virtually forcing their money on the builders and developers'.[16] Does Cardiff bear this out? On the whole it does not, for the resources were used to construct the wrong sort of houses, being of particular assistance to the middle class and the new suburbia rather than the working class. In a sense, Cardiff was too well built, with too many houses which were out of the reach of the working class. The reasons for this are deep rooted in the socio-economic structure of the nineteenth century. If the working class was to have decent housing they had to have higher wages, so long as housing was provided by the free market. As it was, they could not afford new houses at an economic rent, so capital avoided this sector. The suburbs were the strategic component in the housing of the whole urban community. It was the pace of their development and the amount of capital they consumed which determined the provision of housing for the working class. Indeed, it is likely that the flow of private capital into surbuban house building is always at the expense of investment in lower-grade housing, unless modified by subsidies for working-class housing. The important point is not the flow of capital between housing in the U.S.A. and Britain; it is the concentration of capital *within housing* upon suburbia.[17]

The city building process was not quite the success Olsen suggests, and contemporaries were groping towards reform. There could be two effective changes. One was to increase wages and achieve a more equal distribution of income so that the working class could afford to buy or rent the products of a private building industry and give the investors an economic return. There was, however, little sign that the whole socio-economic structure would be altered. Given this, workers could not afford to pay an economic rent so the second possibility was for the municipality to subsidize housing, replacing private and economic provision of housing by public and social provision. This was not very appealing, casting as it did doubts on the efficacy of the free market and of capitalism. In Cardiff, it did seem by 1914 as if the council was nevertheless and reluctantly being forced into such a position.

III
The fact that the estate owners required builders to erect larger houses than they might otherwise have done was regarded by contemporaries

as the basis of the housing problem of Cardiff. Houses were too large and too expensive for one working-class family, so there was a high level of subletting. This feature was noted repeatedly by the Medical Officer of Health, but he believed that overcrowding did not ensue, for each house was large enough for two families. The 1908 Board of Trade Enquiry supported him. Cardiff had only 2·9 per cent of its population in over-crowded tenements (i.e. two or more persons per room), which made it 21st of all towns of over 100,000. However, in 1911 Cardiff ranked eighth in terms of persons per inhabited house. After rising to 1871, the number of persons per inhabited house had indeed declined (table 26).

Table 26   *Persons per inhabited house in Cardiff, 1801–1911*

1801	5·9	1871	7·4
1811	5·2	1871*	7·0
1821	5·5	1881	6·8
1831	4·4	1891	6·3
1841	5·8	1901	5·9
1851	7·2	1911	5·9
1861	7·1	*1875 boundaries	

Source: *Census of England and Wales* 1801-1911

It was true that in 1911, 36·2 per cent of families were sharing houses, but the absence of overcrowding by the census definition enabled most contemporaries to deny the existence of a housing problem. Also, the fact that almost three-quarters of houses had been built since 1871 and regulated by bye-laws made even the most ardent housing reformer, E. L. Chappell, admit that Cardiff had no slums in the strict sense.[18]

However, while Chappell accepted that 'Cardiff is, perhaps, the least "slummy" of the south Wales towns, from the standpoint of excessive rents and the consequent subdivision of dwellings, however, it occupies the most unenviable position'.[19] According to Chappell, of houses let at 18s. a week or less, only 7·5 per cent were available at rentals which lower-paid workers could afford; only 26 per cent could be rented by ordinary working-class families without subletting; while nearly 75 per cent were rented at sums which could be paid only by sharing.[20] Cardiff's housing problem was that the houses being erected were larger and more expensive than could be afforded, but workers had no option but to take them because of the absence of a stock of old, low-rent property (except for the courts in the centre) and because of the failure to build anything cheaper (except by the cottage companies). Chappell calculated in 1913 that if a person took a whole house, the situation was as in table 27. It was obviously impossible to pay such large sums in rent, so houses had

Table 27 Relationship between wages and rents in Cardiff c. 1913

wage	rent	rent as % wage
15*s.* to 24*s.*	6*s.* to 7*s.*	40 to 30
24*s.* to 32*s.*	8*s.* to 9*s.*	36 to 28
32*s.* to £2	10*s.*	32 to 24
£2 to £4	10*s.* to 16*s.*	27 to 20

Source: E. L. Chappell, *Cardiff's Housing Problem* (1913), 6.

to be sub-let. In 1894 an investigation in south Roath found most houses were six-roomed, with rents of 8*s.* to 8*s.* 6*d*, rising to 9*s.* and 10*s.* Men earning 24*s.* to 28*s.* a week lived in these houses, and as one workman said, 'There is not one tenant in ten who does not let unfurnished apartments. That's how they have to do; they couldn't get along otherwise. . . . These are not the sort of building which ought to be put up for working men. . . . They are too large.' This, said the reformers, was the housing problem of Cardiff: 'the Cardiff housing problem consists . . . in providing lower rented dwellings for occupation by single families, who are now in all parts of the city compelled to share dwellings with other families.'[21]

What, then, was the distribution of rents? The Board of Trade Enquiry of 1908 found the situation as shown in table 28.

Table 28 Rents in Cardiff, October 1905

number of rooms	predominant weekly rent
2	3*s.* 6*d.* to 4*s.* 6*d.*
3	4*s.* 0*d.* to 5*s.* 0*d.*
4	5*s.* 0*d.* to 6*s.* 0*d.*
5	6*s.* 0*d.* to 7*s.* 0*d.*
6	6*s.* 6*d.* to 8*s.* 6*d.*
7	9*s.* 0*d.* to 11*s.* 0*d.*

Source: *Board of Trade Enquiry*, 1908, 135.

The majority of working-class houses were, the Report said, six-roomed, and two rooms were often let unfurnished. This applied to half the labourers in the town. The reports of the Medical Officer of Health confirm this and show the sort of sums involved. He inspected 3,208 six-roomed houses between 1911 and 1914. Further, in 1,477 of the houses he inspected two rooms were sub-let. The rentals are given in table 29. This suggests a typical case as follows: a labourer in a six-roomed house paying a rent of 6*s.* 6*d.* to 9*s.* would sub-let two rooms for 3*s.* to 4*s.* 3*d.*, so reducing the amount paid in rent by about half, the proportion of wage

Table 29 Rent of houses and sub-let rooms, 1911–14

rent of 6-roomed houses

(3,208 cases)	percentage
5s. 0d. and less	2·6
5s. 3d. to 6s. 3d.	7·2
6s. 6d. to 7s. 3d.	30·6
7s. 6d. to 8s. 0d.	26·3
8s. 3d. to 9s. 0d.	22·8
9s. 0d. and above	10·5

rent of 2 sub-let rooms

(1,477 cases)	percentage
under 2s. 6d.	4·7
2s. 6d. to 2s. 9d.	11·2
3s. 0d. to 3s. 3d.	27·8
3s. 6d. to 3s. 9d.	33·2
4s. 0d. to 4s. 3d.	18·3
above 4s. 6d.	4·9

to about 15 per cent. In all, 36·2 per cent of families were sharing accommodation in 1911.[22]

The building industry before 1914 was concentrating on even more expensive houses, letting at 9s. to 15s. a week, which was beyond the reach not just of labourers but also of artisans and clerical workers. This in consequence forced 'large numbers of families to occupy dwellings which were hitherto regarded as beyond their capacities'. Jevons pointed out around 1913 that:

> workmen's houses from 6s. 6d. to 7s. per week are not to be obtained. As a result in most parts of the town the apartment system has become the general thing. Hardly can a workman family afford to have a house for himself . . . 9s. or even 10s. is the usual rent for a workman's house. . . . There is in the city a lamentable scarcity of small cheaply rented houses for the lower waged workers. . . . No effort is being made to cater for the needs of the low waged labourers. Practically all the new houses contain six rooms and are rented from 10s. to 15s. a week.[23]

The spread of rents in the city just before the war is shown in table 30.

Table 30 Typical rents in Cardiff c. 1914

Best working-class house	7, 8 rooms	bath	10s. to 11s.
Ordinary working-class house			
30 years old, in short supply	6, 7 rooms	no bath	7s. 6d. to 9s.
Oldest area	5 rooms	no bath	6s.
New houses	6 rooms	bath	10s. to 15s.

Source: N. L. W. Jevons IV 126.

Cardiff's housing problem was not on the whole structural; it was that houses were of the wrong sort, being increasingly larger and more expensive. What was the contemporary reaction to the high rents (or more strictly, high unit cost of housing) and sub-letting which formed the basis of the Cardiff housing problem?

For the greater part of the period there were two reactions. Because Cardiff was not 'slummy', the housing problem did not impinge on the middle-class consciousness. High rents and sub-letting concerned the domestic arrangements of working-class families, of which the middle class need never be aware. Instead they saw areas of sound bye-law housing and concluded that Cardiff had no housing problem, except perhaps the courts in the centre. In a structural sense, the conclusion was correct, and there was little attempt to go further until after 1910. In Cardiff there was none of that continuous activity by middle-class philanthropists and social reformers in the field of housing that there was in many other towns. Housing was *not* central to the liberal definition of the social problem in Cardiff as it was in London; central to the liberal outlook in Cardiff were prostitution, drink and sabbatarianism.[24] Insofar as housing *was* seen as a problem, it was connected with the land question. The need was to tax land values and to enfranchise leaseholders to reduce the rents and rates. These were the two dominant middle-class responses to housing: either to accept the structural soundness of housing as proof of the absence of a problem, or to see the central factor as a land question.

Both views were adopted by the Medical Officer of Health who explained the existence of expensive housing by the level of ground rents, but who also felt that the consequent sub-letting was not a matter for concern. The dominant impression was indeed lack of concern. Indicative of this was the history of the corporation's Housing of the Working Classes Committee. This met in November 1899, when it was resolved to meet on the call of the chairman. A meeting was held in June 1900, and that was the sum total of its work, and although it was reappointed in subsequent years, on no occasion was it convened. Neither was housing an important political question.[25] However, a change in attitudes came quite suddenly at the end of 1910.

During the municipal elections of 1910 housing was not discussed, but at the end of the campaign the *South Wales Daily News* remarked that 'progressive Cardiff has no Housing Committee; it is time it had'. In 1911 both the *South Wales Daily News* and the *Western Mail* commissioned a series of articles on housing conditions in south Wales. The *Western Mail* correspondent was J. A. Lovat-Fraser, a barrister and a Conservative councillor in Cardiff, and he later remarked that what he found came as a great surprise to him, leading to a realization that housing reform lay at the root of the social problem and involving him in the garden city movement. The professor of economics at University College came to a similar conclusion at the same time, for in 1911 H. S. Jevons resigned his chair to become managing director of the Housing Reform Co. And in January 1911 the housing question quite suddenly engaged the attention of the council. The Health Committee, having done nothing for 20 years, went on a tour of houses with the Medical Officer of Health and was shocked by conditions in the central courts. Immediately closing orders were issued, and the M.O.H. and the City Engineer ordered to prepare an improvement scheme. The council was moved to wonder what the M.O.H. had been doing in the past that unfit houses should be discovered only as a result of a special inspection by the Health Committee. In his report for 1905 he had been very optimistic and announced that no improvement scheme was necessary – but in 1911 his optimism went by the board.[26]

The striking emergence of concern for housing around 1910 must be understood in a national context. The work of men such as T. C. Horsfall, E. R. Dewsnup, J. S. Nettlefold, and Patrick Geddes, and the passing of the Housing, Town Planning Etc. Act of 1909 provided the background to the discovery of a housing problem in Cardiff. Also, the local context had changed. As a result of the overbuilding of the 1890s, the percentage of empty houses in 1899 was 6·8; in 1905 it was 4·2; but by 1909 it was 1·8. And it became clear that the building industry was not responding to the changed situation, particularly at the bottom end of the market, for by 1914 the level of empty houses was down to 0·8 per cent of the housing stock. The situation demanded some sort of response.[27]

The Housing Reform Co., with Jevons as its guiding light, reflects one approach to the housing problem. The Company had three objects: to form co-operative societies to own houses erected by the Company to its own designs; to promote the adoption of garden city and town planning principles in its own operations and by advice to landlords; and to introduce new techniques in house planning and construction. As far as the third point is concerned, the Company was agent for a number of new processes of building. It was decided, however, to concentrate upon the first two objects, which were, indeed, combined. The aim was to develop co-operative garden villages. Co-operative societies were seen to have a number of advantages. In the first place they would ensure the continuing attractiveness of housing as an investment, which otherwise had a number of drawbacks. A person who owned one or two houses had to face 'trouble and petty annoyance'. He had the problem of collecting rent weekly, with the danger of defaulting, and he had the question of repairs to consider. There was also the difficulty of limited convertibility of the investment, and its possible depreciation when sold. Housing was therefore felt to be losing its attractiveness as a form of investment to municipal loans and company shares. But the rate of return was said to be better than with safe securities, more on a par with industrial companies producing 5 or 6 per cent, which entailed a risk. According to Jevons, 'what is wanted is some method of arranging investment in house property by which the trouble and risk can be removed without reducing the rate of interest'. Co-operative housing societies were his solution. £1 shares would be issued which would give a safe 5 per cent return, averaging risks of vacancies over a number of houses and being more convertible and less open to the risk of depreciation. In the second place, there were the benefits to the tenants of the houses. Each tenant would be a shareholder in the society, so that the tenants would be perpetually joint-owners of the whole property erected by the society, and would annually elect a committee to control the property. This would have an 'educative influence' on tenant members who would be governing their 'garden village'. 'Further', said Jevons, 'there is the advantage that the committee can exclude persons who are not good neighbours and make rules against common neighbours.' What emerges, therefore, is not just an attempt to maintain the attractiveness of housing as an investment, but also an attempt to replace an amorphous, impersonal urban society by a cluster of self-governing villages in a semi-rural setting – a 'vision . . . of a series of beautiful garden suburbs around Cardiff', with 'the establishment of a happy and pretty little village'. The co-operative garden village movement was seeking more than a solution to the shortage of housing; it was after a new society. This was clear from a brochure of 1913 issued by the Cardiff Workers Co-operative Garden Village which noted that a 'missionary spirit prevails': 'The society has a message to the people of south Wales to promote the spread of a new civilising and uplifting influence. It is a movement of the people for the people, and is to bring them far greater things than merely sound and honest bricks and mortar – though these are often hard to get.' In Jevons's Utopia, co-operative societies would control not only housing; common or joint ownership would apply to everything except a family's household goods. He did not, however, get very far with the restructuring of society, or, indeed, with the provision of 'sound and honest bricks and mortar'.

By 1912 the Housing Reform Co. (or South Wales Garden Villages Association, as it became) had sponsored four garden villages in south Wales. The village at Cardiff was the first and only successful garden village to be formed in the city. The Housing Reform Co. in 1912 took an option on a site to the north of Cardiff. On ten acres, the Cardiff Workers Co-operative Garden Village Society would build 300 houses at rents of 5s. 6d. to 10s. 6d. a week 'for the yues ov wurcing men, solid artisans, clarcs, shop asistants, and urthers ov moderait incums', while on 20 acres the Pentwyn Garden Village Society would build houses at rents of 10s. 6d. upwards. The latter does not appear to have built any houses, while the Workers Society was only a little more successful than its orthography. By 1915 only 60 houses had been erected. The success was indirect, in shaping the planning of the subsequent council estates.[28]

However limited the actual impact of the garden city movement on the housing market, it was nevertheless greater before 1914 than that of council housing schemes, the need for which was also recognized for the first time. At the beginning of 1911 the corporation's policy on housing was still characterized by 'dawdle and drift', and pressure built up for a separate Housing Committee. This met for the first time in January 1912. During that year attention turned from the courts in the centre of town to a realization that low-rent working-class houses were required, and that the council should take action. In June 1912 the Housing Committee instructed the city engineer to draw up a scheme to build small houses on corporation land to rent at 5s. to 6s. 6d. By the end of the year land had been obtained from other committees, and in January 1913 it was decided to build 30 houses at a cost of £170 each and a rent of 6s. 6d. There was to be no charge upon the rates, and in the end the rent had to be fixed at 7s. to break even. It was glaringly obvious that 30 houses at a rent of 7s. a week had not met the need for cheap houses at rents which the working class could afford. Meanwhile, the housing question had become a political issue. In 1912 a few councillors stood on a platform of communal responsibility for working-class housing, urging a large-scale provision of small houses at 5s. 6d. a week. Also in 1912 the Trades Council set up a Housing Sub-Committee which called for houses at a maximum rent of 5s. 3d. and in 1913 made housing a platform question. During 1913 a number of councillors were pressing for large-scale provision of cheap houses and at the end of the year the Housing Committee was instructed to consider the erection of houses at a rental of 5s. a week.[29]

Perceptions of the housing problem had thus changed very markedly. The problem was knowing what to do about it. E. L. Chappell is a good illustration of this. He had located the nature of the housing problem, in a shortage of about 2,000 cottages at rents of 4s. to 6s. The reason for this, he said, lay in the control of the land market. But he was not quite sure what to do about it. He was not a consistent advocate of municipal housing in preference to all other solutions. At one point he suggested co-partnership housing, at another he called for the municipalization of land to reduce ground rents, so permitting builders to supply the houses by breaking down the 'artificial barriers' erected by landowners. Sometimes he thought the municipality could supply houses at rents 25 to 30 per cent lower than currently paid, and still break even; at other times he thought there would have to be some charge upon the ratepayer. So in 1912–13 his solution varied, but with certain fundamentals remaining the same. It was expected that the problem could be solved by tackling the land question, without necessarily having subsidized municipal housing, or even municipal ownership of housing. It was never posited that it was impossible to provide decent working-class housing at a market rent for the simple reason that a market rent was bound to be too high for the working class to afford, given current wage levels. It was far easier to put the blame on the aristocratic landlords for making rents too high than upon the organization of the economic system for making wages too low. What must be stressed is the continuing uncertainty of the best course of action to be taken to solve a problem so defined.[30]

The council showed a similar uncertainty. It wanted to erect houses to let at 5*s*. but had not managed to build under 7*s*. In 1914 it retreated from direct involvement, offering instead to provide cheap land for the private sector, on condition that houses were built at rentals not exceeding 6*s*. 6*d*. But the Master Builders Association was unable to give such a guarantee, and indeed when the Housing Committee decided to develop the land on its own account a rent of 7*s*. was needed to break even, let alone to make any profit which the private sector would have required. Eventually, the council's scheme was modified to reduce rents to 6*s*. 9*d*. and 6*s*. 3*d*., and the construction of 143 houses was about to start on the outbreak of war. Two years previously the Trades Council and interested councillors had realized that rents should be nearer 5*s*. Financial orthodoxy, even with cheap land, could not deliver the necessary houses. By 1914 the activities of the council had shown that the housing problem *was* more than a land question and that it was simply impossible to provide housing at rents which the working class could afford.

The war relieved the council of the unpleasant experience of having to face up to the logic of the situation. The decision was eventually made at the national level, and subsidized municipal housing schemes were to be of major importance after the war. Before the war, there had only been the most tentative beginnings of a municipal policy, the exact basis of which had never been thought out. The sudden change in attitudes after 1910 is interesting, but it must be noted that those involved were only groping towards solutions. Chappell on one occasion suggested subsidized council housing, but then retreated from it; at one stage the Housing Committee retreated from the idea of itself providing houses. Certainly, the Committee never wanted susidized housing, but it was already beginning to appear inevitable, for the council wanted rents of 5*s*., while the best that could be achieved was 6*s*. 3*d*. A tension was building up between what was considered possible and what was seen to be socially desirable. Gradually, the treatment of the housing question as a land question was being superseded as force of circumstances showed the problem to be far greater.[31]

7 Home-owners and landlords

Over a decade ago, S. B. Saul suggested that historians, rather than constructing complex interactions between the British and the United States economies to explain the pattern of investment in housing, should seek a greater understanding of the internal structure of the building industry to appreciate more precisely how the industry did operate and respond to changing market conditions.[1] Such information is now becoming available, especially in the case of London. The preceding chapters add a provincial example. What is still unclear is who bought the houses from the speculative builders, and it is therefore important to take a third step, from the estates as initiators of development and the speculative builders as the agents, to those who purchased the resulting product. This is certainly necessary in order to give some support to the analysis of investment in housing which was suggested earlier.

The source used with this purpose in mind was the municipal rate books, which list, street by street, the rateable value, owner, and occupier of each house in a local government area. In the case of Cardiff, complete sets survive for 1884 and 1914 and these have been studied, along with partial sets for 1894 and 1904. From the rate books it was a simple matter to calculate, for the entire housing stock, the percentage of houses owned by their occupiers at 1884 and 1914. For 1884, the ownership of each *tenanted* house was also recorded – a time-consuming process which could not be contemplated for 1914 when the number of houses had more than doubled. Accordingly, for 1914 ownership of tenanted houses was recorded for only two suburbs. It was felt that it would be inadequate to record information for all houses without differentiation, so ranges of rateable value were selected which would very roughly divide houses by the occupational class of the inhabitants. The following ranges were selected by using the street directories (which list the occupations of most heads of household) to ascertain what sort of person lived in a house of what rateable value:

1. Rateable values of over £35: houses largely of professional class and merchants.
2. Rateable values of £20–34: houses largely of middle class.
3. Rateable values of £12–19: houses largely of artisans and clerks.
4. Rateable values of under £12: houses largely of semi-skilled and unskilled working class.

The methodology has been outlined elsewhere in detail for those who require a justification of such procedures. At present, the concern is with the results which emerged.[2]

I

The first issue to raise is the proportion of houses owned by their occupiers. Professor Bowley has claimed that before 1914 'houses cost too much for the ordinary working-class family to buy'. As far as the middle class is concerned, Professor Sigsworth and Miss Blackman have written that in the 1890s 'the fashionable suburban separate family dwelling [came] within the purchasing power of a whole new class of would-be house owners'. There is, therefore, a suggestion of negligible working-class owner-occupation and an increase in the level of middle-class home ownership before 1914, although by how much and from what initial level is not stated. This forms a useful starting point for discussion.[3]

It might be disputed whether it was so self-evident that workers could not afford to buy houses. Could it not be that the very fact that rent was such a large proportion of earnings encouraged at least regular wage-earners to become owner-occupiers? Dr Chapman has noted that in Leeds in the 1780s, Lancashire in the 1790s and Nottingham in the 1820s the better-off artisans were amongst those who formed building clubs to help one another become property owners. The Royal Commissions on Friendly Societies of 1872 and the Housing of the Working Classes of 1884 both found that the working class in certain areas – especially Yorkshire and Lancashire – was still active within building societies, buying houses not just to occupy but also to let. The urban report of the Land Enquiry Committee in 1914 also found a number of towns in which working-class home ownership was achieved. The topic of working-class home ownership is not, therefore, to be dismissed out of hand. The problem lies in assessing the variation in the extent of ownership over time and between areas, and the degree of fulfilment of 'the love or desire to possess property' which the London Trades Council found among the working class.[4]

That the desire to possess property could in certain areas be fulfilled on a fairly extensive scale is indicated by evidence from the hinterland of Cardiff. Contemporaries were agreed that the miners in south Wales were remarkably successful in becoming house-owners. On the basis of a return made to the Monmouthshire and South Wales Coalowners Association, 19·2 per cent of houses in the whole coalfield were owned by colliery workmen. This overall figure masks variations between different parts of the coalfield. Professor H. S. Jevons, writing in about 1914, noted that

exact figures are not available but the percentage of occupying owners
would appear to vary from about 15 up to 60 per cent in the mining
valleys. . . . A very high percentage (over 60) is stated to be in Ferndale
and Mardy in the Rhondda Fach. Building clubs flourish in Monmouthshire and the eastern valleys of Glamorgan and large numbers of workmen have purchased their dwellings through the medium of such
agencies. In the towns, especially Swansea, building clubs do a considerable business. In the anthracite district where wages on the whole
are rather good most of the owner-occupiers had houses built to their
own plans by local contractors. In this area the building club idea
has not been at all popular.

So not only did the proportion of working-class home-owners vary, but
so did the mode of purchase. Evidence from Monmouthshire confirms
Jevons's claim of 60 per cent owner-occupation. Of houses built upon
land owned by the Tredegar Iron and Coal Co., 76 per cent were owned
by workingmen, 17 per cent by tradesmen, and 7 per cent by others; in
Tredegar as a whole 60 per cent of houses were owned by their occupiers.[5]
If this was the situation in the hinterland, what of Cardiff? If working-
class owner-occupation could attain such levels, what of the middle class?

The answer is given in tables 31 and 32. Two patterns may be noted in
table 31. The first is the decline in the level of owner-occupation over the
30 years. The use of the incomplete series of 1894 and 1904 shows this to
have been a trend over the period as a whole:

Table 31   Percentage of houses in Cardiff occupied by owner

Rateable value	1884	1914
£35+	26·3	22·3
£20–34	18·3	14·9
£12–19	10·3	6·4
Under £12	3·7	1·3
All	9·6	7·2

The level in Cathays fell from 11·8 per cent in 1884, to 9·8 per cent in
1894, to 8·4 per cent in 1904 and 5·2 per cent in 1914. The second pattern
relates to the level of each class. Even disaggregating the figures by
suburb, the maximum level of owner-occupancy of category 1 houses in
any one suburb was just under a third, of category 2 houses a fifth in
1884 and a quarter in 1914. There was therefore a middle-class level of
owner-occupancy below that attained by many south Wales working-
class mining communities. The comparison with the hinterland applies
even more strikingly to a maximum level of owner-occupation in category 3 in any suburb of 15·7 per cent in 1884 and 11·2 per cent in 1914. In
category 4 the maximum was 7·9 per cent in 1884 and 2 per cent in 1914.

Table 32 presents the occupations of 1,005 of the total of 1,291 owner-occupiers in 1884, as recorded in the street directory. The middle class accounted for 48 per cent and the working class for 52 per cent of those located. If the proportion of total owner-occupiers taken by each work-group is compared with the proportion that group formed of the male labour force, then ship repairing and building craftsmen were over-represented. However, the difference was not great and they certainly did not attain the levels of owner-occupancy of the miners in the hinterland.

A number of questions are therefore suggested by the two tables: why the level of working-class and lower middle-class home ownership was much lower than in the coalfield; why it fell from 1884 to 1914; and why more of the middle class were not owner-occupiers.

Table 32   Social composition of owner-occupiers in 1884

Middle class		Working class	
Professions	6·6	Foremen, supervisors	4·8
Mercantile	5·8	Ship repairing, engineering	11·6
Tradesmen	12·7	Building craftsmen	11·4
Builders	6·2	Railwaymen	5·9
White-collar	12·6	Pilots, mariners	3·1
Master mariners	4·2	Dockers	3·7
		Labourers	4·1
		Miscellaneous: skilled	4·5
		unskilled	2·9
Total middle class	48·1	Total working class	52·0

The situation in which a high level of working-class owner-occupation might be expected can be defined on *a priori* grounds. If rents are a high proportion of income, while construction costs are low in relation to average wages, the owner-occupier is in a more favourable position than the tenant, and the incentive and the ability to buy a house will alike exist. Does such an explanation fit the contrast between Cardiff and its hinterland?[6]

Rents were considerably higher in Cardiff than in the mining valleys. Partly this was because of the higher ground rents and rates, but the main reason was that there were more cheap houses in the valleys than in Cardiff. To the investing owner, unit cost of housing was of little consequence provided that he had an adequate return on his capital. If he was getting a net return of, say, 5 per cent on £2,000 invested in houses, it was immaterial whether he had 20 houses of £100 each or 10 of £200 each. But to the potential owner-occupier, unit cost was crucial, making all the difference between whether or not house purchase was possible. In terms of a constant wage, rents were a larger proportion of income in Cardiff than in the valleys, while unit costs of housing were lower in the valleys than in Cardiff. Neither area therefore wholly fits the suggested conditions for high levels of owner-occupation of housing. For persons earning the same wage in Cardiff as in the mining valleys, house owner-ship was more economically *available* in the valleys because it involved fewer years' income than in Cardiff. But rent was a lower proportion of a given income in the valleys than in Cardiff, so that house purchase was less economically compelling. However, can it be assumed that wages were constant between the two areas? The preponderance of miners in the valleys entailed a larger proportion of well and regularly paid workers than in Cardiff. This difference acted to reinforce the availability of house purchase in the valleys, making the relationship between wages and house prices even more favourable.

Home purchase was more economically available in the mining valleys than in Cardiff. The problem becomes why this availability was exploited to the extent it was. In Cardiff, even the workers whose economic position was closest to that of the miners were much less successful in becoming home-owners. The difference is explained by two basic contrasts between Cardiff and the hinterland: first, social structure and attitudes; and secondly, the availability of investors.

The most important avenue of owner-occupation in the valleys was the operation of the building clubs which provided about 25 per cent of all houses in the central coalfield after 1878. The building club was 'an association of potential owner-occupiers', usually of 50 to 60 members.[7] The absence of agencies of working-class house purchase in Cardiff is striking in comparison with the mining communities. The only such agencies were the Starr-Bowkett societies, the first Cardiff branch being formed in 1881, the eighth and final in 1886, each with 500 members. These operated as follows. Suppose 100 members pay a subscription of £2 1s. 2d. *per annum*, of which 1s. 2d. is for expenses. At the end of the year there will be a balance of £200. The members then draw lots, the winner taking the £200 interest free for ten years, repaying it at £20 a year plus his £2 1s. 2d. subscription. When all 100 members had received a loan, after about 31 years, the subscriptions paid over that time, less the expenses, would be returned, so that in 31 years each member re-ceived and repaid £200 with the society refunding £62 of subscriptions. Whilst the building clubs appealed to Liberal ideology as agencies of self-help and thrift, it was feared that the Starr-Bowkett societies had 'an immoral tendency'. They did indeed become financially unstable, and promoted gambling rather than thrift, but for a time they gave at least some chance of home ownership. The societies continued functioning up to 1904 when it was found that their accountant had embezzled a large part of the funds. Apart from the Starr-Bowkett societies, there was an ephemeral body, the British Homes Investment Corporation, which set up a branch in 1897, with the intention of increasing the level of owner-occupation from a stated 1 per cent in Britain to the claimed 50 per cent of the U.S.A. This had the support of a leading Liberal councillor, who 'could not conceive a higher ideal than a prosperous working-man owning his house'. While the speeches presented the Liberal ideology of thrift, self-respect, respectability, and orderliness as an outcome of working-class home ownership, the Corporation's practical effect was non-existent. [8]

There were more conventional building societies apart from the Starr-Bowkett societies. The local newspaper commenting on such societies in 1882 claimed that 'building societies assist men of small capital who desire to become owners of the house in which they dwell and in this way there is a much larger proportion of persons in Cardiff than in many towns residing in their own homes'. But by 1882, the building societies were well on their way from providing for owner-occupiers to providing for investing owners. At first, these organizations had been terminating societies of little significance. The first and most important permanent building society was the Principality, formed in 1860. The *Cardiff Times* considered that it would mean that 'the provident workingmen of the town will have an opportunity of securing for themselves a house at a trifling cost'. When the Society had been formed it had been at least partly a philanthropic concern, 'to foster habits of saving' among the working-class. But the Principality soon succumbed to the general trend which had been noted by the 1872 Royal Commission on Friendly Societies, of providing for the middle class. Whereas in the hinterland building clubs were thriving up to about 1910, in Cardiff the picture is one of *decreasing* availability of agencies of working-class home ownership. [9]

The explanation is probably that building clubs were possible only in the type of society and with the range of social attitudes found in the valleys. Professor I. G. Jones, pointing to the chapels, friendly societies, *eisteddfodau* and *cymanfaoedd canu* – and building clubs should be added to this list – has noted 'to what an extraordinary extent the characteristic institutions of the coalfield were [the miners'] creation. . . . Voluntaryism was the hallmark of the characteristic institutions of the coalfield'. The same statement cannot be applied to Cardiff. The co-operative society in Cardiff was noticeably unsuccessful, and when the Cardiff Labour Party established itself apart from the Cardiff Liberal Association, it failed to elect one candidate to the city council until after the war. Generally, the working class did not provide institutions for itself; it was treated as a social and religious challenge which had to be provided with chapels and recreational facilities. Whereas the miners provided their own chapels and workmen's institutes, the pattern of chapel provision in Cardiff was a colonization of working-class areas by wealthy middle-class congregations, and recreational provision by temperance and religious workers. The contrast is partly to be explained by the relative simplicity of the social structure of the valleys. The absence of any clearly defined middle-class group meant that the role of philanthropy was much smaller. The working class, not being treated as a social and religious problem, was left to create its own institutions to give meaning to the new communities. Further, the working-class in the valleys had a more unitary experience than was the case in Cardiff, being much less differentiated in terms of area of emigration, work-experience, and, above all, religion and its associated ethic. Institutions such as building clubs were more likely to thrive in the less cosmopolitan, shifting and diverse society of the mining communities, and the movement of miners to provide their own houses had important connections with the values of the dominant Nonconformity and the high status it gave to sobriety, respectability, and thrift.[10]

Building clubs were thus more viable in the mining communities than in Cardiff, no matter what the economic analysis might suggest. The miners in any case had little opportunity to calculate the economic niceties. The reason why building clubs flourished in the valleys, but were absent in Cardiff, is explained by the difference in the structure of the housing market between the two area, which also arose out of the difference in social structure. The absence of a large middle-class in the valleys meant that there were fewer investing owners. In the early stages of development of a new mining area, the coalowner had little option but to provide housing. However, his general reaction was to withdraw from the housing market as soon as possible. With the withdrawal of the coal companies, the miners in turn had little option but to provide housing by self-help, for there was no large class of potential investors in housing. Significantly, the inability of the building clubs to surmount the rising costs of building around 1910 compelled the coal companies to re-enter the housing market. The pattern of investment in housing in Cardiff was very different, with widely based ownership. There was no need for self-help to fill the gap.[11]

Before turning to investing ownership, two points still remain: the decline in the level of owner-occupation up to 1914; and the low level of middle-class home ownership. In rateable categories 1 and 2 it is perhaps surprising not just that the level fell between 1884 and 1914, but also that the general level was not considerably higher. In working through the rate books, it is noticeable that wealthy coalowners often did not own their own homes; also, that many investing owners were themselves tenants. E. R. Moxey, a director of Cory Brothers, illustrates both points. He rented the house he lived in, while himself letting eight houses. So far as the well-off were concerned, home ownership was not considered socially necessary, the general attitude being that house purchase for self-occupation was merely another investment and not of any pressing importance. However, the overall decline in home ownership in categories 1 and 2 masks the fact that in areas developed since about 1910 middle-class home ownership was above the earlier levels. It was noted earlier that the best level obtained in category 2 in a particular suburb increased from a fifth to a quarter between 1884 and 1914; indeed, in one sub-area it reached 35·8 per cent. This was in the new developments to the east and west. In the most significant areas of category 2 housing which had been built by 1884, the level of home ownership had fallen from about a fifth in 1884 to about 12 per cent in 1914. There is, therefore, a pattern of decline in old areas and rise in new areas. Perhaps for the new houses being built before 1914 investing owners were not forthcoming, so prospective inhabitants were obliged to purchase. Possibly, the decrease in the size of the middle-class family was significant, requiring a more modern type of house and freeing resources to take out a mortgage.

A decline in working-class home ownership between 1884 and 1914 could be explained in terms of the building cycle. In 1914, after a prolonged depression in building, there was severe pressure on housing and a shortage especially in the cheaper working-class sector. The level of empty houses was 0·8 per cent. On the other hand, 1884 was a year of peak building activity. There is therefore a contrast between 1884 and 1914 in the availability of houses, and with the stagnation in real wages after 1900 and the rise in building costs and house prices, the prospects of working-class house purchase went into decline. The snag is that the figures for Cathays indicate a decline in each decade from 1884 to 1914, although building activity was high in the early 1890s and empties considerable before 1904, and although working-class wages had improved in the 1880s and 1890s. It is difficult, therefore, to account for a *continuous* decline between 1884 and 1914. Probably, it is necessary to consider working-class attitudes to home ownership, and possibly the fact that the size of the working-class family did not fall as did that of the middle-class may be of some significance.

Clearly, after the war the overall decline in home ownership was reversed, and the change found in the new middle-class areas before 1914 gained momentum. To indicate the extent of change, a 20 per cent systematic sample was taken from the rate books for 1934, for private-sector housing. The rateable categories were upgraded to £50+, £25 to £49, £15 to £24, and under £15, in order to maintain comparability. The result is shown in table 33.

*Table 33   Percentage of private-sector houses in Cardiff occupied by owner, 1934**
Rateable category

1	79·2
2	56·2
3	32·7
4	9·3
all	35·4

*20 per cent sample

Nationally, the level of owner-occupation in 1939 was 35 per cent. In 30 years the level of owner-occupation had increased five-fold. The *Daily Telegraph* could justifiably remark that 'it would be difficult to exaggerate the influence of this silent social revolution on the habits and outlook of the population'. The *Telegraph* saw it as leading to thrift, security, self-dependence and a sense of having a 'stake in the country' which would create national stability. Mark Abrams felt the effect was the same, but saw it from a different political stance:

> in its economic interests and fears, and in its political values and ambitions [the block of owner-occupiers] forms the urban equivalent of a European peasantry. Its way of life is governed not by an attachment to the soil but by an investment in suburban bricks. . . . But, like the landowning peasantry of, say, France, it lives outside of and blurs the classical social dichotomy of proletariat and capitalist.

If so, it might be wondered how south Wales miners before 1914 viewed their situation. However, it is necessary to leave such speculations and move on from a consideration of owner-occupiers to an analysis of investing owners.[12]

II

In 1884, 90·4 per cent and in 1914, 92·8 per cent of houses in Cardiff were inhabited by tenants rather than owner-occupiers. Who were the landlords? How many houses did they typically own? How popular was investment in housing?

Professor Bowley has suggested that the housing investment market was 'primitive and out of line with other investment markets'. It was local, local people investing within their own area, and a fall in the rent of one house meant a fall in the rents of all the investor's houses; the investment was difficult to realize, and the units were inconveniently large. 'Its survival probably depended on the belief that it was possible to know all about the local market but not about the other opportunities of investment. . . . Sooner or later it might be expected to die out like other primitive institutions.' This, Bowley argues, occurred after the First

World War. But the report of the Land Enquiry Committee suggested that already by 1914 housing was becoming less popular as an investment. It was noted that although foreign investments might be attractive,

> there is another fact which has an even greater influence upon the small investor than an increase in the return obtainable on foreign, and even British, securities with which he is not familiar, namely that facilities for the investment of small sums near home have greatly increased [through] the enormous growth of the co-operative movement, the popularity of municipal stocks held in small quantities, the increase, especially in the textile towns, in the number of small joint stock undertakings.

'This tendency to invest outside bricks and mortar', it was said in the case of Sunderland, 'has undoubtedly the effect of permanently widening the outlook of the small investor.' The activity of H. S. Jevons in sponsoring co-operative garden villages was, it has been seen in the previous chapter, inspired by a realization that the same might happen in south Wales. In other words, there is evidence that, at least in some areas, in the years leading up to 1914 the compartmentalization of housing investment was lessening. What then, was actually happening in one town in the period before 1914?[13]

The first point which can be made is that company provision of housing was unimportant. The cottage companies and employers, such as the Great Western Railway and D.I.C., provided 3·8 per cent of all tenanted houses in 1884 and 4·1 per cent in 1914 (table 34). Clearly, the over-

Table 34 Company ownership of housing in Cardiff, 1884 and 1914

	1884	1914
Cardiff Workmen's Cottage Co.	348	334
Glamorgan Workmen's Cottage Co.	99	250
Railway Cottage Co.	18	59
Cathays Workmen's Cottage Co.		70
G.W.R.		36
D.I.C.		222
Avoca Estate		85
Roath Park Cottage Co.		36
	465	1,092
% all tenanted houses	3·8	4·1

whelming bulk of tenanted houses were owned by individuals. The next point to consider is the number and distribution by size of these individual investors. The data for 1884 is presented in table 35. This is done on a suburb-by-suburb basis only, to reduce possible errors introduced by

Table 35 *Percentage of investing owners of various sizes and percentage of tenanted houses owned, 1884*

Houses owned	1	2	3	4	5	6	7	8	9	10	11–15	16–20	21–50	51+	n.a.	mean investment
Canton																
owners	35·6	24·2	10·6	7·7	4·8	3·1	1·6	2·6	1·5	1·8	2·8	1·5	2·2	nil	–	3·8
houses	8·2	11·1	7·3	7·1	5·5	4·3	2·6	4·7	3·0	4·2	8·0	5·8	15·0	nil	13·0	
Grange																
owners	25·8	22·6	11·9	11·7	3·8	4·4	3·1	3·1	3·8	1·9	5·0	0·6	1·8	1·2	–	
houses	4·9	8·5	6·8	8·1	3·6	5·0	4·2	4·7	6·4	3·6	12·6	1·9	9·5	20·3	–	5·3
Cathays																
owners	31·1	22·6	9·3	10·9	5·4	4·1	1·9	1·9	1·9	1·9	4·9	2·2	1·9	nil	–	4·2
houses	7·4	10·9	6·7	10·5	6·5	5·9	3·2	3·7	4·1	4·6	14·7	8·9	12·9	nil	–	
Centre																
owners	36·9	21·2	10·5	8·5	6·0	2·7	2·7	2·7	1·7	2·2	2·0	1·2	1·2	0·2	–	3·7
houses	9·0	10·4	7·7	8·3	7·3	4·0	4·7	5·4	3·8	5·5	5·8	5·3	7·7	5·4	9·6	

1. The development of Cardiff

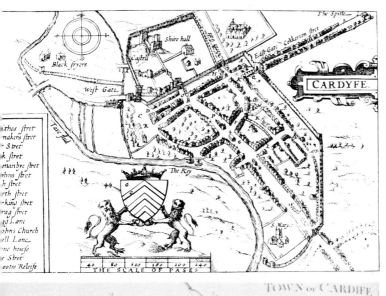

a. Plan of Cardiff in 1610, from Speed's map of Glamorgan (from a reproduction in Cardiff Central Library).

b. Cardiff in 1824 (by courtesy of the Glamorgan Record Office).

c. Cardiff in 1849 (by courtesy of Cardiff Central Library).

1. The development of Cardiff

d. Cardiff in 1869 (by courtesy of the Glamorgan Record Office).

1. The development of Cardiff

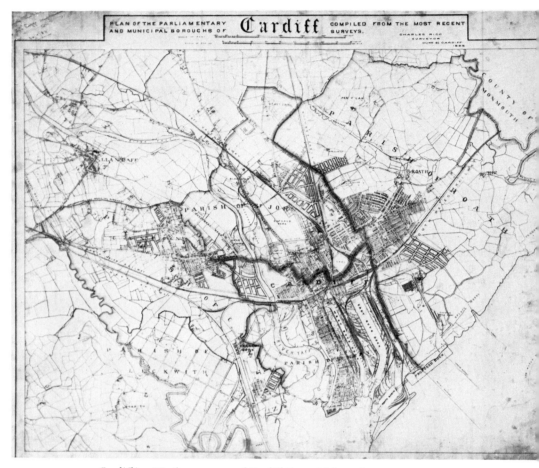

e. Cardiff in 1883 (by courtesy of Cardiff Central Library).

PLAN of CARDIFF.

f. Cardiff in 1897
(by courtesy of
Cardiff Central
Library).

g. Cardiff c. 1907
(by courtesy of
Cardiff Central
Library).

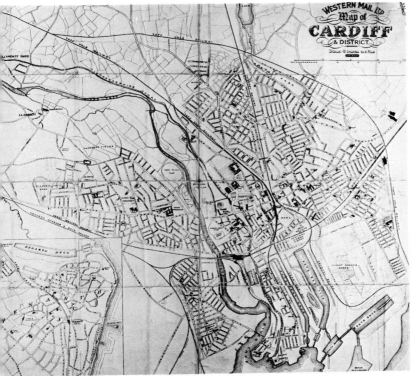

2. The Freehold Land Society: housing development

The map shows the development of the northern section of the Freehold Land Society property in Canton. The point to note is the irregularity compared with the leasehold property elsewhere in Canton. The photograph of Severn Grove (the street on the east of the map) shows the variety of house styles which could result.

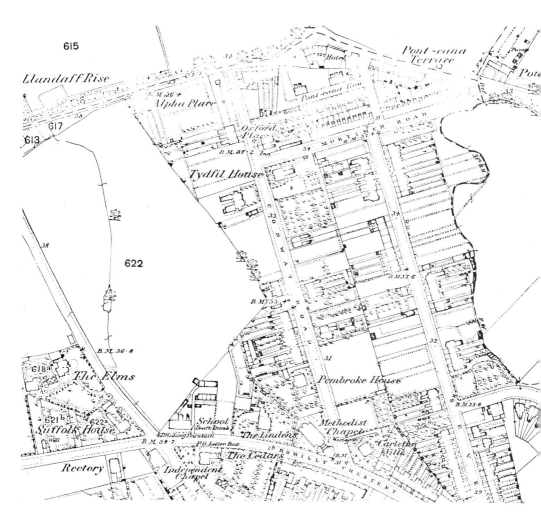

a. 1880 25 inch Ordnance Survey map (reduced): Freehold Land Society development in Canton.

b. Severn Grove

3. The Bute estate: housing development

This group of illustrations indicates the style of Bute development which came to the fore after the completion of Butetown. Senghennydd Road was a Bute enclave in Cathays, developed to a higher standard than the surrounding streets. The same applies to Bute land alongside the Taff in Grangetown and Canton (see map 2). The Bute land in Canton ran from the Freehold Land Society property in the west to the Taff on the east. The orderly, uniform development of this area – exemplified by Plasturton Avenue – contrasts with the irregularity of the freehold land. Cathedral Road to the east was one of the prime residential locations, with open parkland stretching eastwards across the river to the castle, and north to Llandaff Fields and the Cathedral – a massive incursion of open space into the heart of the town.

By about 1910, development had moved to the periphery of the city, around Roath Park to the north-east, Gabalfa to the north, and Victoria Park to the west. The typical speculative house then being erected was of a predominantly large kind. The photograph of Gabalfa shows both a Bute garden development of this period and also this currently popular house type, which men like E. L. Chappell claimed was inappropriate to the needs of the working class.

a. 1920 25 inch Ordnance Survey map (reduced): Senghennydd Road.

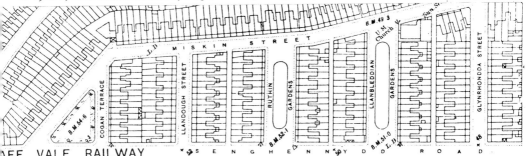

b. Bute development in Cathays, built in the 1880s.
c. Plasturton Avenue, built in the early 1890s.

d. Cathedral Road, built in the 1890s.
e. Gabalfa: Bute development around 1910.

4. Other estates

The Tredegar estate developed part of its land in Roath from the 1850s as a high status area known as Tredegarville. But until the development of the Roath Brook area before 1914 – when the Bute estate had established the strategy – the Tredegar estate concentrated on ordinary working-class housing built to a rigid grid plan on its holdings to the south-east. It was a sound, orderly, regular development, but always somewhat below the standard on the Bute estate. The same contrast is apparent in the Plymouth estate's developments: a high status area outside Cardiff at Penarth, and predominantly working-class development at Grangetown.

Where the market would permit it, some of the medium-sized landowners did develop to a higher standard, as the Homfray estate at Canton. Plate 4f shows the large houses on St John's Crescent, while plate 4g shows the houses in the area to the west, which also serve to illustrate a predominant house type being erected by speculative builders towards the end of the nineteenth century.

On the whole, the usual pattern on the small and medium-sized estates was one of sound property built under the control of 99-year leases to a grid system. The Bute estate was generally followed – with the exception of the Freehold Land Society and the centre – so far as the use of 99-year leases and a control of the activities of the speculative builders went, but the market catered for was more often working class than middle class. The Mackintosh estate is an example of this pattern.

a. 1880 25 inch Ordnance Survey map (reduced): Tredegarville.
b. Tredegar estate: houses in Partridge Road, built in the 1850s.

c. 1880 25 inch Ordnance Survey map (reduced): working-class housing on the Tredegar estate.
d. Housing on the Tredegar estate, East Moors, 1880s.

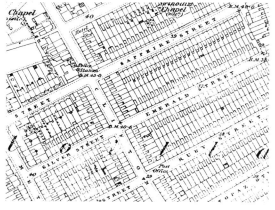

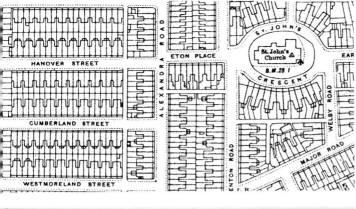

e. 1920 25 inch Ordnance Survey map (reduced): the Homfray estate at Canton.
f. St John's Crescent, Homfray estate.
g. Houses on the Homfray estate.

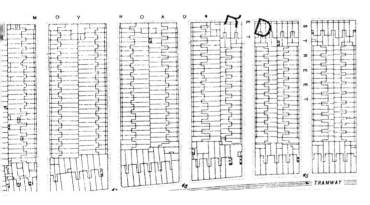

h. 1920 25 inch Ordnance Survey map (reduced) part of the Mackintosh estate.

i. Upper Kincraig Street, Mackintosh estate, built in the 1890s.

5. Roath Park

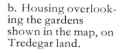

a. 1920 25 inch Ordnance Survey map (reduced): part of the Roath Park complex, which developed along the Roath Brook.

b. Housing overlooking the gardens shown in the map, on Tredegar land.

c. Housing overlooking the main park, on Bute land.

6. Housing reform

These three photographs show three schemes other than those carried out by speculative builders. The municipal housing at Canton owes much more to the style of the earlier cottage companies than to the contemporary garden village at Rhiwbina, which *did* establish the style of inter-war municipal housing schemes.

a. Glamorgan Cottage Company Property at Grangetown, erected in the early 1880s.

b. Municipal housing in Canton, completed in 1914.

c. Rhiwbina Garden Village.

7. Central courts

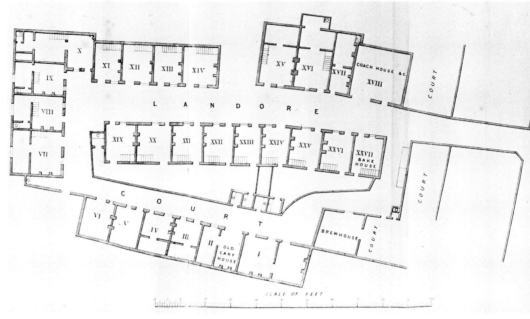

a. Plan from Rammell's Report to the Board of Health of 1850, showing the development of Landore Court, one of the burgage plots in the central area (by courtesy of Cardiff Central Library).

b. Landore Court: photograph taken in 1891 (by courtesy of Cardiff Central Library).

8. The docks

The coal trade was always highly mechanized, advancing from the simple gravity drops of 1839 to hydraulically-operated tips after 1858; these reached their final stage in the Queen Alexandra Dock of 1907. The majority of Cardiff's trade needed little labour; the minor trades were like the ordinary line of dock work in being labour-intensive and unmechanized.

a. The Bute docks in 1907 (by courtesy of Cardiff Central Library).

8. The docks

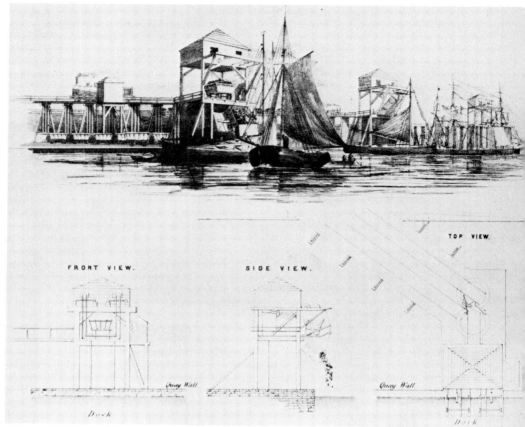

b. Coal drops at Cardiff, 1839 model (by courtesy of Cardiff Central Library).

c. The coal tips, Queen Alexandra dock, 1907 model (by courtesy of Cardiff Central Library).

Stacking pit props
Cardiff docks *c.* 1910
(courtesy of
Cardiff Central
Library).

Sailing ships in the
Bute docks around
1870, showing the
extreme congestion of
the docks (by courtesy
of Cardiff Central
Library).

Loading steam
ships in the Roath
Dock about 1910 (by
courtesy of Cardiff
Central Library).

9. Change in the central area

a. The Royal Hotel, St Mary Street, around 1870. The building of the Royal Hotel was an incursion into a street of modest houses; by the time the photograph reproduced here as plate 9b was taken, the hotel had itself been dwarfed (by courtesy of Cardiff Central Library).

b. St Mary Street around 1910. The Royal Hotel is in the middle distance on the left (by courtesy of Cardiff Central Library).

c. The Royal Arcade, opened in 1858. The series of arcades running between the shopping streets are a feature of the central area.

Bute																
owners	36·1	21·3	16·5	8·2	2·8	3·4	3·1	1·7	1·7	0·6	1·7	1·1	1·7	nil	–	3·4
houses	10·1	11·9	13·8	9·2	4·0	5·7	6·1	3·8	4·2	1·6	6·0	5·8	14·0	nil	3·8	
Splott																
owners	37·8	15·5	6·7	4·4	6·7	11·1	4·4	nil	nil	2·2	4·4	nil	2·2	4·4	–	16·8
houses	2·2	1·8	1·2	1·1	2·0	4·0	1·8	nil	nil	1·3	3·4	nil	3·3	77·8	–	
N. Roath																
owners	44·0	21·3	15·5	5·8	4·4	2·0	0·9	0·7	0·4	0·7	2·2	0·7	1·3	nil	–	2·9
houses	14·2	13·8	15·1	7·5	7·2	3·9	2·0	1·7	1·3	2·1	8·7	3·7	13·6	nil	5·2	
S. Roath																
owners	34·6	24·4	12·6	8·5	3·9	4·5	2·7	2·6	1·5	0·8	1·7	0·9	1·2	nil	–	3·3
houses	9·4	13·2	10·2	9·2	5·3	7·4	5·2	5·6	3·7	2·1	5·5	4·5	9·4	nil	9·2	

common names. If John Thomas owns 10 houses in Cathays, is this the same John Thomas who owns 5 houses in Canton? Of course the 'John Thomas' in Cathays might be one person or ten, and this problem accounts for the exclusion of a certain proportion of houses in some suburbs. The figures are, however, sufficiently accurate to support some general points.

Ownership of tenanted houses was widely diffused. Between 71 and 91 per cent of landlords in the various suburbs owned 5 houses or less; excluding Splott, these small investors owned from just under a third to just over a half of all tenanted houses. Splott was exceptional, for out of 756 houses the Cardiff Cottage Co. owned 348 and Charles Fox 247. Generally, about a quarter to a third of houses were owned by investors holding over ten houses each. The number of really big owners in this group was small. Within only three of the eight areas were there any owners possessing over 50 houses. Table 34 indicates that two of these large owners were companies; individuals owning over 50 houses throughout Cardiff are shown in table 36. In the whole of Cardiff, only six men owned over 50 houses each. Of these Charles Fox was exceptional. He was a builder, and it would appear from the plans register that he built all the houses he owned. Possibly, he was in 1884 waiting for an opportunity to sell recently erected houses, although the fact that in 1914 – when his estate was being wound up – he still owned over 100 houses shows that there was no pressing necessity in this. The same remarks apply to the smaller-scale activities of Henry Marshall and Thomas Gough. The other three large owners had different backgrounds. Solomon Andrews had arrived in Cardiff from Trowbridge in the 1850s and moved from selling pies in the streets to exploiting all chances of profitable investment in a rapidly growing town. He built up a chain of over 20 shops; owned cabs, trams and buses in Cardiff, London, Manchester, Plymouth and Portsmouth, and built the vehicles in his own workshops; he was a property developer, building offices and shops in the centre of Cardiff and being responsible for the development of Pwllheli; late in life he bought a colliery. His interest in housing, which he had built on his own behalf, was only a small part of his wider interests. F. C. Vachell was the grandson of an apothecary who came to Cardiff in 1790 and who had bought land which had been developed intensively in a series of courts in the first phase of urbanization. Such property accounts for most of his 112 houses. Solomon Blaiberg was a moneylender and pawnbroker at the docks, who left £95,120 on his death in 1909.[14]

The small group of large owners was of diverse background. The success rate in locating the bulk of smaller owners was low, making an accurate analysis of their social composition impossible. Unless the investing owner was also an owner-occupier, his address is not known from the rate books and he is therefore not easily located in the street directories

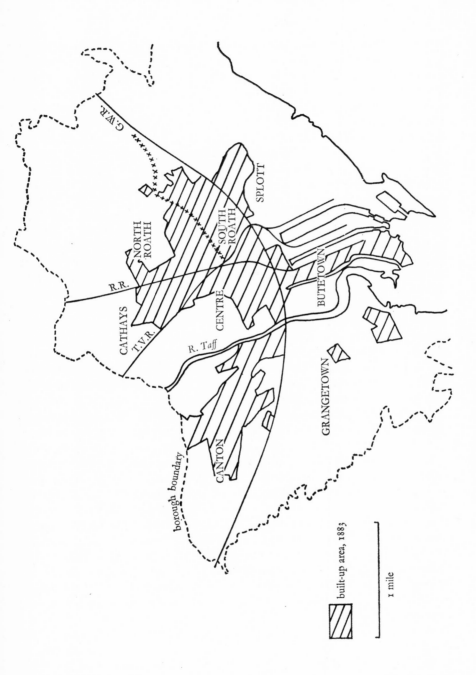

Map 3. Division of Cardiff into areas for analysis.

*Table 36   Number of houses owned in the whole of Cardiff in 1884 by individuals
holding over 50 houses*

Charles Fox	builder	401
F. C. Vachell	land owner	122
Solomon Blaiberg	pawnbroker	86
Henry Marshall	builder	72
Solomon Andrews	retailer, bus owner, property developer	65
Thomas Gough	builder	52
% of all tenanted houses		6·5

to ascertain his occupation. The exception to this was in part of Splott and
Roath where the clerk did note the addresses of a proportion of owners,
so that a rather better success rate was achieved in this area in determining
the occupations of investors from the street directories. Some impressions
did emerge, in particular the width of the social composition of ownership.
Although tradesmen were of importance, house ownership was not their
exclusive prerogative. There was at the top a number of wealthy merchants investing in houses, and at the bottom a group of working-class
owners. It would also appear that those speculative builders who did not
become bankrupt were likely to retain the ownership of a proportion of
the houses they had erected. As a very rough indication of these points,
table 37 presents the occupations of a 10 per cent sample of those investors
in housing who were located in Splott and Roath in 1884.

So far a static analysis of investing ownership in 1884 has been presented. On the basis of the two suburbs which were studied in 1914,

Table 37   Sample of investors in housing in Splott and Roath, 1884

Dairyman	Builder (4)	Mason
Grocer (3)	Engineer	Carpenter (3)
Coal dealer	Architect	Railway guard
Beer retailer (4)	Accountant	Engine driver
General dealer	Solicitor	Labourer
Hosier	Commission agent	Docker
Confectioner	School proprietor	Foreman
Hatter	Landowner	Tinsmith
Jeweller	Clerk	Boilermaker
Nurseryman		Shoemaker (2)
Butcher		Shipbroker (3)
Boat builder ⎫		
Coach builder ⎬ employers		Shipowner
Waterproofer ⎭		
Ships chandler		

there was a trend towards a wider diffusion of ownership. But it was only marginal before 1914. An analysis of the two suburbs in 1934 showed that the trend went much further in the inter-war period. Between 1884 and 1914 it is fairer to characterize the situation as one of stability (see table 38). There is no evidence of an increasing concentration of ownership, which might be expected if small investors were switching to other means of investment; neither was the move to increased diffusion of ownership so marked as to suggest that large owners were moving from housing. This pattern is probably explained by the absence of attractive alternative *local* investments which, rather than foreign investments, was the issue of importance. The attraction of housing as an investment was that it was safe and local. Shipping companies were open to local investment but were notoriously risky. The railway companies in the area did pay well but otherwise it is difficult to think of any avenue of local investment more attractive than housing.

The rate of return on housing has been calculated for a number of properties managed or owned by John Jenkins, a local accountant (table 39).[15] Cairns Street was a typical terraced working-class street in Cathays and Ruby Street a similar street in south Roath, both built in the 1880s. Leckwith Road was a working-class street in Canton developed at different times in a variety of styles. Dudley Street was an old street in the centre and showed the best net return because of the low capital cost of the old house and the low ground rent resulting from the early date of development. In the other cases, rates took 16 to 21 per cent of gross return, repairs 11 to 19 per cent, and ground rent 14 to 16 per cent, giving a net return of 4·6 to 6·6 per cent. As Professor H. S. Jevons remarked in 1912, 'house property still maintains its pre-eminence as a real, solid basis of investment. It produces higher rate of return upon capital than the safe securities of the Stock Exchange, and is more on a par with industrial companies producing 5 or 6 per cent interest on capital invested in them.' The problem as Jevons saw it was not that housing gave an inadequate return, but rather that 'owning and managing house property is so full of trouble and petty annoyance that there is little wonder that it is losing its popularity as a form of investment'.[16]

Perhaps the most sensible conclusion would be that housing was remaining an attractive investment in Cardiff but that there were already before 1914 indications that investors would switch to municipal loans and the like which did not involve the troubles of collecting rent, making repairs, securing reliable tenants. Above all, quite small investors are involved. The figures presented above support the impression of *The Land* that 'a very considerable proportion, probably much more than one-half, of the total number of working-class houses are owned by people who have less than £5,000 at their death'. What attracted such people was

Table 38 Structure of house ownership for investment in Cathays and Grangetown, 1884 (%)

Houses owned	1	2	3	4	5	6	7	8	9	10	11–15	16–20	21–50	51+	n.a.	mean investor
Cathays (1884)																
investors	31·1	22·6	9·3	10·9	5·4	4·1	1·9	1·9	1·9	1·9	4·9	2·2	1·9	nil	–	4·2
houses	7·4	10·9	6·7	10·5	6·5	5·9	3·2	3·7	4·1	4·6	14·7	8·9	12·9	nil	–	
Cathays (1914)																
investors	42·8	20·9	8·1	7·1	4·4	4·5	1·8	1·3	1·2	1·4	2·9	1·6	1·8	0·2	–	3·6
houses	11·7	11·4	6·6	7·8	6·0	7·4	3·5	2·8	2·8	3·8	9·9	7·5	13·5	4·1	1·0	
Cathays (1934)																
investors	65·6	14·1	6·8	2·2	3·5	1·5	1·0	1·3	0·7	0·3	1·5	0·4	0·8	0·1	–	2·3
houses	24·8	10·7	7·8	3·4	6·6	3·5	2·6	3·8	2·4	1·1	7·3	2·9	8·7	2·9	11·5	

Grouped subtotals (investors / houses):

Cathays (1884): columns 1–5 = 80·3 / 42·0; columns 6–10 = 11·7 / 21·5; columns 11+ = 9·0 / 36·5.

Cathays (1914): columns 1–5 = 83·3 / 43·5; columns 6–10 = 10·2 / 20·3; columns 11+ = 6·5 / 35·0.

Cathays (1934): columns 1–5 = 92·2 / 53·3; columns 6–10 = 4·8 / 13·4; columns 11+ = 2·8 / 21·8.

Grange (1884)															
investors	25·8	22·6	11·9	10·7	3·8	4·4	3·1	3·1	3·8	1·9	5·0	0·6	1·8	1·2	—
houses	4·9	8·5	6·8	8·1	3·6	5·0	4·2	4·7	6·4	3·6	12·6	1·9	9·5	20·3	—
Grange (1914)															
investors	32·7	25·4	8·9	8·5	3·8	3·6	2·7	2·7	1·8	1·7	2·9	2·1	2·4	0·6	—
houses	6·8	10·6	5·6	7·1	4·0	4·6	4·0	4·6	3·4	3·5	8·1	7·6	15·0	14·1	1·0
Grange (1934)															
investors	56·1	17·3	8·8	3·8	2·6	2·1	1·1	1·2	1·4	0·5	1·1	0·9	2·0	0·9	—
houses	14·6	9·0	6·9	4·0	3·4	3·3	1·9	2·5	3·2	1·2	3·3	4·3	14·5	21·3	6·4

Grange (1884) — investors: 74·8 / 31·9, 16·3 / 23·9, 8·6 / 44·3, 5·3

Grange (1914) — investors: 79·3 / 34·1, 12·5 / 20·1, 8·0 / 44·8, 4·7

Grange (1934) — investors: 88·6 / 37·9, 6·3 / 12·1, 4·9 / 43·4, 2·7

Table 39   Return on four house properties, 1894–1910

	9, 10 Dudley St	159, 161 Cairns St
Gross return *p.a.*	19·2	12·2
Percentage of gross return taken by:		
rates	22·2	19·5
repairs	6·9	10·7
ground rent	4·4	14·9
Net return *p.a.*	12·6	6·6
	81 Leckwith Rd	41, 43 Ruby St
Gross return *p.a.*	9·6	10·9
Percentage of gross return taken by:		
rates	15·8	20·8
repairs	14·9	18·6
ground rent	14·4	15·8
Net return *p.a.*	5·4	4·6

not the rate of return compared to foreign investments, but the 'facilities for the investment of small sums near home'. It was the availability of these facilities which was the key to the flow of investment into housing, and the importance of the alternatives varied between areas. The underlying block of capital which had been peculiar to housing was in some areas being whittled away before 1914 and becoming integrated into the wider capital market. But generally speaking change was as yet slight – it was a gradual erosion in some places, not a disappearance. The real breakthrough came after the First World War. Professor Bowley is certainly right to state that between the wars the attractiveness of housing as an investment permanently decreased as other forms of investment became more attractive, and the local investment market in housing died out like other primitive institutions.[17]

8   Shapes on the ground

'Segregation by class was the most important social effect of urbanization.' Certainly, the change in the spatial patterns of the city in the nineteenth century amount to a revolution in land use, and a central concern for the urban historian across time, as it has been for the urban sociologist and geographer at a point in time, should be the 'reciprocal relationship between the social structure and the spatial structure, between physical distance and social distance'. Historians have largely neglected this relationship and its development, or looked at it incidentally – through the development of suburbs and public transport – rather than centrally.[1]

Contemporaries reacted strongly to the emergence of physical distance as a reinforcement of social distance, seeing in this a major threat to the stability of urban society. Leon Faucher, writing on Manchester in 1844, complained that the merchants and manufacturers left the town as soon as business ended, and pointed to the dangers of this 'local absenteeism' which 'abandons the town to the operatives, publicans, mendicants, thieves and prostitutes'. The result was, as was said of Leeds in 1856, that the town 'is deprived of all those civilizing influences and mutually respectful feelings which are exercised when rich and poor – employer and employed – know more of each other than they possibly can under present arrangements'. How, it was wondered, was social control possible if the residents of east and west London, 'on the occasions when they came into contact, which were but seldom, surveyed each other with much the same curiosity and astonishment as would nowadays be exhibited by a native of this town at the appearance of an Esquimaux in Hyde Park or Regent Street'? It was C. F. G. Masterman who in 1901 summed up this plaint about the city. He saw the creation of a physically and mentally 'new city type' which was 'stunted, narrow-chested, easily wearied; yet voluble, excitable, with little ballast, stamina or endurance – seeking stimulus in drink, in betting, in any unaccustomed conflicts at home or abroad'. The 'new city type' was completely segregated from the higher classes, 'cut off within a different Universe of Being from the London that thinks and talks and chatters'. This Universe

is the Ghetto, the enclosure into which is penned our labouring popu- lation. Outside, some incredible distance beyond its borders, is the world that counts; those that look before and after, meditate, design and aspire. Within are those to whom the twentieth century belongs; who appear in the sunshine upon occasional days of national festivity, fatuously cheerful in the daylight, drunken, sodden and abusive when darkness falls. All round the edge of this incomprehensible region are the homes of those who have crawled out of it: the residents of the villas, the clerks who are sustained in their long hours of unhealthy toil by the one triumphant thought that they have not yet fallen back into the abyss below.[2]

This is not a very attractive view of the Victorian city, but it was one with a very real justification, created by very real fears, for 'at the most fundamental level, the separation of classes had led to a breakdown of social relationships and traditional methods of social control'. It was something the more socially aware members of the middle class sought to modify. The Charity Organization Society was an attempt to reintroduce social obligations into the receipt of charity which had been destroyed by the fact that 'in a large urban area, where rich and poor had been separated, the social power supposedly inherent in the gift had disappeared because the poor no longer knew and respected the rich'. Going further, the settlement movement tried to end the physical separation by bringing the well-off and educated back into the working-class areas. This clearly did not appeal to the majority who had escaped to suburban complacency where they could forget the problems of the city and of the poor: 'every day, swung high upon embankments or buried deep in tubes underground, he hurries through the region where the creature lives. He gazes darkly from his pleasant hill villa upon the huge and smoky area of tumbled tenements which stretches at his feet.' But for men like Arnold Toynbee or Edward Denison or Samuel Barnett it was a practicality. Stedman Jones has with sarcasm but some accuracy summed up their approach: 'London was to be reconstructed along the lines of an old Arcadian myth; the capital city would be turned into a gigantic village, and its poor would be led back to manliness and independence under the firm but benevolent aegis of a new urban squirearchy'.[3]

Such an approach has survived to the present day in planners' ideology. In the wartime and post-war theory of town planning, which was implemented in the new towns, a central concept was the 'neighbourhood unit', seen as 'the modern urban counterpart of the village', with a socially balanced population which would provide leaders and help create a viable community life. As L. E. White put it, this was 'a conscious endeavour to recover much that was worth while in the old village tradition and translate it into modern times'. It would not be too much of an exaggeration to see continuity between the settlements of the 1880s, the garden suburbs after 1900, and the new towns post-1945. The 'old Arcadian myth' which Stedman Jones derisively refers to in the 1880s was not very far away from the comment of the chairman of Stevenage Development Corporation in 1947: 'We want to revive that social structure which existed in the old English village where the rich lived next door to the not-so-rich and everyone knew everybody.'[4]

When an attempt is made to move from these middle-class perceptions to the historical reality, a void appears. Of course, the building of suburbs and the development of urban transport is a part of the process of residential segregation, but the changing extent and character of that process has not been studied directly for the Victorian city, at least on this side of the Atlantic. This is unfortunate, for the Victorian city experienced a change from one type of differentiation of land use to another. Two ideal types may be created to indicate the changes. In the pre-industrial city, the limits of inter-city transport and of the economic base created a tightly compact physical form, whilst the limits of intra-urban transport created a 'walking city'. There was a lack of segregation by class or occupation; if there was a primitive segregation, it was if anything the reverse of the later pattern, with the well-to-do concentrated in the centre and the poor on the fringes. But what was more remarkable than any segregation, was the general mixing together of diverse social groups. Even if the city were large, there were a number of relatively distinct component parts conforming roughly to a standard unit set by the possible radius of walking. The mode of social control resulting from these features was informal, arising from the unity of everyday life which held the town together. In the industrial city, inter-city transport and the economic base were revolutionized, and spatial bonds in consequence loosened. Although the city remained a discrete entity, the compact nature of the pre-industrial city was broken. Urban transport was revolutionized, segregation developed and single-class areas came into existence. Social control of the informal type collapsed with the increase in size and the rise of segregation, and had to be formalized. The history of the Victorian city is the history of the change from the one ideal type to the other. It was not a sudden change but took the whole century, for there was a lag in the chronology of change between the parts of the ideal types. The economic base and inter-city transport were revolutionized in the early nineteenth century, while the change in urban transport and segregation was slower, only gradually filtering down the social scale over the whole of the nineteenth century.[5]

The stages of the change have been suggested by S. B. Warner in an American context. The town in the eighteenth century closely fitted the first ideal type. With the onset of the first phase of industrialization and rapid urban growth, most areas of what he terms the 'big city' remained a jumble of occupations, classes, shops, houses, immigrants and natives.

The city was not yet segregated: 'only a primitive specialization in respect to urban land existed, and the neighbourhoods and districts of the big cities were highly mixed in their activities, ethnicity and class.' However, even before the development of segregation, the 'informal neighbourhood street life' of the eighteenth-century town had been destroyed by the increase in scale. The big city of the period 1820–70 was thus half way from the first ideal type to the second. The process was completed during the years from 1870 to 1920, when pronounced segregation developed, with urban land becoming highly specialized, allocated by income and ethnicity. The change from the eighteenth-century town to the segregated city had taken a hundred years to complete.[6]

The process in Britain was broadly similar but probably followed a different chronology. Up to the mid-nineteenth century, segregation was probably ahead of America. London, for example, or the other mercantile cities of the eighteenth century – Bristol, Newcastle, Liverpool – would be like the American mercantile cities of the years up to the mid-nineteenth century. True, the poor were concentrated on the fringes and the well-to-do in the centre. But the segregation was by no means complete, and what was more remarkable was the general mixing together of diverse social groups, even within one house. This was indicated by a commentator on London in 1795:

> First then in order of all those who occupy only parts of houses stand the tenants of stalls, sheds and cellars, from which we take our flight to the top of the house in order to arrange in the next class the residents in garrets, from thence we gradually descend to the second and first floor, the dignity of each being in the inverse ratio of its altitude.

As Vance says, 'given such a residential structure, class organisation of city space was not so obvious as it is in urban areas today'. It started to become obvious in the British city ahead of the American city. The American 'big cities' of the mid-nineteenth century were still mercantile with small-scale industry, whereas an English town such as Manchester with large factories had already started to segregate quite noticeably by the time Engels wrote in 1844. Segregation was ahead of the U.S.A. in the mid-nineteenth century.[7]

In the late nineteenth century, however, segregation proceeded far more rapidly in the American city, and moved ahead of the pattern found in Britain. This can be seen in the more rapid development of urban transport in the U.S. Urban transport was late in being revolutionized, moving beyond the pre-1825 position of the railways, of horse-drawn vehicles on rails, only in the late nineteenth century in either country. The railways themselves were not important agents of urban transport, interconnecting the towns rather than supplying them with a useful means of internal transport. However, they did have a large impact upon the inner city. They defined the central business district, and in the inner districts crossed by the lines created an area of industry, warehousing and low-status residence. But the railways compressed the city rather than spread it. Population was forced out of the centre by their incursion and the development of a central business district, whilst fares were not cheap enough to take workers out further. They were therefore compressed in the inner area within walking distance of the casual labour market. Only gradually did it cease to be a 'walking city' as transport slowly filtered down the social scale.

The changes in transport technology were taken up sooner and on a much larger scale in the American than in the British city, and with a much greater influence on spatial patterns. The horse omnibus came to the English cities around 1830, at more or less the same time as in the U.S.A., although not on the same scale. The real lag started with the horse tram. This developed spectacularly in American cities in the period 1852–60. The tram did not even appear in England until 1860, and then failed. It did not develop in the English cities until the late 1860s. Similarly, electric trams were introduced in the U.S.A. from 1888, and by 1902 97 per cent of mileage was electrified. At that date, the process had hardly started in England. The first effective electric tramway in England came in 1895, the real breakthrough only after 1900. The difference was not only in timing. Ownership was also different. In America, electrification led to consolidation of ownership, but it remained private; in England, it led to municipalization. In American cities, lines proceeded ahead of the frontier of development; in England, they were simply fitted into the existing built-up area and had a much less positive impact. And the scale of development was much greater in the American cities. In England in 1898, 618 miles of track served $7\frac{1}{2}$m. people in the largest cities, carrying 474m. passengers a year. In the Boston area alone, 316 miles of track served a million people, carrying 181m. passengers a year.[8]

The reasons for this difference are not hard to find. In part, it was the result of a difference in the phasing of the building cycle, so that changes in transport technology had a different relationship to building activity. But this cannot be a full explanation. It might explain why when British trams were electrified after 1900 they did not go beyond the built-up area, for building was simply not active enough. What it cannot explain is the failure to electrify in the 1890s when building *was* active. More important than the fluctuations was the underlying trend. Generally, British cities had experienced their most rapid growth in population before 1850, whereas American cities were experiencing their most rapid growth later in the century. Tramways in the English cities were being inserted into an already established and relatively rigid urban pattern; in the U.S.A. it was still flexible and expanding. The chronology of rapid growth and transport technology was therefore different, the context in the U.S.A. being much more favourable than in England for confident investment and for extensions beyond the built-up area. However, this cannot be applied to Cardiff, which was one of the few British towns growing rapidly in the late nineteenth century. Two other factors must be introduced. One was that urban transport in itself was not very profitable. This was certainly so of the Cardiff system, and the local companies resisted extensions even up to the limit of the already developed area. In American cities, profits could be made by the transport concerns themselves engaging in land development, or being subsidized by the developers. This did not happen in England, and instead the systems were municipalized to secure the investment which private concerns were not willing to make, and even then – as in Cardiff – the low rate of return led to a very conservative policy. The second factor was the difference in the socioeconomic structure. The American cities had more middle-income families which were able to escape to suburbia. In England, given the demand for suburban living, perhaps the amount of land available did not need to be greatly extended. In the American city, electrification took the limit of the city from about $2\frac{1}{2}$ miles to 6 miles; in England it was simply not necessary to develop the land beyond $2\frac{1}{2}$ miles from the city centre, at least until the private housing boom of the 1930s. It was only then that the English city attained the pattern of the American city before 1914.[9]

There is nevertheless a basic similarity: in neither country did public transport become generally available. Perhaps only 20 per cent of the American urban population could move out and achieve a new life-style in the low-density suburbs. Another 20–30 per cent could settle in the older inner suburbs, with the remainder trapped in the central city. The same applies to Britain. The short-distance coach served the upper levels of the middle class; the omnibus and the horse tram reached down through the middle class to, possibly, the most highly-paid and securely-employed workers. The wealthy and then the well-off middle class left the central areas, but for long the lower middle class and artisans were tied to the same areas as the semi-skilled and unskilled. For the lower classes, the 'walking city' survived to the late nineteenth century. Segregation in this situation would be by place of employ rather than by level within the working class. All employed at one location – skilled, semi-skilled and unskilled – would need to be within walking distance. The casual poor and artisans were both forced to share urban space and this created social anxiety, both on the part of the middle class who feared the two might draw together (a threat seen by some in London in the 1880s), and also on the part of the status-conscious artisans. The trams gradually permitted the various social levels of the working class to separate out. Cardiff at 1871 was at the end of one stage – division by place of work but not by level of skill. The further process of division by strata of the working class had not started seriously, for the first tram came only in 1872. However, the extent of change in the late nineteenth century was nothing like that in the U.S.A. because of the more limited scale of development of transport facilities.[10]

The development of segregation reflects somewhat more than transport technology – it was a physical expression of the inequality of income distribution. In analysing housing, it was pointed out that the allocation of capital was concentrated upon suburbia rather than upon working-class housing; there were slums in a sense because there was suburbia. And of course the same sort of point applies to transport. The investment in urban transport benefited – at least directly – those able to afford the fares, who got the cheap land and the new houses available on the periphery. The benefit to the working class was indirect; they were left with the vacated middle-class housing in the inner city, although they were excluded from the cheap land and lower densities of the suburbs.[11]

It is not enough merely to measure the degree and chronology of segregation; it is also necessary to enquire into the nature of social relationships *within* areas of the city. The early theories on residential segregation were very ambiguous about the definition of these areas, whether geographical or social. Were the residents an interacting group, with the area defined by the interactions; or were the areas defined by their physical boundaries, with the inhabitants simply a statistical aggregate? Park was obviously right to suggest that time is an important variable in the definition, so that

> in the course of time every sector and quarter of the city takes on something of the character and qualities of its inhabitants. . . . The effect of this is to convert what was at first a mere geographical expression into a neighbourhood, that is to say, a locality with sentiments, traditions and a history of its own.

The close-knit pattern of communal life based on kinship networks found in Bethnal Green in the 1950s, for example, was the outcome of a population established over several generations. It has been suggested that the key difference between such an old working-class area as Bethnal Green and the new council housing estates, such as Dagenham, is not some intrinsic feature which leads to communal solidarity in one and fragmentation of life in the other. Rather, *in time* the council estate becomes like the old working-class area.[12]

Since it is impossible to study the relationships between inhabitants of areas of nineteenth-century cities at first hand in order to discover the extent to which they formed an interacting group or merely a statistical aggregate, a measurement of the length of residence is a useful surrogate.

Masterman wrote in terms of a 'ghetto', which suggests that the inhabitants were trapped. Studies such as those of Bethnal Green in the 1950s, Robert Robert's reminiscences of pre-1914 Salford, and Richard Hoggart's analysis of the Leeds of his childhood, suggest how this immobility then made the inhabitants into an interacting group. Hoggart gives a vivid picture of a working-class area of Leeds which had some of the features of a ghetto but also the cohesiveness of a village:

> To a visitor they are understandably depressing, these massed proletarian areas. . . . But to an insider, these are small worlds, each as homogenous and well defined as a village . . . One knows practically everybody, with an intimacy of detail. . . . Unless he gets a council-house, a working-class man is likely to live in his local area, perhaps even in the house he 'got the keys for' the night before his wedding, all his life. He has little call to move if he is a general labourer, and perhaps hardly more if he is skilled. . . . He is more likely to change his place of work than his place of living; he belongs to a district more than to one works. . . . Life centres on the groups of known streets, on their complex and active group life.

But how applicable is this to the period before 1914, or, rather, to the period before rent control gave an incentive to remain as long as possible in one house? Evidence presented to the Royal Commission on Local Taxation suggests the applicability is doubtful. Tenants apparently changed address so often it was almost impossible to follow them to secure payment of the rates. Nevertheless, Charles Booth largely supports Hoggart, for the movement was of a particular type:

> In many districts the people are always on the move; they shift from one part of it to another like 'fish in a river'. . . . On the whole, however, the people usually do not go far, and often cling from generation to generation to one vicinity, almost as if the set of streets which lie there were an isolated country village.[13]

Certainly, if the experience of British cities was one of residential stability or movement confined to a small area, this was in very marked contrast with the volatility of nineteenth-century American cities. Recent research has replaced the idea of immigrant and working-class ghettoes in which 'a settled population, trapped in misery, huddled together in some sort of "culture of poverty".' The general impression is of 'a dizzying rate of population turnover'. The significance of this work has been suggested by Stephan Thernstrom:

> In no American city has there been a large lower class element with continuity of membership. You can identify more or less continuously

lower class *areas*, but *the same individuals do not live in them very long* . . . The bottom layer of the social order in the nineteenth- and twentieth-century American city was thus a group of permanent transients, buffeted about from place to place, never quite able to sink roots and to form organisations.

Does this rather than the picture presented by Hoggart apply to the Victorian city in Britain?[14]

There are thus two related problems to consider. One is the degree of segregation. This must be considered not just between rich and poor, which is what primarily concerned contemporaries, but also within the working class. John Foster has shown that the frequency with which labourers and craftsmen lived next door to each other in early nineteenth-century towns varied, and he has used this as an indirect measure of class consciousness.[15] Even if his explicitly Marxist approach is rejected, the measure of residential differentiation is a useful (if indirect) measure of aspects of the urban social structure. It has been suggested that up to 1850 traditional distinctions among the labouring poor gradually broke down, and then from 1850 distinctions within the working class were consolidated and sharpened, in particular a labour aristocracy separated out, with a fluid boundary with the lower middle class and rigidly differentiated from the rest of the working class. This change in social structure might be expected to have a spatial reflection, particularly as transport became available to lower groups, although even earlier there could be streets of various social complexions within the inner city. In particular, it is interesting to see whether the labour aristocrats lived among the lower middle class or with other segments of the working class.

Leading on from this, the second question relates to the social relationships within the areas. Are they geographical expressions or something more? Was it segregation of stable unchanging groups, or of different people with the same characteristics? This makes a great difference to the type of society resulting from a given pattern of segregation. Did the inhabitants remain long enough in a part of the city to turn an area into a neighbourhood? So having made three steps – from the initiators of development, to the builders, to the purchasers – a fourth step is now to be taken, to the residents of the houses, asking how they were located and for how long they remained.

II

In order to measure the pattern of residence, two indices are available: the index of dissimilarity and the index of segregation. The index of dissimilarity compares one group with another group, and states the percentage of the one group which would have to move if it was to have the same pattern of residential distribution as the other. The index of segregation measures the degree of residential separation between one group and the remainder of the population, and states the percentage of the group which would have to move if it was to have the same pattern of distribution as the rest of the population.[16] The data used were the 1871 census enumerators' books, from which the occupation of every male head of household was extracted and then coded for occupation and social class on the lines suggested by W. A. Armstrong, that is, using Charles Booth's classification for occupations and the 1951 Registrar-General's classification for social class.[17] The resulting indices of segregation and dissimilarity by occupation and social class are presented in tables 40 and 41. What can be deduced from this data?

Table 40   Indices of segregation, Cardiff 1871

(a) Occupations	%
Seamen	53·4
Shipowners and brokers, coal merchants	50·2
Irish	43·7
Law and medicine	40·2
Ship repair and supply	34·1
Clerical and financial	32·0
Railwaymen	30·5
General labourers	28·1
Building workers	25·5
Dock workers	25·5
Iron and steel	21·0

(b) Class	
I Professional	38·4
II Intermediate	35·1
III N Skilled, non-manual	23·0
III M Skilled, manual	15·1
IV Partly skilled	19·6
V Unskilled	21·2

It is an easy matter to read off the tables and say '44 per cent of the Irish would need to move if they were to have the same distribution as the rest of the population', or that '38 per cent of railwaymen would have to move to have the same distribution in the city as dockworkers'. But what exactly does this entail? Are these figures high or low? Certainly, groups in Cardiff in 1871 were more segregated than comparable groups in Philadelphia in 1860, where the highest figure was 47·3 per cent for negroes, the Irish figure being 19·8, building trades 16·4.[18] The fact that

Table 41 Indices of dissimilarity, Cardiff 1871

(a) Occupation (%)

	Shipowners	Ship repair, supply	Railwaymen	General labourers	Building workers	Dock workers	Iron and steel	Clerical and financial	Law and medicine
Seamen	58·1	35·6	59·0	62·9	63·4	48·4	50·0	54·0	70·3
Shipowners, etc.		52·5	60·8	63·7	59·3	60·4	55·6	28·9	51·3
Ship repair, supply			36·6	48·2	42·0	31·9	33·7	45·5	60·9
Railwaymen				35·6	32·1	37·8	33·5	47·1	55·4
General labourers					26·6	40·3	29·4	46·7	50·1
Building workers						39·3	24·8	39·3	49·2
Dock workers							33·6	49·3	52·1
Iron and steel								38·2	51·2
Clerical and financial									43·0

(b) Class (%)

	II	IIIN	IIIM	IV	V
I	32·5	35·4	40·6	45·8	45·1
II		30·4	36·8	39·2	43·8
IIIN			24·9	25·6	31·1
IIIM				19·9	18·0
IV					23·8

the Irish in Cardiff were almost as segregated as negroes in an American city does suggest that the level of segregation was high rather than low. As suggested *a priori*, the British city was in mid-century ahead of the American city in its level of segregation – and this is true even of a town like Cardiff which was mercantile rather than industrial. Further, and again as suggested on *a priori* grounds, segregation was higher in terms of occupation than of class. The trend to 1914 was probably to reverse this, making segregation higher by class than by occupation.

In 1871 cheap public transport had not yet affected the residential structure of the town. The first tramline did not operate until 1872, and development thereafter was slow, lagging well behind the growth of the town: the Provincial Tramway Company started its first Cardiff line in that year, serving the route from the centre to the docks only; in 1878 the system was extended to Roath and Canton. The company was in 1878 being criticized by the council for failure to provide $\frac{1}{2}d$. per mile artisan trams, and for being disinclined to make the extensions in Canton and Roath to the full extent desired by the council. At the end of 1879 work-men's trams were introduced from Canton to Roath and the docks, and from 1881 Grangetown was served by the Cardiff District and Penarth Harbour Tramway run by Solomon Andrews. The Provincial Company considered further extensions to Cathays in 1883, and in 1884 the council was pressing for extensions in Roath and Canton. The problem was that severe competition from the omnibuses run by Andrews both in Cardiff and other towns was cutting profits, so that in 1886 and 1887 no dividend could be paid. The company was in consequence disinclined to make extensions. In 1885 $1\frac{1}{2}$ miles was announced to be built to Cathays, and $\frac{3}{4}$ mile in Canton and Roath, as a result of compulsion from the corpor-ation, but the company complained bitterly of the effect of Andrews' competition. The extensions opened in 1886, and negotiations also started to buy out Andrews. By mid-1887 he had agreed to sell, and this led to a proper and regular timetable, ending the system whereby a bus had 'nursed' a tram, so that in effect two vehicles had done the work of one. By 1896 there were 8·73 miles of line, which were then increased by municipal lines erected under the 1898 Corporation Act. In 1902 the whole system was brought into municipal ownership and electrified. The operation of the municipal tramways was a major problem up to 1914, for it had been overcapitalized which led to reluctance to make further extensions; and there was also a continuing debate as to whether it should be run as a public service or as a profit-making concern.[19]

Generally, therefore, the public transport system of Cardiff did not exert a major influence on the shape of the town. However, by the end of the century it had freed some of the inhabitants from the need to be quite so close to their place of work. The skilled and unskilled in any occupation

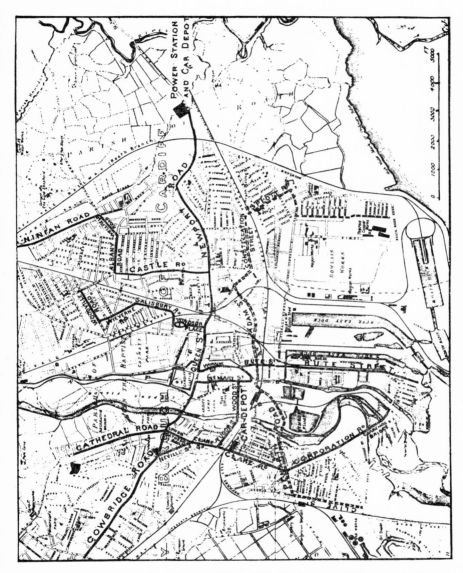

Map 4. Tram routes in Cardiff, 1902 (Electrical Engineer, *16 May 1902*). *Routes completed are shown by a solid line, routes in course of construction by a broken line; the route of the Cardiff District and Penarth Tramway, then about to be purchased and reconstructed for electric traction, is shown by a double broken line.*

could then become residentially distinct, so that segregation by occupation might fall, while segregation by class would rise. In 1871, even the wealthy merchants were still close to the commercial centre – at the docks, in the central area, and in Roath. By 1914, they were further out, usually outside the city boundary. This is indicated by the distribution of residence of members of the Chamber of Commerce who were traced in local directories.

Table 42   Residence of members of Chamber of Commerce

	1875	1891	1911
Living in Cardiff	96	110	105
Living outside Cardiff	15	78	148

Source: Annual Reports of Chamber of Commerce, 1875, 1891, 1911; Butchers, J. Wright and Co., Daniel Owen and Co., and *Western Mail* Directories of Cardiff.

The middle class was moving to the new suburbs on the fringe of the town, where they might become owner-occupiers, and the respectable working class would also appear to have moved out from the centre and Butetown to Canton and Cathays. Probably the result was a greater segregation between middle class and working class, between skilled and unskilled working class.

The indices of dissimilarity are perhaps more interesting, allowing an analysis of who was differentiated from whom. Skilled manual workers were less differentiated from the groups below them than from the non-manual workers above them. The non-manual workers were in turn less differentiated from the skilled manual workers below than from the class above. That is, in terms of residence the skilled manual workers were closer to the rest of the working class than to the bottom of the middle class, while the bottom of the middle class was residentially closer to the skilled and semi-skilled working class than to the rest of the middle class. Further, the various working-class occupations were quite highly differentiated from each other in terms of residence. The mean index for each working-class category in respect to the six other working-class categories, is shown in table 43. The level of residential differentiation

Table 43   Mean index of dissimilarity between working-class occupations

Seamen	53	Building	38
Labourers	40	Dockers	37
Railwaymen	39	Iron and steel	34
Ship repair	38		

within the working class in terms of occupations was thus as high as the differentiation between the middle class and the working class.

The population of Cardiff was quite highly segregated by occupation and class. Does it necessarily follow that inhabitants were trapped in their area, so that there were virtual ghettoes of the various groups? In order to establish this, a 10 per cent systematic sample was taken from the directory for 1884 and traced through the directories up to 1894.[20]

It was possible first of all to calculate the length of stay at the original address of 1884 (table 44, a–c). The fact that half the inhabitants had left their original address in four years immediately cast doubt on the picture of stability presented by Hoggart. No particular area formed an enclave of stability – at least 73 per cent of the sample members in each area moved from their original homes in ten years. An analysis of four social groups showed that the group at the bottom of the scale was over twice as stable as the total sample – almost a third of the labourers did stay at the same address for ten years.

In ten years, 87 per cent of the sample members moved from the original address. What proportion of them remained in Cardiff? And how many remained in their original area, so that it can be judged if the movement was short-distance, within the same neighbourhood, or involved a break with the neighbourhood. Table 44, d–f, presents figures on residential persistence. The rate of population turnover for the town as a whole was directly comparable with the level in American cities, for in ten years the proportion remaining in the city had fallen to 41·2 per cent. The persistence within any one area of the town was somewhat lower than for the town as a whole, ranging from just under a quarter to just over a third. An area such as Splott was unlikely to develop into a local Bethnal Green, for only 26 per cent of the population remained after 10 years. Certain occupations were stable – over half of the labourers and building craftsmen did remain for ten years – but this did not carry over to create stable areas which could develop the sort of cohesive society remembered by Hoggart. More applicable are the words of H. P. Chudacoff on the American situation: 'the low permanence rates leave the impression not only of weak attachment of people to their places of residence but also of weak holding power of neighbourhoods on their residents.'[21]

What can the movement of 60 per cent of the population away from Cardiff in ten years explain? Certainly, the organizations requiring a relatively stable population were unsuccessful: the co-operative movement failed, there were no working-class building clubs such as were found elsewhere in south Wales, and there was a poor record of working-class political organization. There *is* a danger of trying to explain too much. It is perhaps fair to say that variations in the level of turnover of population might provide a more or a less favourable environment for various organizations, given the presence of other factors. On the whole, it is fair to accept Willmott's point that a key variable in the degree of community life is length of residence, so measurement of residential persistence is important in this respect. Certainly, it is necessary to study mobility alongside segregation, for it is important to know if the segregation was in terms of areas with a stable population or of areas of changing inhabitants with the same characteristics. The pattern of mobility can

Table 44   Residential persistence in Cardiff

(a) Total sample, percentage remaining in each year at original address

1884	100·0	1890	23·8
1885	74·5	1891	20·1
1886	55·9	1892	17·2
1887	44·5	1893	14·9
1888	33·5	1894	13·2
1889	28·1		

(b) Occupational groups, percentage remaining in 1894 at original address

Lower middle class	16·4
Ship repair trades	15·2
Building crafts	27·3
Labourer	31·3

(c) Areas, percentage remaining in 1894 at original address

Canton	10·6	Bute	20·2
Grange	15·5	Splott	11·8
Cathays	15·4	N. Roath	22·7
Centre	21·1	S. Roath	13·9

(d) Total sample, percentage remaining in Cardiff at each date

1884	100·0	1890	55·5
1885	88·4	1891	52·7
1886	78·6	1892	48·5
1887	72·2	1893	44·2
1888	64·0	1894	41·2
1889	60·0		

(e) Occupational groups, percentage remaining in Cardiff in 1894

Lower middle class	49·1
Ship repair trades	44·1
Building crafts	62·1
Labourer	57·8

(f) Areas, percentage remaining within area in 1894

Canton	37·1	Cathays	26·9
N. Roath	31·9	Splott	26·4
Centre	31·1	Bute	25·8
Grange	27·6	S. Roath	23·7

offset the class consciousness or communal solidarity which may otherwise be deduced from a particular pattern of segregation.

There is here a danger of reading too much into precise figures. Some of the American 'new urban history' has done just that. It has been seduced by quantification, deducing from figures states of social consciousness which could have been studied in their own right.[22] And it is important to look at intangibles – not just physical distance and social distance, but also mental distance. That is to say, how was the city perceived?

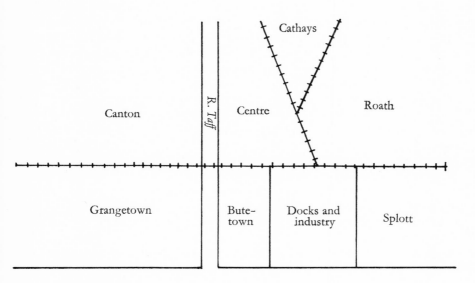

Certainly, distinct geographical areas were immediately apparent. The ground landlords had defined the character of areas as respectable or not, as working-class or middle-class. There was the high status area of Roath Park, the sound working-class terraces on Tredegar land, the Bute street-gardens, and so on. Physical constraints then moulded the area. The city was divided by two barriers, the river north to south and the Great Western Railway east to west. The two easterly segments were further divided by the docks and the Taff Vale and Rhymney Railways. This is presented schematically above. Some of these areas did appear to be isolated socially and physically from the wider city. The railways formed formidable physical barriers; the routes into Splott, Cathays, Butetown, and Grangetown were limited and these areas were geographically distinct. Certainly they were geographical expressions – but did the inhabitants make them anything more?

Cathays possibly did become more. Distinct it certainly was, cut off between the tracks. It was also the centre of working-class Liberalism. The Cathays Liberal Association was dominated by railwaymen, building workers, and other artisans and was well known to be the main centre of Lib-Labism within Cardiff Liberalism. It was also the centre of railway unionism. It was in Cathays that the meetings were held during the 1900 Taff Vale strike; it was to Cathays that captured blacklegs were taken. Occupationally, it was an area 'where such a large proportion of mechanics and engineers resided'.[23]

Splott and Grangetown were also physically distinct, and given a definable character, Splott by the steelworks and Grangetown by the designs of the Windsor estate. Splott had much more unity, with a major employer, and a more undifferentiated social character. Grangetown, on the other hand, ranged from the 1850s working-class terraces to the Bute street-gardens of the 1890s, and did not have a major employer within the area. Like Cathays, both had Lib-Lab councillors, but it does not seem likely that the areas became much more than geographical expressions.

The other physically distinct area – Butetown – was *sui generis*. It had failed to survive as the socially-balanced community originally planned, and by the late nineteenth century was divided between a business area to which clerks and merchants commuted during the day, and the 'sailortown' of Tiger Bay. The business district was part of the wider urban society; Tiger Bay was an alien enclave, both literally and metaphorically. It was like the 'sailortown' of any other port, having little connexion with the rest of the town. As Little remarked in his pioneer study of race relations in Butetown in the inter-war period, 'merchant seamen probably constitute in themselves a relatively "isolated" section of our society. By virtue of their employment they tend to be separated not only spatially and physically, but in actual pyschological terms.' The seaman was often an alien, with vague and transient social relations and few responsibilities. Many were doubly isolated, as seamen and as foreigners – not just Europeans, but also Lascars, Chinese, and blacks. Before the war, the isolation had scarcely led to a feeling of communal identity. The area was very rigidly segregated, geographically, socially, and psychologically, both by internal dynamics and external prejudice, but there was little internal solidarity because of the racial tensions between groups in the area. This was to change between the wars, when a large number of Moslems and Afro-West Indians were being openly discriminated against by the blatant misapplication of the law on the employment of alien seamen. Differences started to be submerged and a definite sense of group consciousness to emerge. So any internal cohesiveness developed only in the inter-war period. Before 1914 there is, however, no denying the area's separateness; to the inhabitants of Butetown, the area north of the G.W.R. was another world, rarely entered. This was the red light district of boarding houses, brothels, foreigners, in constant flux. With some exaggeration, one commentator remarked that 'the white man desirous of penetrating to the real Bute Town has a harder task before him than ever faced Livingstone'.[24]

The central area was, like Butetown, undergoing social transformation. The mixed residential and business streets were becoming entirely devoted to business use, and being rebuilt on a larger scale. Courts were being replaced by shopping arcades, stores and offices. The middle class abandoned its houses for use as offices. This is simply to say that from about 1880 the central business district took on a modern form, very largely with the same shape and many of the same buildings which survive at present.[25]

Canton and Roath are much more heterogenous. Socially, each was a mosaic; geographically, they had no easily definable and immediately apparent shape. Both had a working-class area and a small upper-class area, but were most notable for their respectable artisan and lower middle-class character. The distinction developed by Dr McLeod in the case of London is useful in understanding the life style of these areas in comparison with the more distinct and single-class areas. McLeod discerns three conceptions of the community to which an individual belonged, representing three distinctive patterns of life. These he terms 'neighbourhood-centred', 'district-centred' and 'national and international'.

Neighbourhood-centred life was particularly characteristic of the unskilled working class, 'tied to a narrowly defined area by poverty, insecurity and ignorance of any wider world. This small community provided not only personal contacts with potential employers or foremen, but concentration of friends, kin who could help in times of need, credit-giving landlords and retailers, sympathetic pawnbrokers. . . . The result was extreme parochialism.' At the other end of the scale was the 'national' and 'international' life of the wealthy, with town houses, country weekends and Continental holidays. Between the two extremes was a large and heterogenous section, with a district-centred life-style, characteristic of the suburbs and especially of the middle class:

> The distinguishing features of the 'district-centred' pattern were local ties looser than those of most of the working class, but still far more concentrated than those of the upper class; the focus of social life on the nuclear family and on formal associations; and life in 'residential streets', often at a considerable distance from the main places of work. One determinant of this style of life was intermediate income: enough to travel to work, to occupy a whole house, to employ some sort of domestic servant, to pay school fees and to take a summer holiday. A second was a clearly defined career structure: usually beginning with

a period of what was in effect apprenticeship in which a young man would be quite likely to live in lodgings at some distance from the parental home; followed by a period in which he would be looking for promotion, either by securing the approval of his present employer or by moving, perhaps some distance, to take a more promising position; and by the achievement of maximum income relatively late in life.

Certain parts of Cardiff were at least regionally oriented, with coal merchants with interests throughout south Wales. The Irish and the working-class areas like Splott and south Roath were neighbourhood-centred. Butetown was an odd mixture, being cut off from the rest of Cardiff whilst part of a world-wide network of similar fringes to ports. Canton and north Roath were characterized by the 'district-centred' conception of the community.[26]

There is one group which stands out very clearly in its attitude to the city: the Irish. They were separate by their places of residence but more than other groups were conscious of their distinctiveness, which they sought to express institutionally. The number of inhabitants born in Ireland fell from 5,990 in 1861 to 3,124 in 1911, as the original immigrants died and the children born in Cardiff became undifferentiated in the census. The size of the Irish population is therefore difficult to assess. Certainly, they were residentially distinct, had a common class position and often place of work. They were united by religion, by nationalism, and by institutions such as the Hibernian Society. A good example of this separateness was the Catholic School Board. Each area of fairly compact Irish settlement provided its church and then its own school, and later secondary schools were set up for the whole of Cardiff. In 1877 a Catholic School Board was established to work parallel to the official board in supervising Catholic education and raising money. Although two Catholics were elected to the first School Board – a priest was top of the poll – and representation was continued on each Board, the representatives also stressed the independence of the Catholics:

> we have a School Board of our own, for the support of which our people most willingly tax themselves, and this Board, we trust, will look after our very poorest children, and send them into school, and pay their school fees, whenever their parents are unable to do so, by being out of work. More than this we do not require. The Catholics of Cardiff are far from expecting their children to be educated at the expense of the ratepayers.

Similarly in politics the Irish saw themselves as a distinct grouping to be organized as a separate pressure group. The problem was that they were torn between two issues, of home rule and education, as Irish patriots and as Catholics. Generally, the Irish National League supported the Liberals on the first issue. After many grumblings about being ballot fodder for the Liberals without a share in power, which led to a collapse of the alliance in 1880 and 1892, they were rewarded by the election of a candidate in 1895. The Catholic Registration Society supported the Conservatives on the second issue. The Irish vote swayed between the two according to circumstances, with sometimes the rank and file of the C.R.S. overruling the priests and middle-class leaders to vote with the I.N.L., while in 1903 the I.N.L. supported the Conservatives on education.[27]

The Irish, then, formed an extreme, being residentially, socially, and mentally segregated. Butetown is similar in some respects, a mysterious world which was impenetrable to outsiders. So far as other areas are concerned, what is called for is a measure of the attitude of the ordinary town dweller to his environment and the width of his perception of his surroundings. Geographers are starting to consider the physical side of this in the new sub-discipline of perceptual geography.[28] Historically, Richard Sennett has made a pioneering attempt to analyse the social and psychological responses to the environment in his study of late-nineteenth-century Chicago.

In the mid-nineteenth century, Sennett argues, communities had diverse primary group networks, with face-to-face social contact. This changed in the latter decades of the nineteenth century, as the old network of primary group associations and multiple avenues of face-to-face contact disappeared. The home became the main focus of a new kind of private, isolated and intensive family life, at the expense of diverse primary group contacts. Sennett argues that men were seeking to defend themselves from the disorder and diversity of the city, retreating to areas where everybody was like themselves. The family became the instrument of defence against the complexities and uncertainties of city life, 'a retreat from perceived disorder'. The retreat into a small and intimate pattern of relationships was a shelter from the impersonality and complexity of the city. The suburbs were the locale of this intense family life. The intense family depended upon a simplification of community life, a move away from the multiple contact points of the inner city. This was precisely the value of suburbs – closer family ties were more possible in suburbs where everyone had the same life style and social status. In the suburbs, all unknowns and unforeseen social conditions of surprise could be minimized, creating a sense of long-term order and continuity on which family intensity could be based. The intense family and the suburb were, Sennett argues, mutually dependent. This all needs much more rigorous testing, and there is a large element of nostalgia for an encompassing, warm, friendly central city which might contain more myth than reality. But it is an imaginative attempt to ask what the development of segregation meant in social terms for those who were being segregated, approaching the subject not in impersonal terms of transport technology but in the personal terms of the experience of the city dweller.[29]

Something of the same process might have been happening in the 'district-centred' life in England. It is contained in Masterman's picture of the suburbanite who 'gazes darkly from his pleasant hill villa' at the chaos of the city. It is confirmed by the existence of a small group which reacted against the general pattern by joining the settlement movement or by 'slumming'. And there is no doubt that the middle-class family was in flux in the late nineteenth century. Further, as will be shown in a later chapter, the predominant middle-class response to the city in Cardiff was to purify it, to remove its diversities, to impose conformity. Life in the neighbourhoods was different. Very often, on first arriving, immigrants would settle within easy reach of relatives who would guide them into the community. At least in some working-class areas the family remained what it had been earlier in the century in the U.S.A. – not a retreat from but an avenue into the community.

These are merely speculations, but it is important to ask what segregation meant to the segregated. This is to take a fifth step, if only in a very stumbling manner. The previous steps were from the landowner to the builder to the purchaser to the spatial patterns of inhabitants. The fifth step is to ask exactly how people responded to and lived in the environment which was created. It is a question which can be more readily asked than answered.

Part three   Society and politics

Asa Briggs once remarked that much as the urban historian studies the common problems faced by all towns, his main interest will be in the differences between communities. This can be an invitation to antiquarianism, to stressing what is peculiar to one town rather than generic to all. Certainly the variations between towns are important but they must be placed within a framework which can establish where a particular community stands in relation to others. The next three chapters contain such an analysis. The broad questions are obvious: who held power in the town; what was the nature of social relationships; what was the dominant ideology? In answering these questions, an attempt will be made to place Cardiff in relationship to other communities which have been studied. So having approached Cardiff as an economic unit and as a physical structure, our concern now shifts to its social and political life.

9 Merchants and 'economists'

'Analysis of an urban élite . . . implies consideration of its community function as well as its internal structure.'[1] The internal structure has already been analysed in chapter 4. In the present chapter our concern is with the community function of the élite, something which varied greatly between towns according to its economic interests and its social attitudes.

The starting point for any discussion must be the work of E. P. Hennock.[2] He has illustrated the variation in the community function of the élite by a detailed analysis of Leeds and Birmingham, and has also suggested that there was a general process at work in all Victorian cities which affected élite participation in urban government. The particular may be taken first. Birmingham was governed in the 1850s–60s by a group well below the élite, dominated by small retailers and the drink interest. In the 1870s the élite returned to the council, to provide the background to the municipal career of Joseph Chamberlain. In Leeds, the changes were virtually inverse, the élite losing control in the 1870s and not re-entering until the 1890s. Clearly, both in Birmingham and Leeds the community function of the élite was changing over time and the study of the urban élite cannot be confined to its internal structure. Further, this fluctuation in élite representation is claimed by Hennock to be intimately linked with a key process in the nineteenth-century city, the cycle between brief periods of expenditure and lengthy periods of retrenchment.

Élite control and municipal expansiveness, lower-middle-class control and retrenchment, are largely synonymous in Hennock's analysis. He argues that élite communal leadership in English cities was under constant threat from groups further down the social and economic scale. The thesis is that the narrow basis of municipal finance, almost entirely falling upon real property, meant that there was 'nemesis built into the functioning of urban local government'. Rates were assessed on the rental value of premises and while for a merchant or shopkeeper the rental of the office or shop bore little relation to profits, for the owner of house property, rates were directly levied upon the income from rent. Further, these house owners were generally small men (a supposition amply confirmed in the case of Cardiff). 'The system of local government finance tended therefore to push a section of the inhabitants, often a predominantly lower middle-class section, into municipal politics . . . hostile to the professional men and the large merchants and manufacturers, who were the *natural leaders* of the community [my italics].' According to this analysis a programme of municipal expenditure and rising rates would lead to the formation of a ratepayers' society led by small property owners, which would fight elections, replace the previous leaders and inaugurate a period of 'economy'. This process usually involved the replacement of members of the business and professional élite by lower-middle-class representatives, for Hennock considers that a period of expansiveness usually required the presence of big businessmen and professionals with a wider perspective and greater financial expertise. A deterioration in social status was thus closely linked with a decline in the standards of municipal decision-making.

Two assumptions in Hennock's analysis are open to criticism: that élite rule was 'natural', and also that it was superior. It can be argued that Hennock has reversed what was natural in the circumstances of the nineteenth-century city. After all, was it rational in many cases for merchants and industrialists to serve on the council? The actions of the council were quite marginal to many industries, particularly in the earlier stages of industrialization. The council did not affect their efficiency and it did not make them pay for the social costs which were passed on to the community. The industrialist was concerned with the relative costs of that particular urban location and the external economies it provided for him. Industrialists might have an incentive to enter the council if the external economies started to decline and the powers of the municipality could be used to check this by providing better roads, modernizing the central business district and improving the water, gas, and electricity undertakings. There might also be pressure for industrial concerns to pay for some of the social costs incurred by the community. These incentives to council membership would exist particularly later in the century as factories in the centre of cities faced problems of congestion and an outmoded infrastructure. A cynic might wonder if this was not an element in the change in Birmingham in the 1870s, alongside the religious ethic stressed by Hennock. For merchants, involvement would very much depend upon whether the municipality owned the docks. If it did, they had an obvious incentive to be represented. So it can be argued that the élite only provided the 'natural' leadership in certain circumstances.

Surely the groups below the élite were much more the natural leaders. They formed Chadwick's 'dirty party' of slum-owners with a vested interest in opposing expensive sanitary reform, 'the shareholders and connexion of shareholders in bad water companies, who profit by the monopoly of inferior supplies; chimney owners who talk of political enlightenment and befoul the population with soot; shareholders and connexions of foul trading interests: as well as the class of owners for which exorbitant rents are exacted.'[3] It was more rational for such groups than for the élite to be the permanent, 'natural' leadership. Hennock's approach should be reversed: what has to be explained is, not the replacement of the élite as natural leaders by lower groups; it is why the lower groups as natural leaders might sometimes be replaced in certain circumstances by the élite. And Hennock makes a second assumption which might be queried. This is that élite government is not only natural but also better and with a broader approach to urban problems. In his analysis, small businessmen are narrow-minded, big businessmen broad-minded. At the very least, this is unproven and is certainly open to doubt. Big businessmen could be – and often were – simply interested in the 'efficiency' of local government, in tighter accounting procedures, in treating municipal concerns like the private sector. Their arrival could simply replace one kind of economy by another, and it might be lower social groups which had a wider conception of municipal functions. Cardiff is a very good illustration of both of these points of dissension from Hennock's essentially conservative analysis.

I

The first question must be, who exactly was on the council? The composition of the council, by economic interest group for the 30 years from 1884 to 1913 inclusive, is shown in table 45.

The heading 'Shipping, coal' covers the dominant branches of commerce upon which the mercantile élite was based. The maximum representation was seven, or 17·5 per cent, of the council. But this is undoubtedly an exaggeration of élite participation, as a biographical analysis of the group made clear. In all there were 19 individuals under this heading over the 30 years, and while the élite was based on these trades, it does not follow that all 19 were part of the élite. Only six were of leading importance: John Cory the shipowner, Richard Cory the coalowner, the Morel Brothers, Edward Nicholl, and John Gunn the shipowner and dry dock proprietor. Three were very marginal figures who must be excluded: the Beavan brothers were mainly engaged in exporting house coals, which was a minor part of the coal trade, and were forced out of business by the pressure upon middlemen, and W. J. Trounce was a shipbroker who became essentially a travel agent. If another four doubtful cases are also excluded, representation of the merchants was 2·5 per cent for 4 years, 5 per cent for 5 years, 7·5 per cent for 14 years, 10 per cent for 6 years, and 12·5 per cent for 1 year. Between the six leading figures and the marginal characters at the bottom there were small and middling shipowners, and middlemen coal exporters and colliery agents. There was only one coal *owner*. Of the six leading figures, two served for only one term or less, two were on the council for somewhat longer but without taking an active role, and two were long term members: Richard Cory, who was a largely negative force, and Thomas Morel, who during

Table 45 Composition of Cardiff Borough/City Council, 1884–1913

	Drink	Building	Tradesmen	Medicine	Law	Finance white collar	Union	Shipping, coal	Misc. commerce
1884	4	7	11	4	1	3	—	6	4
1885	5	7	10	3	1	3	—	7	4
1886	6	9	11	2	1	2	—	6	3
1887	5	8	11	3	1	2	—	7	3
1888	4	7	11	4	2	2	—	7	3
1889	5	8	13	3	1	2	—	6	2
1890	4	8	14	3	—	2	—	6	2
1891	5	9	9	2	1	4	1	7	2
1892	8	6	10	2	1	3	1	6	2
1893	7	6	10	1	2	4	2	6	2
1894	7	5	9	1	4	4	2	6	2
1895	7	9	4	2	4	4	2	6	2
1896	6	8	4	2	4	4	2	7	3
1897	6	7	4	2	4	4	4	6	3
1898	7	7	4	—	3	5	4	6	4
1899	6	5	4	—	5	7	3	6	4

Year									
1900	7	5	4	—	5	7	3	6	3
1901	6	5	5	1	4	7	3	5	4
1902	7	4	6	1	4	7	3	5	3
1903	6	5	5	2	4	7	3	4	4
1904	6	6	6	2	3	6	3	5	3
1905	6	5	4	3	3	7	3	5	4
1906	6	7	5	3	4	4	3	5	3
1907	5	4	4	3	5	7	3	6	3
1908	2	4	6	3	6	7	3	7	2
1909	3	2	8	3	6	7	3	7	1
1910	2	2	10	3	8	7	1	5	2
1911	1	2	9	3	7	9	1	5	3
1912	1	3	9	3	6	10	—	6	2
1913	2	3	9	3	8	10	—	3	2

Source: The occupational breakdown of the council was derived from nominations printed by the local press; the returns of members elected in the Council Minutes; lists of members in the Borough (City) of Cardiff Year Books; and street and commercial directories.

his year as mayor did try to make the council more dynamic. The élite, then, was politically marginal. The economically dominant branches of commerce were poorly represented, and such council members as they did supply were either not the leading figures or they were not very active.

'Miscellaneous commerce' covers all engaged in branches of commerce other than coal and shipping, and in servicing coal and shipping trades. It comprised 15 individuals. Four were timber merchants, each in a fairly substantial way of business, even if not comparable with the leading coal shippers. Three were officials of transport undertakings, namely the engineers of the Bute docks and Taff Vale Railway, and the manager of the Glamorganshire Canal. Two railway wagon concerns were represented, and the remaining six provided various port services.[4]

'Tradesmen' covers non-commercial, non-dock trade, and 'Finance, white collar' the middle class, non-manual occupations. Together they

Table 46   Councillors in 'tradesmen' and 'finance, white collar' categories, 1884–1914

Tradesmen

Coffee tavern proprietor (2)	Hotel manager
Undertaker (2)	Draper, outfitter (5)
Shoemaker/retailer (3)	Chemist (2)
Grocer (2)	Hay and corn merchant (2)
Miller (2)	Butcher
Produce merchant (2)	Furniture maker
Ironmonger	Auctioneer
Music seller	Oil distiller (2)
Newspaper proprietor (2)	Haulier
Coal dealer	Cab proprietor
Paper merchant	Veterinary surgeon
Bus and tram owner, property developer	Laundry proprietor
Fell monger	
Coach builder	

Finance, white collar

Bank manager	Building society secretary (2)
Insurance (5)	Stockbroker (2)
Teacher	Secretary of provident fund
Political agent	Technical adviser
Accountant	Railway clerk
Rentier	

Source: Drawn from occupational data calculated for table 45.

made up a minimum of 20 per cent and a maximum of 47·5 per cent of the council: 5 years 40 per cent and over; 16 years 30–39 per cent; 9 years 20–29 per cent. The 'finance, white collar' group consisted of respectable middle-class occupations but not the élite. The 'tradesmen' group consisted of 41 individuals, of whom eight were well-to-do and the remainder small retailers. Finally, if the legal and medical professions are considered together, their representation varied between 7·5 and 27·5 per cent, being under 10 per cent for six years, 10–19 per cent for 17 years and 20 per cent and over for 7 years.

The most important finding relates to the relative importance of 'docksmen' and 'townsmen'. Interests completely unconnected with the docks – drink, building, tradesmen, finance/white collar, law and medicine – dominated the council, fluctuating around three-quarters of the membership (maximum 87·5 per cent, minimum 65 per cent, three-quarters or above for 15 years). On the broadest definition of 'docksmen' – all 'Shipping, coal', added to 'Miscellaneous commerce' – the peak was 27·5 per cent for one year, and this is a definite exaggeration, for it will become clear that the real difference in practice was between the mercantile élite, whose interests were not specifically tied to Cardiff, and those of the townsmen, which were. By this criterion, a large part of the miscellaneous commerce group was very definitely tied to Cardiff with investments within the town and their interests peculiar to it. While the 'townsmen' dominated the council, the 'docksmen' dominated commerce. Political power did not parallel economic power, and groups below the élite always provided the governors of the town.

II

In Cardiff the commercial élite of shipowners and coal shippers was *not* the 'natural' leaders of the town. These leading merchants did not consider they had any leadership function within Cardiff; their attitude towards the town was very different from that of the groups which dominated the government, and this was most strikingly apparent over the issue of dock extension. As a general rule, it was a conflict between the Chamber of Commerce on the one hand, concerned for dock provision but not necessarily at Cardiff, and the council on the other hand, concerned that the docks should be extended only at Cardiff. As a corollary to this, it was a conflict between those wishing to provide for coal and those wishing to diversify the local economy. One councillor in 1880 put his finger precisely on the matter:

The corporation represents people who are more directly interested in this question than all the shipowners and merchants at the docks put together. Every man in Cardiff who has a house or shop or business depends for the value of his investments upon the amount of shipping done at the Docks. If the Docks were closed tomorrow, Cardiff would be a ruin as literally and lamentably as was Carthage of old. Meanwhile, those gentlemen who constitute the Cardiff Chamber of Commerce, and others like them, would speedily transfer their capital to other districts, would find means of registering their steamers and sailing vessels at fresh ports, and conveying the mineral treasures which lie at the back of Cardiff to Newport, Swansea and elsewhere. To the Cardiff Chamber of Commerce the Cardiff Docks are a convenience and economical means of carrying on their business. To the ratepayers of the town they are an absolute necessity of existence.[5]

The difference in approach was most clearly seen in the early 1880s. The Chamber and the town council had jointly negotiated with Bute and decided in 1881 that he should build a new dock provided that the existing scheme was extended, and charges were not raised. Both conditions were broken, but by 22 to 8 the council supported the Bute Dock Bill of 1882. The interests of the merchants were brushed aside by the overpowering desire for a dock in Cardiff, no matter on what terms:

the corporation has got nothing to do with the freighters terms. They would take care of themselves. . . . What the corporation wants is to get the docks made. . . . It was not for the corporation to throw the slightest obstacle in the path of the marquis, for by increased dock accommodation the town would be benefited considerably. . . . Anyone who fought against the bill was an enemy of the town.

The merchants were obviously traitors, for by 59 to 1 the Chamber of Commerce came out against the bill. As one speaker said,

there were now unfortunately two great parties antagonistic to one another in regard to dock accommodation. He meant the corporation, who were in favour of the new dock regardless of terms and at any cost, and there were the colliery proprietors and merchants and others who were opposed to the new dock unless the terms were fair and equitable.

The corporation made an error, for by making any critic of the terms of the proposed new dock into 'an enemy to the town', they forced the merchants into taking action which undermined the position of the Cardiff docks. Later in 1882 the merchants selected a site for a new dock outside the town. As critics of the corporation pointed out, the corporation had told the freighters to look after their own interests and had repudiated them as part of the borough entitled to representation. Now the freighters had taken the advice of the council and would build their own dock outside Cardiff:

the freighters urge that the corporation of Cardiff, by supporting the Bute Dock Bill, imposed, or allowed others to inflict a tax upon them, of £60,000 a year . . . As the corporation declined to consider their welfare, they violate no breach of faith by studying their own interest in the construction of the proposed dock, and they are, therefore, justified in selecting a site most favourable to themselves, without regard to the prosperity of the town.[6]

The conflict over the Bute Dock Bill of 1882 was merely the most important and striking of the different approaches of council and Chamber of Commerce, of 'townsmen' and 'docksmen'. It appeared also in the various moves towards a harbour trust during the 1890s. The aim of this was to free the trade of Cardiff from dependence upon one commodity, to make the docks more than a shipment point for coal which could be transferred elsewhere without undue hardship to the merchants but with untold consequences for Cardiff. Instead, it was hoped to encourage an import trade and factories: 'once you induce merchants and manufacturers to build works and warehouses you have practically linked them to the port, for even with fluctuations of trade they cannot move their buildings from one port to another.' The basis of the harbour trust movement was the ambition of the 'townsmen', with all their interests in Cardiff, to encourage trade and manufacturing firmly tied to the port; not simply to provide facilities required by the coal exporters but rather to increase 'the business and wealth of our tradesmen'. The docks, they thought, should be more than the 'convenience' of the coal trade.[7]

It was obvious that the attitude of the leading coal shippers and shipowners to Cardiff was simply dictated by speed of despatch and cheapness compared with the other coal docks. They had no reason to be tied to Cardiff where they had no investment. The mercantile élite had no firm ties with the town. Archibald Hood (1823–1902) is a good example. His father was a colliery overman in Scotland. Whilst working as a miner he qualified as an engineer and became mineral agent for a Scottish firm. He acquired an interest in south Wales, forming the Glamorgan Coal Co. in 1860, and settling in Cardiff in 1867. He continued to live in the town, but all his investment was to the north. He was not troubled if his coal went elsewhere, and he was, indeed, a promoter and deputy chairman of the Barry Dock and Railway Co.[8] Other leading coalowners – men such as David Davies of the Ocean Co. – scarcely even set foot in the town. They could leave the merchanting to commercial managers like Thomas Webb of the Ocean Co. Webb (1830–1908) was born in Herefordshire and was a journalist before becoming Davies's private secretary. He rose to become a partner and director in charge of the commercial department, and was also a director of the Barry company. He left £374,651 net – but none of this was tied to Cardiff.[9] Some coalowners like D. A. Thomas and the Corys did play some role in the local society, but there was no real necessity for them to do so. They lived outside Cardiff, their investments were in the coalfield and in coaling stations throughout the world. It was shown in chapter 4 that the 'legitimate' middlemen in coal had world-wide investments and were often part of national rather than purely local concerns. Louis Gueret with his investments in France and in the coalfield, his directorship of the Barry Dock and Railway Co. and an estate of over £400,000, represents the 'legitimate' middlemen, even if he went further than most in living across the Bristol Channel at Weston-super-Mare.

The shipowners were similarly distant from the local society. They paid rates only on a small office, and the corporation had no power over the efficiency of the docks. There was no economic necessity to seek representation on a council which was quite peripheral to their interests. T. R. Thompson (1846–1919), for example, was born in Newcastle, moving to Cardiff in 1856 when his father established a firm of ship-brokers and coal exporters. In 1864 he became sole owner of the company. He had interests in Tyneside collieries, Sunderland shipping, and was director of the Barry Dock and Railway Co., and chairman of a Barry dry dock firm.[10] These examples could be expanded, but the basic point is clear: these men were *in* but not *of* Cardiff, they had an office there but no real economic interest. It would not particularly have harmed these men if Cardiff *did* become 'a ruin as literally and lamentably as Carthage of old'. To them Cardiff docks were indeed no more than 'a convenience and economical means of carrying on their business'.

The absence of élite representation on the council might be explained by the recent arrival of these men and their need to establish their businesses in the first generation. However, this explanation does not hold up very well. Most who *did* serve were first-generation residents, and there is no sign that participation increased as firms and families became established. It was not so much a matter of lack of *opportunity* as lack of *relevance*. If they wanted to enter politics, it was more likely to be at the national level. As many or more members of the Chamber of Commerce were M.P.s or parliamentary candidates as were local councillors. The interests of the Chamber of Commerce were at least regional – the south Wales coalfield – and because of the importance of coal as an export commodity, often still wider, most obviously in the campaign against the export duty on coal.[11]

It was in fact 'natural' that groups below the mercantile élite controlled local government in Cardiff. It is misleading to start from the assumption that élite members were the natural leaders of the community, and then have to discuss how élite control was abdicated or overthrown. Rather it should be asked, did the élite see urban government as part of its natural function or its self-interest? In Cardiff, the answer was that it did not. The interests of the élite of Cardiff were at least regional, and in some cases international, not limited to the town, and neither did the élite see its functions of political and social leadership as confined to Cardiff. Membership of the council fell predominantly on those whose interests were specific to Cardiff. This is true of the drink, building, and trade groups especially, but also of the 'miscellaneous commerce' groups. Unlike the coal shippers and shipowners who had no major investment in Cardiff, the miscellaneous commerce group did – and for that matter, so did the Morels and Gunn as dry dock owners which might in part explain their presence. Timber merchants had considerable establishments within the town, as did railway wagon builders. The transport representatives were also, of course, firmly tied to Cardiff: the fortunes of the T.V.R., B.D.C., and canal company were indeed synonymous with the fortunes of Cardiff. Attitudes in the council toward dock extension and the harbour trust faithfully reflected the interests of these groups which formed the 'natural' leadership of urban government. Their concern was with the continued prosperity of the town, with control of municipal expenditure, and with docks *at Cardiff regardless of terms*.

If the corporation had controlled the docks, it might have been different. As it was, Cardiff had come into existence around a private dock, and the efficiency of that dock in exporting coal was the dominating concern of the mercantile élite. They were simply interested in efficient docks, *on the right terms and not necessarily at Cardiff*. The élite's interest in the economic efficiency of Cardiff was an interest in the ability of the T.V.R. and Bute docks to bring coal from the collieries to the ships as quickly and cheaply as possible. The government of Cardiff could not affect the efficiency of this in any way, so the élite had no concern to direct council policy. If a harbour trust had been established, attitudes might well have changed, for as one coal shipper said, 'it would be nothing short of a disaster if the docks were to be controlled through the town or by the municipal authorities, because, with one or two exceptions, all the essentially up-town gentlemen know nothing as to the needs of the coal or shipping trades.'[12] In the absence of a harbour trust, however, the composition of the council scarcely mattered. Neither was there any need from the coalowners' and shippers' point of view to control the level of municipal expenditure.

III

Was local government in Cardiff always narrow and uninspired, given the absence of élite control? Contemporaries did express alarm at the unwillingness of 'the merchant princes at the docks' to serve on the council so that Cardiff was 'under the disadvantage of having a portion of its governing body of less than average ability'. In 1876, it was complained that

> It is unquestionably a sad spectacle to see a town growing in commercial prosperity and increasing rapidly in population, so destitute of public spirit among its leading men . . . Take . . . our iron and coal masters, our merchants and brokers and try if you can count half a dozen out of the whole number who take a prominent part in any movement either of a religious, social or political character. They are certainly not to be found in the Town Council.

This was a constant theme, and it raises the question of what exactly *was* the difference between those councils adopting a policy of expenditure and those adopting a policy of economy. As a prelude to establishing this, we must examine the timing of the cycle of economy and expenditure.[13]

The first period of expenditure came with the Improvement Act of 1875 which extended the borough and gave the corporation powers to undertake improvements. Comments in 1880 were certainly correct:

> the work which the Cardiff corporation undertook to carry on either as a corporate body or as an urban sanitary authority, before [1875] . . . bears but a feeble comparison with the work which has been accomplished since 1875. The whole routine of business seems to have undergone a complete change. . . . The old system of procrastination and delay ceased with the extension of the borough.

The corporation had been inactive since the 1850s. An Improvement Act had been obtained in 1871, but was so truncated as to be useless. The early 1870s had been marked by 'culpable indifference and neglect'. When in November 1874 the council resolved to obtain powers to extend the boundary, purchase the gas and water companies, buy land for parks and a cemetery, and make street improvements, clearly something had changed.

The council's increased activity for the next few years was indeed striking. Expenditure on permanent improvements between 1875 and 1880 amounted to £230,925 or 90 per cent of the total expenditure incurred before 1880. The purchase of the gas company was dropped, but in 1879 an Act was obtained to buy the water company for £300,000. In the early 1880s the need to extend the supply of water was discussed, and in 1883 the decision was for the most expensive and forward-looking scheme against the arguments of short-term economy. The decision of 1883 to build reservoirs on the Taff Fawr to the north of Merthyr was the terminating point of this period of municipal expenditure.

The remainder of the 1880s was a period of retrenchment. The reservoir

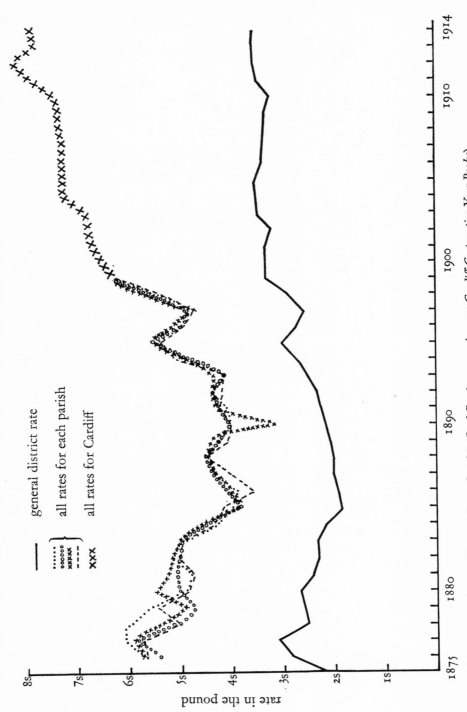

Figure 6. Rates levied in Cardiff, 1871–1914 (source: Cardiff Corporation Year Books).

was being constructed (it opened in 1892) but new commitments were avoided unless absolutely necessary. On two occasions the purchase of the gas company was raised, but the dominant attitude of caution meant that nothing was done. Rates fell until about 1890. When they started to rise after 1893, there was a revolt on the council in 1895, a victory for the 'economists' who purged the Finance Committee and trimmed all estimates. Rates fell heavily in 1896 and 1897. This was the last victory of municipal economy before a second period of heavy expenditure.

The roots of the second period of municipal expenditure went back to 1893 when a committee was appointed to consider purchase of the existing tramways. Up to 1897 the idea was merely to buy the lines and then to lease them back to the tramway company. In 1897 there was a basic change when another committee looking at the question of electric tramways recommended that the present company should not make any extensions, but that they should instead be made by the corporation and operated by the municipality separately from the existing system. This was accepted by the corporation, which also took the view that the existing tramways would in time be taken over in one system to be operated by the municipality.

This strategy was contained in the Corporation Act of 1898, which was also concerned with the construction of a new civic centre. This issue had been under discussion since 1890 without anything being settled. But in 1897 Bute's offer of 58 acres of Cathays Park was accepted. The 'economists' on the council were appalled at the decision to proceed immediately with building a new town hall and law courts. In 1898 the 'economist'-dominated Finance Committee was desperately trying to cut expenditure as rates rose to the highest level since 1877. But now 'the voice of the financial economist in the Cardiff Town Council is as the voice of one calling in the wilderness'. £800,000 was raised for the new civic centre, for electrified extensions to the tramways, for a new sewer to serve the west of the town, and a new asylum. Then in 1899 the corporation finally decided to buy the gas company. However, the company refused to negotiate and the plan had to be dropped. The Corporation Act of 1898 is thus directly comparable with 1875 as a watershed in local government policy.

By 1903 the economists were beginning to return from the wilderness, and they soon took over control. They reduced the 'reckless and extravagant' expenditure as much as possible, in what was termed the 'wave of economy'. A Departments Committee was set up in 1905 to investigate the running of each department so as to secure the maximum economy, which did lead to a reorganization of chaotic accounting procedures and the introduction of a more centralized administration. But while efficiency was improved, the dominant attitude was of 'retrenchment wherever possible', of 'being chary before committing themselves to even legitimate expenditure'.[14]

IV

The chronology of council activity is fairly clear-cut. There was a failure to do much to meet the problems of rapid urbanization before 1875. The lost ground was made up in a spurt of activity between 1875 and the early 1880s. This was followed by a retreat into retrenchment until the late 1890s, when there was an interlude of expenditure between 1898 and 1903. The period from 1903 to the war was dominated by the 'economists'. Why, then, did these changes occur? If the cycle of economy and expenditure was not a cycle of élite absence and presence, what was it? Was it a social conflict of any kind, or a conflict between different economic interests? Was it associated with the activities of ratepayers' associations acting as pressure groups outside political parties, based upon the lower-middle class; was it perhaps a party political conflict, based either upon pragmatic adoption of popular policies or upon different ideologies; or was it a cross-party question, based upon the social position of councillors or upon house ownership as Hennock would suggest?

On the face of it, 'nemesis' was built into local government in Cardiff to a high degree, for municipal finances were heavily dependent upon the rates. The corporation did not own the gas works to help out, and the tramway and the electricity undertaking which it did own were not profitable concerns. The only non-rate revenues were a few thousand pounds from markets, and about £1,500 a year from harbour dues. This dependence upon rates for revenue would appear to threaten an especially speedy nemesis for any scheme of municipal extravagance. However, the cycle cannot simply be explained in a deterministic manner by the buoyancy or stagnation of rateable value, or by the prosperity of the town as measured by trade figures. Rateable value was rising in the 1870s, but the break in trend to a lower growth rate did not come until the mid-1890s, just as the second period of expenditure was developing. So the situation was more favourable in the late 1880s and early 1890s for a policy of expenditure, when in fact they were years of economy. As far as trade is concerned, the period 1875 to the early 1880s was buoyant, but the low growth which set in from the 1880s persisted to 1914, with no break in trend to explain the revival of expenditure after 1898. The explanation must be more than the degree of flexibility in the basis of municipal finance and the prosperity of the local economy.[15]

The size of the group of house owners in Cardiff, and the wide diffusion of investment in housing would, if Hennock's approach is valid here, suggest an almost complete downfall of the advocates of expenditure. On the council of 1884–5, three-quarters did own houses as an investment.

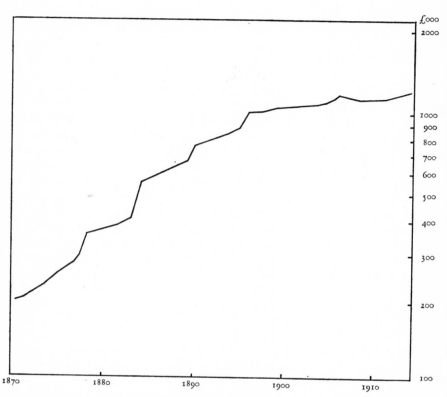

Figure 7. Rateable value of borough of Cardiff, 1870–1914 (source: Cardiff Corporation Year Books).

At least ten of the 40 councillors owned 11 or more houses. So Hennock's revolt of small property owners at first sight appears to be very plausible. But if the ten non-owners are compared with the ten councillors owning 11 or more houses, the similarity between the two groups is remarkable (table 47). If there was a conflict based upon house ownership, then, it was not between two different social classes. Could house ownership give two groups of similar social composition a different attitude towards municipal expenditure and be the key to the situation? Or was house ownership only a marginal factor, the key division being elsewhere? Clearly, the conflict could not be between a lower middle-class group of house owners and 'the large merchants and manufacturers who were the natural leaders of the community', for the simple reason that in Cardiff the large merchants did not see community leadership as part of their function. So if house ownership was a central feature in explaining the changes in corporation policies, it must explain changes in council attitudes which did not involve *major* changes in social composition. It seems unlikely that it could bear the main weight of explanation.

The house owners certainly did not create a powerful separate organization. They did not dominate the ratepayers' associations, which were in any case of little significance; there was no permanent ratepayers' organization until the very end of the 1890s. A number of earlier bodies had brief existences without achieving anything. But opposition to the Act of 1898 and subsequent schemes created first an *ad hoc* and then a permanent body, the Cardiff Ratepayers and Property Owners Association of 1900. It might have had some influence in the return of economy in 1903, but was probably only marginal. The membership was not wide, and its appeal was limited by its extreme ideology, which was far more dogmatic even than most 'economists' found necessary. It was certainly not getting backing from the expected quarters, for in 1908 it dropped 'Property Owners' from the title because no support was forthcoming. Such support as it gained came not so much from groups below the élite as from élite members who had some sympathy with the Association's extreme anti-socialism and denial of any public economic role. In 1907 the Chamber of Commerce pledged its allegiance, and Amon Beasley of the T.V.R. became a leading spokesman. The strident ideology of the Ratepayers Association did encourage the formation of more moderate bodies. In 1901 the Cardiff House Owners Association was formed to guard the interests of property owners, but it was defunct by 1903. The point of view of house owners was also presented by the Cardiff Ratepayers Federation of 1912, an ephemeral body of no significance. Small traders and clerks, rather than house owners as such, were represented by the Cardiff Ratepayers Non-Political Association of 1909 and the City of Cardiff Ratepayers Association of 1910. These were based upon feelings of middle-class outrage

Table 47   Social composition of property owners and non-property owners on council, 1884–5

Owning 11 + houses	Owning no houses
Civil engineer	Dock engineer
Bus, tram proprietor etc.	Tramway manager
Licensed victualler	Wine merchant
Building society manager	Insurance manager
Colliery proprietor	Ship broker
Lime merchant	Corn merchant
Dyeing works proprietor	Manufacturing chemist
Timber importer	Fell monger
Sanitary engineer	Surgeon
U.K.A. agent, retired coal exporter	Temperance coffee tavern proprietor

Source: Rate books for 1884 and analysis of council membership.

against paying for expensive social reform to benefit the 'idle and the thriftless', so that 'at present the oppressed classes of this country are the middle-classes'. It was believed that 'the brain worker, the shopkeeper and the man with a limited income are rapidly having their vitality crushed out of them'. Their desire was 'the application of sound commercial principles to municipal finances, municipal trading and municipal enterprise'. But whilst this view dominated the council before 1914 it was certainly not because of pressure from the ratepayers' associations working outside the political parties. As pressure groups, their role was minimal, and none of them ever became an independent political force before 1914. In 1911 the City of Cardiff Ratepayers Association did plan to put up candidates jointly with the Chamber of Trade, but nothing came of it. A series was published on 'Men who ought to be on the City Council' – but none ever were, and action was limited to protests and deputations of little effect.[16]

The ratepayers' associations in Cardiff were ephemeral bodies of minor importance which never became centres of political power outside the party system. Neither was their appeal particularly to owners of 'small house property'. Attempts to reach house owners were of little significance The process of nemesis suggested by Hennock might on *a priori* grounds have been expected to be strong, but in fact it was weak, not so much nemesis as a grumbling discontent. If the force for economy did not come from ratepayers' associations backed by house owners, could it come from the political parties, either as a straight party political conflict between one party adhering to economy and the other to expenditure, or between segments of both parties? A party political conflict does in fact fit the first cycle of economy-expenditure-reaction quite well.

When the change to a policy of expenditure came in 1875 it was not marked by anything so striking as Joseph Chamberlain's mayoralty in Birmingham at the same time (1873–6) and a concomitant change in the *social* composition of the council. What marked it was a change in the *political* composition of the council – from 15 Conservatives and 9 Liberals in 1869 to 13 Conservatives and 27 Liberals in 1876. The Liberals provided a simple explanation of the upturn in municipal activity: 'instead of an overwhelming majority of Tories, whose sole idea of municipal responsibility was humbly to bow with cap in hand to Cardiff castle . . . there is now a body of representative men as intelligent and independent as are to be found in any town council in the kingdom'. Without accepting that Liberals were by definition more intelligent, nevertheless the change around 1875 was the outcome, almost by accident, of a political struggle between Conservatives and Liberals in the early 1870s *on other issues.*[17]

About 1870 the municipal elections took on for the first time the character of a full-scale Liberal-Conservative contest. The foundation of the Constitutional Association in 1868 was followed by that of the Liberal Association in 1869. The Liberal Association certainly started from the position that it 'did not intend to mix in municipal matters' and it was not until 1878 that the Liberals established ward committees and 1880 that responsibility was taken for municipal elections. But despite the slowness of its institutionalization, municipal elections had become party political by 1870. This 'party politicization' of municipal elections after 1870 formed the background to the change in the council's policy in mid-decade. To a large extent it was linked to Liberal opposition to a Bute/Conservative fusion.

There is no doubt that the Bute estate had controlled the corporation and the parliamentary representation of the borough in the early nineteenth century, and that this pattern was not disturbed by the reforms of 1832 and 1835. However, during the minority of the third marquis after 1848 control had gradually been undermined. The parliamentary representation was lost in 1852, and in 1857 Bute's solicitor resigned as town clerk in the belief that the two roles were not compatible. Bute influence ceased to be a matter of particular concern. But this changed in the late 1860s. In 1868 the Bute estate had thrown its full weight behind the Conservative candidate in the parliamentary election. There were now references to 'the great stronghold of Toryism – Cardiff castle'. In the 1869 municipal election, 'supporter of the castle' had become a synonym for 'Conservative'. This change in attitudes was linked with an attack on Bute attempts 'to wield absolute power', a 'protest against the agents of Lord Bute nominating candidates for the Town Council'. It was the Liberal attack upon what was seen as a dangerous Bute/Conservative fusion which changed the council from a lethargic institution to one with a greater awareness of its functions in the growing town. This was a particular case of the general pattern which emerged in the aftermath of the 1868 election in Wales, when the retaliation (actual or supposed) of Tory landlords against tenants who voted Liberal was important in developing a political consciousness.[18]

The importance of the combination of an attack upon Bute/Conservative power with widening perceptions of municipal functions appears very clearly in the 1872 municipal election. Liberal concern then was with the 'specious designs and aggressive policies of Lord Bute's agents', who were 'resolute in the determination to wrest power from the burgesses'. The Liberal task was to prevent this, and, further, an opposition to Bute influence, real or imagined, was seen as part of an attempt to increase the activity of the council:

> Influential and wealthy as his lordship is, there are other matters to be considered, and nobler purposes to be subserved, than the development of his property and the extension of his influence. Cardiff is a rising place and the corporation must keep pace with the times. The lighting and general condition of the streets, the sanitary defects of many houses, the want of adequate attention to the improvement of the appearance of the town, and a lack of public institutions, all indicate a sluggish action on the part of the corporation, and the absence of that healthy public spirit and zealous pride in local affairs on the part of municipal authorities which are of far more value to a borough than a dozen noblemen and an army of obsequious agents.[19]

Municipal inefficiency was another stick with which to beat the Conservatives and Bute. It was not that Bute influence was the reason for indifference, or even Conservative control *per se*. But the council had become a lethargic backwater, and this situation was ended by the attack on Bute and the Conservatives which made control of the council a matter of vital interest. To complete the analogy, the politicization of the council flushed out the backwater, brought it into the mainstream of the life of the town.

The changes coalesced in 1874. The Conservatives were linked by their opponents not only with Bute's 'benumbing and paralysing influence' but also with the gas company whose high charges and large profits were leading to agitation for municipalization, with the drink interest, and with opposition to the formation of the School Board. With such a range of support in 1874 a Liberal pressure group was formed – the Ratepayers Protection Association – which was hailed as 'the first break of sunrise in the long night of corporate darkness'. The aim was to return men who, when discussing the Improvement Bill, would not owe allegiance to Bute or to the gas and water companies, whose allies it was claimed had controlled the council in the past. Three seats of the four contested were won.[20] There had certainly been an infusion of 'new blood' into the council, to use the contemporary term. The phrase was a Conservative jibe at the Liberal entrants of the early 1870s, who willingly accepted it:

> a more appropriate and more honourably suggestive appellation than 'the men of the new blood' could not have been given to those members of the council who have regenerated the atmosphere of the council chamber and have destroyed much and will yet destroy more of that old and bad system of preference and privilege and favouritism and exclusiveness. . . Cardiff is now being benefited by her new blood.[21]

This change in the political composition of the council meant a change in personnel, as Conservatives lost seats to Liberals and as new Conservatives replaced those who did not wish to face hard-fought campaigns. And this change in personnel brought in its wake a change in the perception of the council's role.

When the council had stood outside party political conflicts membership had been left in the hands of a relatively static and closed group with only occasional agitation. One of the dominant figures of the old static council was James Pride, a member of a small clique which did most of the council's work. In 1825 he had started business as a wharfinger on the old town quay before the building of the railways and docks. He was elected to the council in 1846, and with one gap remained until 1877. From 1858 he was chairman of the Public Works Committee and a member of the Finance Committee. He was also a director of the gas company, and, as his obituary pointed out, 'one who feared to go forward *pari passu* with the rapid strides which Cardiff has made for several years'. This applied as much to the Liberals as to the Conservatives on the 'unregenerated' council. Was there perhaps a split between an old and a new élite? Pride would fit this theory, being a member of the élite of the old market town, but very minor in terms of the new mercantile élite. So would C. W. David, a tanner, who was another member of the ruling clique. He was mayor five times, and was following the example of his uncle, whose business he had taken over. Again, there were the Vachells, who had moved to Cardiff in 1790 as apothecaries and established themselves as landowners and professionals in the town. They were virtually constant figures on the council, as were the members of the Bird family which was closely linked to the Bute estate as legal advisers. There had been a small market-town élite dependent on Bute, which was to be upset by newcomers attracted to the growing port.

The leader of the attack upon the old pattern was John Batchelor, 'the Friend of Freedom'. He moved from Newport in 1843 to establish a shipyard. He entered public affairs in 1845, becoming a Liberal councillor in 1850 and mayor in 1853. From 1868 he was chairman of the Liberal

Association. He was also the Liberals' martyr, bankrupted, it was said, by a Bute vendetta. Already by the 1850s, then, the old and the new existed side by side, but conflict on such lines was of minor importance by the 1870s. The old élite had by then been very diluted by more recent immigrants. And the 'new blood' was in any case not from the mercantile élite but from the men attracted to Cardiff to service the growing town – a newspaper proprietor, builder and undertaker, building society manager, oil distiller, laundry owner. So the change of the 1870s was not the replacement of an old market-town élite by a new mercantile élite. Some of the old élite survived, and one member of the new élite was elected, but essentially it was the supersession of one group of 'townsmen' by another with a similar function of servicing the town. It was the outcome of a party political conflict between groups which were not basically divided between an old and a new élite, or indeed, between élite and non-élite.[22]

The election of Liberal councillors of 'new blood' created a contrast between the Liberals and Conservatives on the scope of municipal policy. Similarly, the change back from expenditure to economy in the early 1880s was associated with a loss of Liberal control. The Conservatives were in an increasingly strong position because of their ability to equate Liberalism with high expenditure, and the use of their links with Bute to suggest that Conservative councillors would be able to secure the new dock so urgently required in the early 1880s. From 1880 the Conservatives moved to a more aggressive policy. In 1881, for example, with support from Bute officials, they were urging electors to vote for them 'and the new docks' rather than the Liberals 'and no more docks'. This was linked to an attack upon high municipal expenditure. The Conservatives were winning back control on this platform, the two planks of which were mutually reinforcing. Those whose interests were entirely within Cardiff – in housing, building, trade – were aligned in support of the Bute Dock Bill, that is, of a dock in Cardiff on any terms. Further, it was the supporters of more docks in Cardiff, who had all their investments in the town, who would also support a policy of retrenchment on the council. The Liberal domination of Cardiff was thus under a severe threat in the early 1880s as tradesmen switched to the Conservatives. While they were by no means united, any opposition to the Bute Dock Bill and any support for the Barry bill, did come from the Liberals. The Conservative/Liberal divide on the dock issue, as on expenditure, was clear enough to make the Liberals unpopular with those with investments within Cardiff. By 1886 the Conservatives controlled the council by 24 to 16.[23]

Conservative control was short-lived. The parties were level by 1887, and Liberals regained control in 1888, to maintain it until 1898 when representation was again level. Liberals immediately returned to power until 1904. After this, the Conservatives had control until 1909, which they regained in 1913 after a period of stalemate.[24] It is therefore easy to make a connexion in 1883 and 1904 between the movement from economy to expenditure and the change in control of the council from Liberal to Conservative. However, the years from 1888 to 1897 were years of economy *and* Liberal control, while the change to a policy of expenditure in 1898 came only when Conservative representation increased. A simple Conservative-Liberal divide is therefore only a partial explanation for the second cycle of economy-expenditure-reaction. The analysis must be refined further to explain the second cycle and this is attempted in the next section.

Before moving on from the simple Conservative-Liberal conflict, however, it should be enquired if there was any marked contrast between the representatives of the two parties. The data is presented in table 48 below.

A number of differences were obvious and expected. The drink interest was Conservative, the union representatives Liberal. Less expectedly, the Liberals generally had a majority of the building and trading interest and of the finance/white collar group, while the Conservatives generally had a majority of the shipping and coal interest and of the medico-legal group. That is, the Conservatives were more likely to be professionals or members of the commercial élite, the Liberals in groups with narrower interests. Liberals were also more likely to be house owners. In 1884 seven Liberals and three Conservatives owned 11 or more houses, while seven Conservatives and three Liberals owned no houses.[25] So taking Hennock's assumptions, the Liberal party was more likely to be economy-minded, as indeed it was at times. But looking at the debate over council policy more closely it became apparent that these assumptions did not apply and that there was no necessary relationship between the business and professional élite and imaginative responses to urban needs, and lower middle-class representatives and limited responses to urban needs. In analysing the second cycle of economy-expenditure-reaction it emerged that there was not simply an alternation of two attitudes to municipal policy, but rather a more complex interplay of three approaches, with the élite *less* likely than lower social groups to support the more expansive option. In explaining the second cycle it became necessary to go beyond a simple dichotomy of economy and expenditure accounted for by a conflict between two groups, be they élite and lower middle class, or Conservative and Liberal, for such an approach obscured major changes at work in the late-Victorian city.

V

In the years up to the 1880s, a simple contrast of economy and expenditure is apparent. This was the conflict between what Chadwick called the

Table 48 Occupations of Liberal and Conservative members of council, 1884–1913

		1884	1887	1890	1893	1896	1899	1902	1905	1908	1911
Drink	L	1	1	1	1	–	–	–	–	–	–
	C	3	4	3	6	6	6	6*	6	2	1
Building	L	5	5	6	5	5	3	3	2	2	1
	C	2	3	2	1	3	2	1	3	2	1
Tradesmen	L	5	6	9	7	3	3	6	3	5	6
	C	6	5	5	2*	1	1	–	1	1	3
Medicine	L	2	2	3	1	2	–	1	–	–	1
	C	2	1	–	–	–	–	–	3	3	2
Law	L	–	–	–	–	–	1	2	1	3	4
	C	1	1	–	2	4	4	2	2	3	3
Finance	L	2	2	2	4	4	6	6	5	4	5
	C	1	–	–	–	–	1	1	2	3	4
Union	L	–	–	1	2	2	3	3	3	3	1
	C	–	–	–	–	–	–	–	–	–	–
Shipping, coal	L	4	3	2	2	4	3	2	2	2	2
	C	2	4	4	4	3	3	3	3	5	3
Misc. commerce	L	2	1	1	1	2	2	2	2	–	1
	C	2	2	1	1	1	2	1	2	2	2

*1 Independent

Source: Drawn from occupational data calculated from table 45.

'dirty party' and sanitary reformers, between the vested interests of the public utility companies and slum owners on the one hand, and those demanding a safer and more efficient urban environment on the other. But by the 1890s two reform attitudes must be distinguished, what might be termed 'structural reform' and 'social reform'. The structural reformers were continuing the earlier tradition, the social reformers moving beyond them. In Cardiff, the second cycle of municipal policy was based upon a conflict between structural and social reformers, with the 'dirty party' (if it may still for convenience be called that) making noises off. This last group was associated with the Cardiff Ratepayers and Property Owners Association and in particular with Sam Hern, an estate agent, and Amon Beasley, manager of the T.V.R. They saw socialism in every municipal enterprise, and aimed at reducing the role of the municipality to a bare minimum. The structural reformers of both parties denounced their approach. The Liberal press was supporting the 'wave of economy' but came out in strong opposition to Hern and Beasley, for it did 'not intend to permit Cardiff to be counted among the reactionary places of the earth'. And the editor of the Conservative paper had been working with Hern in opposition to the schemes of 1898 until he denounced him for having 'marshalled all the forces of that crass, stupid and selfish immobility which have for so long frustrated the efforts of some of the best of Cardiff's citizens to improve and beautify the town'. Hern and Beasley were without doubt supporters of the most extreme economy. They were the Cardiff equivalents of Archie Scarr of Leeds and Joseph Allday of Birmingham. But in the return to economy after 1903 it was not their attitude which triumphed. Simply to talk in terms of economy misses the point. Hern and Beasley did not just want the economical running of services, for in their view the very existence of the services was wrong, as agencies of socialism.[26] The structural reformers wanted the services to be run economically, but accepted that the services were part of the municipal function. The leaders of reaction on the council from 1903 were in fact the reformers and opponents of the 'dirty party' of 1875–83, or their successors who had extended the scope of municipal action, and it is a misreading of the situation to confound the two under the one head of 'economy'.

The reformers of 1875–83 and the Liberal supporters of reduced expenditure after 1888 and after 1903 had some continuity of membership and certainly had a continuity of policy, what they called in 1874 'retrenchment and municipal improvement'. There was a direct line of descent from the 'new blood' of the 1870s to the Departments Committee of 1905. Structural reformers wanted a policy of business efficiency, opposing the old pre-1875 régime for its incompetence and inefficiency, but equally seeking economy. They reacted to the 'culpable indifference and neglect' of the roads, sewers, and water supply, but then called a halt. The Liberal 'new blood' of the 1870s became the 'old Liberals' of the 1890s onwards, and a group of 'new Liberals' or progressives emerged which wanted to go on a stage further. Structural reforms did not necessarily mean pennypinching, for, as with the new reservoirs of 1883, the largest scheme might prove more economical in the long run. What it did mean was getting the best value for the middle-class ratepayer. The 'new Liberals' were interested rather in social reform directed towards the working class. They wanted an expansive municipal policy and an extension of municipal functions to cater for the needs of the urban poor and to put the Liberal-labour alliance on a new footing.[27]

The Conservatives, after the upheavals of the years 1875–83, were also largely structural reformers, with a few members of the 'dirty party' on the fringes. The attitude of most Conservative councillors was virtually identical with that of a structural reformer on the Liberal benches, based upon what a leading Conservative called 'a state of efficiency with a consistent regard for economy' and opposition to 'all unnecessary expenditure upon unremunerative schemes'.[28] Both Liberal and Conservative structural reformers wanted business efficiency on the part of the council, and any differences would be over questions of Nonconformist rights or temperance or sabbatarianism. However, for a time after 1898 the Conservatives were prepared to go further than business efficiency might dictate, out of party political motives. They were attempting to exploit civic pride and Cardiff's desire to become the capital of Wales, as a vote-catching device. This was the motivation behind Balfour's decision to make Cardiff a city in 1905, and the Conservative mayor, Robert Hughes, was a leading supporter of the movement to secure the national museum and library for Cardiff.[29] But a more important explanation of the cycle lies in the changes within the Liberal party which also took the Liberals for a time beyond structural reform.

The social reformers formed a group within the Liberal party, and in the 1890s were pushing the party further than the structural reformers – the old Liberals – wished. The result was a conflict within Liberalism between what one commentator distinguished as the 'Village Party' and the 'Metropolitan Party'. The 'Metropolitan Party' or social reformers recommended to the Liberals the London progressives' 'noble idea of municipal life' from a platform of two splinter groups formed in 1892, the Cardiff Progressive Labour League (backed by the unions), and the middle-class Cardiff Radical Democratic Union. Both supported the same programme, backed the same group of politicians, and indeed represented an attempt to preserve the Liberal-Labour alliance on a new basis. The culmination of their 'warfare with the old gang' came in 1897 with the adoption of a definite municipal programme based upon the extension of municipal functions. Progressives were elected to the council, and one – a Lib-Lab representative – summed up the attitude of the Metropolitan Party':

> the cry for economy and keeping down the rates – though a very plausible and popular one – is to my mind very often a false and meaningless cry. Progress cannot thrive upon a parsimonious policy. . . . Conditions of life and comfort, better sanitation, healthier and cleaner dwellings, open spaces, parks and pleasure grounds, the extension of the library system, and the erection of public baths, lavatories, gymnasiums and other rational forms of amusement cannot be undertaken or carried out by any cheese-paring policy or thimble-rigging of corporation finances.

This belief in a progressive municipal policy directed towards the working class was not influential for long. Most Liberals remained structural reformers and were soon back in the ascendant.[30]

The leader of the old Liberal reaction in 1903 was F. J. Beavan. He was the leading 'economist' on the Finance Committee, becoming chairman in 1903. Also, from 1912–13 he was president of the Liberal Association. At the same time as he was leading the 'wave of economy' he was opposing a move to consult the Trades Council on the choice of a parliamentary candidate. It would, he said, be a humiliation. He resigned as president of the Liberal Association in opposition to an attempt to direct Liberal councillors to vote for 'social betterment'; to him, it could only be a financial question. He and his brother Ebenezer represented that type of Liberal which defined its ideology in terms of temperance, sabbatarianism, Nonconformist rights, and the old Gladstonian notions of public expenditure. Labour might be integrated into such a movement, but was not to be recognized as an independent force with its own separate aims, to be conciliated by social reform. Ebenezer Beavan was agent for the United Kingdom Alliance, published books in support of the Sunday Closing Act, and fought on the council for the maintenance of the sabbath with the fervour and vocabulary of an Old Testament prophet. Richard Cory, the wealthiest councillor of all, was a member of this group, the main backer of temperance bodies in the town. Again, F. H. Jotham – an outfitter – was a Liberal councillor who combined being treasurer of the Liberal Association with his presidency of the Chamber of Trade, from which position he urged the need for non-political councillors to represent traders, and to apply sound commercial principles. Whilst men of this type reacted against the situation of the 1870s, and in the 1880s favoured giving the working classes a role within old Liberalism, they were very much opposed to a policy of expenditure to cater for the working class. An illustration is the response of one of the 'new blood' of the 1870s to a park scheme in the 1890s. Cardiff 'was not yet ripe for such things – let them keep the evil within as narrow limits as possible'.[31]

In the return to economy after 1903 the old Liberals were firmly in control of the party and opposed Conservatives not with an alternative, progressive attitude but with the argument that they were just as economy-minded. The pressures which had existed within Liberalism to push it towards the Labour movement and social reform were not active or successful in Cardiff after about 1900. The possible alienation of the working class was offset by the potential loss of the middle-class vote if expensive municipal policies were adopted. After the defeat at the second general election of 1910, it was complained with justice that the Liberal executive was a self-perpetuating clique of Whigs opposed to the government's reform measures, that 'new Liberalism was much different from old Liberalism. At meetings the older Liberals spoke of politics of 25 years ago rather than the present time.' Conservatives and Liberals converged as structural reformers after 1903, backing 'a sound and wholesome policy of retrenchment whilst at the same time not interfering with the efficiency of local government'. The watchword was 'economy with efficiency', an attitude which was best expressed in the Departments Committee of 1905 which was backed by both sides of the council. This was not based upon the Hern-Beasley philosophy. The aim of the Committee was to secure the most economical working compatible with the efficient administration of the various departments of the council. Throughout 1905 an exhaustive enquiry was carried out, and in particular it was found that the accounting system was chaotic and antiquated. Accordingly the accounting procedures were modernized and centralized, and the power of the Finance Committee increased. The organization of the corporation was placed on a more rational, manageable, and businesslike footing, and it was this which was the main characteristic of structural reform.[32]

Was there a difference in social composition or economic interest between social and structural reformers? Insofar as big businessmen were interested in municipal affairs, they were structural reformers approaching the operation of corporation undertakings in much the same way as they ran their own businesses. The Chamber of Commerce and merchants at the Exchange passed a number of resolutions urging the council to be more businesslike, and W. H. Renwick – a coal exporter – was elected as a Conservative councillor on a programme of 'strictest economy' with backing from the commercial interests. Generally, the attitude of the big businessmen was to oppose the social reformers, to object to overtures to the working class. It was the exceptional big businessmen like D. A. Thomas who believed such an attitude was short-sighted and who consistently criticized the failure of the local Liberal Association to recognize the interests of labour in selecting parliamentary candidates. More usual was the attitude of Clifford Cory of Cory Brothers who was president of the Liberal Association from 1906 to 1912. In looking for a parliamentary candidate he simply wanted a man of commercial influence, without regard for his attitude on social questions. He was more interested in the religious politics of his Welsh Protestant League of 1898, a rabidly anti-Catholic and anti-ritualistic organization. Thomas was very much the exceptional opponent of such an approach among big businessmen, the vast majority of whom – if they had any interest at all – were structural reformers. Of course, the majority of structural reformers were not big businessmen even if the majority of big businessmen were structural reformers. Most were figures like Jotham or F. J. Beavan who were in a much smaller way of business but equally rigorous adherents to the application of strict business methods to the work of the council.

The social reformers were not drawn from the élite, that much is clear. In other words, contrary to Hennock, the élite did not opt for the most expansive option. Some were indeed small businessmen like Edward Thomas, a coffee house proprietor, although his background as a carpenter and bard made him somewhat unusual. Some were obviously working men, like F. A. Fox who was a union official before joining the employers' federation as a technical adviser. Most characteristically, social reformers were members of the non-trading middle class: Lloyd Meyrick, J. H. Jones, and Allen Upward were solicitors, Morgan Morgan an estate agent, Morgan Thomas a parliamentary agent. As Hobsbawm remarked of the Fabians – and these members of the Cardiff Radical Democratic Union were very similar – they were the 'self-made professionals . . . the "new men" rising through the interstices of the traditional social and economic structure of Victorian Britain'. Alongside them were the 'members of the traditional middle classes who had developed a social conscience, a dislike of bourgeois society', of whom perhaps the best representative was H. M. Thompson, a member of the family owning Spillers' flour mills. However, the exact social basis of the reform movements of late Victorian and Edwardian England is something of which little is yet known, the ideological debates and political conflicts having been studied more than the underlying socio-economic features.[33]

The conflict within the Liberal party thus involved not just attitudes to municipal finances but also relations with the labour movement. The difference between social and structural reformers was also largely a matter of different approaches to the Liberal-labour alliance. It was a difference between those who defined Liberalism as Nonconformist rights and those who wanted to widen the appeal of Liberalism to the working class, pushing it in the direction of progressivism. Put in these terms, rather than simply in terms of municipal policy, it is self-evident that it was not the élite which was going to be in any inevitable way the leaders of municipal expansiveness – almost on the contrary. The nature of the alliance between Liberals and labour is considered in detail in the next chapter, which analyses both the political and the industrial experience of the working class in Cardiff.

There was a seeming paradox in Cardiff between extreme tension in labour relations in the key occupational sectors, and loyalty to moderation in the political sphere. The turmoil on the railways culminating in the notorious Taff Vale strike and decision of 1900–1, and the upheavals on the waterfront in the early 1890s and the years leading up to 1914, were remarkable for their bitterness and intolerance. But the labour movement in Cardiff was slower than in other areas in south Wales and slower than many other urban areas of the same size, in making a successful move from Lib-Labism to an independent political stance. Lib-Lab councillors emerged at roughly the same time as elsewhere – Cardiff in 1890 compared with, for example, Sheffield in 1886, Liverpool in 1889, Bradford and Manchester in 1891. But Cardiff did not move from this stage to an independent labour political stance when others did; when it finally did move, it was without any electoral success. Halifax had four Independent Labour Party councillors by 1892 and Bradford one; Manchester Trades Council in 1897 established a joint party with the I.L.P. and the Social Democratic Federation; the Birmingham Trades Council had been permeated by 1893. In Sheffield, the I.L.P. had split from the Lib-Lab Trades Council and by 1914 had two I.L.P. members on the council alongside two Lib-Labs. Leeds had an I.L.P. member on the council in 1906, which E. P. Thompson describes as 'a remarkable example of arrested development'. In Cardiff, no representative of the Labour Party was elected before 1914, and neither were there any Lib-Labs left on the council after 1910. The central concern of this chapter is to explain why this should have been so, which raises a major theme in late-nineteenth-century social history.[2]

It is generally accepted that the mid-Victorian years were marked by a 'viable class society' or a 'society in equilibrium'. The alarms of the 1830s–40s had been settled and the working class, or at least the labour aristocracy, 'liberalized', brought within the system, in a manner which is the subject of much debate.[3] The outcome, however, is clear. As Tholfsen says:

> mid-Victorian urban culture rested on a tacit agreement among the classes as to values and roles. All groups in the community were devoted to a common purpose: social, moral and intellectual improve-

ment. Within that framework, however, there would be considerable variation from class to class. The bourgeoisie would assist the working classes to advance themselves, but without in any way disturbing power and status relations. Workingmen were to be encouraged to strive to achieve bourgeois values, but always in a form appropriate to their station.

There was, he believes, 'perfect congruence between these cultural values and the ideology of Liberalism'. They formed, indeed, a 'total cultural pattern', an 'irrefragable ideology'. If urban culture had such a basis in the 1870s, when did it start to be challenged, and how successful was the challenge? When did the irrefragable ideology fall apart? In the case of Birmingham – which Tholfsen is essentially writing about – the reorganization of the Liberal Association in 1868 marked the completion of the process of institutionalization of the integrated urban culture and of working-class and middle-class acceptance of that culture. But by 1893 the I.L.P. had permeated the Birmingham Trades Council and was undermining the concord between labour and Liberalism. The point of interest is the variation between towns in the date and the success of the challenge to the mid-Victorian urban culture and the institutionalization of working-class politics.[4]

In the late nineteenth century there were two related political debates: between the new and old Liberals within the middle class; and within the working class between the Lib-Labs and those demanding independent labour representation. And this has important connexions with two other debates: between economy and expansion in municipal services; and about the nature of urban culture. To a large extent they were interdependent. The move to an independent labour position could come because of the rigidity and irrelevance of old Liberalism; new Liberalism could be an attempt to maintain a previous alliance with the working class or to forge one where it had not existed. Municipal expansiveness could be a way to retain working-class support, and clashed with the Gladstonian ideals of retrenchment found among the old Liberals, with their definition of Liberalism as religious rather than social politics. And religious politics sought to impose a particular morality upon urban culture which created complicated cross-cutting forces. Many members of the working class – and most of the leaders – accepted this morality although they might be moving against the old Liberals on other grounds. But many others were committed to the life-style which was under attack.

These related debates mean that two ideal types can be constructed for Cardiff. On the one hand stood the old Liberal, perhaps a member of the 'new blood' reacting against aristocratic rule and municipal inefficiency. He wanted the town to be an efficient economic unit in the same way as his business – but he no more saw it as the function of the municipality to provide social welfare beyond what was needed for the efficient running of the town than it was the function of his business. He was willing to give labour a place within Liberalism, defined as an extension of the franchise and Nonconformist rights, but always under middle-class guidance. His interest was in temperance, sabbatarianism, in cleansing the city of vice and disorder (which involved an attack upon the life-style of a large part of the working class) rather than in social reform and welfare schemes. On the other hand, there was the new Liberal or progressive, linked with various Liberal splinter groups. He was prepared to cater for specifically working-class needs, and to support labour representation based upon a separate institutionalization of working-class politics rather than simply a subsidiary voice within middle-class bodies. He had a programme of social reform and a widened view of municipal functions going beyond what was strictly necessary for the efficiency of the town. He did not simply attack the working-class life-style, but sought in a positive manner to provide better avenues of recreation.

This comes back to the difference between structural reform and social reform, which is here extended beyond municipal policies to attitudes towards labour representation and urban culture. Some individuals did fit each ideal type exactly – say, F. J. Beavan the first, Lloyd Meyrick the second. But in other cases the neat pattern of the ideal types was complicated. The Conservatives sided with the old Liberals in seeking business efficiency, but they did not go along with the attack on the working-class life-style and the attempt to impose a particular view of morality. There was also, of course, division within the working class. At one extreme were those who sided with the Conservatives who defended their life-style, who were interested in the outlook of neither old nor new Liberals. At the other extreme were those wanting social reform and independent labour politics – the progressives who sided with the new Liberals or went beyond them into socialism. These were certainly a small minority. In between were men who accepted the old Liberal religious ethic, who had been prepared to accept a subordinate role within Liberalism but who were starting to move towards political independence. They were caught in the tensions as the 'irrefragable ideology', the 'total cultural pattern', cracked.

The approach to municipal policies was discussed in the last chapter; attitudes to urban culture will be analysed in the next chapter. For the present, our concern is with the third element, attitudes to the labour movement. Obviously, this cannot be approached simply through the eyes of the middle-class structural and social reformers. It is necessary to analyse how the debate between the middle-class approaches reacted with the debate within the labour movement between the Lib-Labs and the advocates of independence. And although E. P. Thompson has argued that class is a relationship which 'evades analysis if we attempt to stop it dead at any given moment and anatomize its structure', it is surely fair to say that the nature of the relationship is largely determined by the structure of the two interrelating groups.[5] Was there a great social distance between them? Were they homogenous or heterogenous? The next section analyses the structure of the working class, looking at the nature of the labour market and industrial relations.

I

The main characteristics of the working class in Cardiff were fragmentation and a heterogenous experience of industrial relations. No single occupation was able to give a lead. Further, in the sectors characterized by bad labour relations and militancy, fragmentation of the workforce made continued organization extremely difficult, so that after a brief spell of activity the movement collapsed into quiescence with no basis for political action. On the other hand, those who had a favourable position in the labour market and could maintain continuity of organization, secured recognition and had little incentive to renounce moderation. The occupational structure of Cardiff was loosely articulated, so that events in one sector set up only a limited repercussion in other groups. An analysis of each occupation will make this point clearer.

The occupational structure of the town is shown in table 49. The figures for 1901 and 1911 were compiled on a different basis from those for 1871 to 1891 but have been made as comparable as possible. The key occupational sector – both because of its size and its strategic importance – was transport, which employed between a quarter and a third of occupied males. Manufacturing took between a fifth and a quarter. Within manufacturing the largest single category was ship repair, but it is difficult to specify clearly those employed in that sector. All those engaged in iron and steel, ship-building, and engineering accounted for about 10 per cent of the workforce. This included employees in the railway wagon works, the engine works of the Taff Vale Railway, and the steel plant. The remainder of the manufacturing sector was made up of a wide variety of small-scale occupations, the largest being clothing, which accounted for 4·1 per cent of occupied males in 1871 and 2·6 per cent in 1891. The remaining occupations were much as would be found in any large town – building workers, shopkeepers and their assistants, the professional and industrial services.

The starting point for the analysis must clearly be transport. This was, of course, the *raison d'être* of the town – the transfer of coal from the railway wagons to ships. This sector was torn by some of the most bitter

Table 49 Occupational structure of Cardiff (occupied males %)

	1871	1881	1891	1901	1911
Agriculture, fishing	1·9	1·6	0·6	0·9	0·8
Mining	0·9	0·9	0·7	0·8	1·7
Building	9·0	12·9	11·5	11·7	8·6
Transport	34·2	24·9	26·4	28·4	29·9
Docks	(4·1)	(4·2)	(5·7)	(7·8)	(9·1)
Seamen	(26·0)	(14·7)	(13·1)	(8·3)	(7·2)
Railways	(2·7)	(3·6)	(3·9)	(5·7)	(6·7)
Dealing	13·0	12·4	12·4	} 36·9	38·5
Manufacture	21·8	22·3	23·6		
Machinery, ship-build- ing, iron and steel	(10·4)	(9·2)	(10·3)		
Iron and steel, engineering				(11·2)	(10·8)
Industrial service	13·9	18·2	17·4	14·0	12·2
General labour	(11·7)	(14·0)	(11·8)	(5·5)	(2·8)
Public service, professions }	4·3	5·2	5·2	6·0	6·6
Domestic service	0·9	1·6	2·1	1·2	1·5

Source: Census for 1871 to 1911. The figures for 1871–91 were analysed as suggested by W. A. Armstrong, 'The use of information about occupation', in E. A. Wrigley (ed.), *Nineteenth Century Society: Essays in the Use of Quantitative Methods for the Study of Social Data* (1972).

struggles experienced anywhere – the notorious Taff Vale strike, the conflicts between the seamen and the Shipping Federation, and between the dockers and the Bute Docks Company. But the transport sector, for all its militancy, failed to provide the basis for a strong and stable labour movement. The fragmentation of the transport workers was a barrier to effective organization, and was much more than a simple split into railwaymen, dockers, and seamen. Sectionalism was rampant within each.

The problem was most serious with the seamen.[6] Cardiff was, of course, largely an export port. The result was that ships would discharge their cargoes and pay off their crews in the import port, which might be London, Liverpool, Bristol, Amsterdam, and would then proceed to Cardiff in ballast with a skeleton crew, to pick up a cargo of coal. Before leaving Cardiff, the ship would therefore have to sign on a new crew: this generally amounted to 30,000 signings a year on foreign-going British ships, which made Cardiff one of the most important ports in the country for signing on men. A new wage bargain was made for each ship, so the labour market was highly fragmented and also virtually completely open.

There was a Cardiff Shipowners Association, but this denied that it had any role in fixing wages. Neither was any single company large enough to establish a wage pattern. In Liverpool, for example, the structure of the shipping industry changed away from many small firms in which a basic wage rate 'emerged' towards one in which a few large firms dominated and controlled the rate.[7] In Cardiff, despite the undoubted trend to concentration, this did not happen. In any case, most ships signing on crews were not even registered at Cardiff. The structure of the labour market was thus unfavourable to union organization.

Further, Cardiff was a 'hard-up' port. Many seamen went to Cardiff to sign on for a voyage, arriving with no money after having been paid off at the major import ports. Boarding-house keepers or 'boarding-masters' were prepared to give them credit to the value of the advance note of one month's pay which seamen received when signing on for a voyage, but no more than this. So when this credit ran out, seamen were virtually obliged to sign on, possibly against union wishes. The boarding masters thus had an important role in the control of the labour supply. Initially in 1889 the N.A.S.F.U. (National Amalgamated Sailors and Firemen's Union) and the C.B.M.G.A. (Cardiff Boarding Masters Guarantee Association) agreed to co-operate, but in 1890 the boarding masters sided with the Shipping Federation, supplying it with 'free labour'. This was because union attempts to exclude foreigners and non-members was threatening the precarious economy of the boarding masters. The union attempt to set up its own boarding house in 1891 to free the seamen from the boarding masters was a failure and the union was defeated on the issue of free labour. Although a number of attempts at a *modus vivendi* were subsequently made, they did not succeed. Boarding masters obviously refused to keep destitute seamen indefinitely, while the union was unable to pay them to do so, and consequently had great difficulty in controlling the entry of labour onto the market. During the strike of 1911 the novel solution was to set up a seamen's camp, to take the men out of the hands of the boarding masters, and this had a part in the success of the union in that year.

The seamen's union was not strong enough alone. It needed the support of the rest of the waterfront. The key to the defeat of 1891 was that the Dockers Union, having come out in sympathy, was itself broken. The key to the success of 1911 was that the support of the rest of the waterfront was won unofficially, at grass-roots level, creating a rank-and-file movement which was sufficiently powerful not to be broken, and to force the shipowners to give in.

The union's unaided control of the labour market was too weak to do more than achieve short rises in wages. The union could at most make wages responsive to upturns in freight rates but could do little to prevent falls in wages when freights turned down. The major weakness was that gains were not reflected in alterations in a fixed port wage rate. The union repeatedly sought this, but did not get it until 1911. The response of the Shipowners Association was always that 'the inexorable law of supply and demand governed wages', so that a port or rate wages board was useless. The inexorable law certainly favoured the shipowners. With a mass of seamen being virtually forced to sign on, and wage bargains being made repeatedly as each individual seaman signed on each ship, wages tended towards the minimum the market would bear. Further, the owners could circumvent union pickets seeking to control the supply of labour by signing on men on board the ship with the compliance of the Board of Trade (despite the doubtful legality of this manoeuvre) and with the active support of the dock company, which prevented union members from entering the docks.

Failure to establish an agreed rate before 1911 was the great weakness of the union. It meant that each ship had to make a new wage bargain, so any gain was not institutionalized and formalized. With the extreme fragmentation of the labour market, the power of the employers and of the boarding masters, there could only be short-term gains unless the owners conceded recognition and a fixed port rate. This they would not lightly do. The existence of a Shipowners Association certainly made it possible, but it was simply not in the interests of the owners. Eventually, and temporarily for three years only, recognition and a port rate were achieved by the revolt of the waterfront in 1911. The real breakthrough came during the war when the Shipping Federation was forced to allow the National Maritime Board to fix national rates, and the union used its membership of this body to enforce a closed shop which finally did give control of the labour market.[8] Prior to this, there was a completely open labour market and a constant turnover of men. For a short time in 1889–90 and 1911 a closed shop was attained, but it was something which in the absence of craft controls and a stable workforce was by definition an unusual event. For the rest of the time it was very difficult for the union alone either to control entry to the labour market or to stop the shipping and hence the docks, the railways and coalfield. Labour relations in shipping could hardly have been worse, but lack of permanent organization – to say nothing of a stable body of potential members – meant that the experience of the seamen was peripheral to the general outlook of the working class of the town. It was something happening almost in a world of its own, inscrutable to the outsider, a feature of 'Sailortown' or 'Tiger Bay', with its own laws and norms.

The situation on the rest of the waterfront was just as complex. In 1891 the docks employed 7·5 per cent of the adult male workforce. The main branch of dock work was loading coal from tipping appliances, which was a process mechanized to an extent unusual on the waterfront before 1914. This set up a division between the tippers, who operated the machinery on the quayside, and the trimmers, who stowed the coal on board ship. The two branches were organized separately and, what is more, the Dockers Union lost control of both of them, thus failing in its ambition to overcome the fragmentations of the workforce.

The trimmers had their own union, formed in 1888.[9] The employment structure was very complicated, and the union's success lay in manipulating this structure without exposing the fact that the role of trimmers was becoming more and more limited. The trimmers were jointly employed by the shipowners and coal shippers. The shipowners actually paid for the trimming, but through the coal shippers as intermediaries – and it was the latter who controlled the trimmers and fixed the rates. The need for coal trimmers was decreasing from the point of view of the shipowners from at least the 1880s, and after 1900 there was, as far as they were concerned, little necessity to trim cargoes. But trimming of coal had some – albeit marginal – benefits for the coal shippers, who were not actually paying. The union could exploit the division between shipowners paying for a service they did not want, and the coal shippers who had some reason for continuing a service about which they did not have to be cost-conscious. Hence the favourable tariff of 1907, when the coal shippers sided with the union against the shipowners, who since 1900 had been pressing for a drastic revision of the tariff. Hence also the union stress upon respectability and moderation, and its refusal to give any assistance to the Dockers Union or to join the Transport Workers Federation. Any militancy or strike action would have exposed the decline in the strategic importance of trimming and united the two groups of employers against the union.

The internal structure of trimming itself was also fractured. There were three groups: the foremen, supposedly paid by the coal shippers but in fact also sharing in the earnings of the working trimmers; the members of the gangs, an exclusive group assured of regular work; and the hobblers or casuals employed by the gangmen at odd times. The foremen and gangmen had controlled entry to trimming before 1888, charging premiums for membership of gangs of 8–12 men. Payment for a cargo was determined by the number of tons loaded, not the number of men employed. Gangmen shared equally in this payment, and foremen also took a share in most cases. It was in their interest to keep the number sharing the lump sum to a minimum, and to limit the number of gangmen to the number which could be assured of constant work; they would then employ hobblers as required and pay them by the hour. The hobblers thus had a very irregular employ solely at the convenience of the gangmen. This created many tensions. In 1888 the union institutionalized the control of trimming by gangmen and foremen, but there was a danger – made real on several occasions – that the hobblers would revolt and undermine union control of the labour market. Attempts therefore had to be made to conciliate the hobblers, which were not welcomed by the gangmen who were always very reluctant to surrender any of their privileged position. But gangmen for their part did not exactly welcome foremen's deductions, and periodically action was taken against the foremen. However, the union had to consider the importance of the foremen in controlling the entry of labour. The union did attempt to establish controls alone by its own methods, but in the last resort had to accept the role of the foremen in controlling hiring.

The Cardiff Coal Trimmers Union, uniquely on the waterfront, secured acceptance and recognition. It was virtually untouched by the fluctuations experienced by other sectors. By juggling with the interests of foremen, gangmen, and hobblers so that they remained more or less in line, whilst ensuring the shipowners and coal shippers did not come together, the C.C.T.U. turned fragmentation to its advantage and found a niche of stability. In 1890–1 the Dockers Union tried but failed to take over representation of trimming, and the trimmers remained aloof in their studied moderation.

The Dockers Union also lost control of the other side of coal loading – tipping – largely as a result of serious tactical errors.[10] Tippers were regular employees of the dock company. The Dockers Union moved into Cardiff in 1889, and by mid-1890 was in a strong enough position to submit a list of demands. When a strike occurred on the railway these demands were waived. The move was tactically sound, for the employers were hoping to fight both dockers and railwaymen at the same time on the general principle of free labour. By standing aside, the dockers enabled the railwaymen to fight on the justice of their claims. But the situation was subsequently misjudged. The agitation of 1890 had not been brought to a satisfactory conclusion, and ran into confusion. The tippers became impatient, and in unofficial negotiations were outmanoeuvred by the Bute Dock Company. Then in 1891 the tippers struck – officially – to back the seamen's attempt to exclude non-union labour, without giving notice and without submitting their own demands. The tippers had played into the hands of the dock company, which soon had all tips working with 'blacklegs', and with the trimmers remaining at work. The confusion between specific grievances and the free labour question was avoided in 1890, but not in 1891. A strike which started on behalf of the seamen became one for the survival of the Dockers Union, which suffered a massive defeat. It had been a serious tactical error. The claims of 1890 had been allowed to drag on too long, and then the strike was called at an inopportune time which effectively lost the men what they had been claiming. As one tipper remarked, 'we made a mistake, a very serious mistake – we now acknowledge it. What we ought to have done was not to strike on account of the [seamen] but to strike for our own demands which were acknowledged to be very reasonable.'[11]

The original intention of the Dockers Union had been to unite the whole waterfront. In this it had failed. The trimmers at one time moved towards the Dockers Union, but at the crucial point remained loyal to the C.C.T.U., refusing to help the Dockers Union in 1891. When the tippers were reorganized in 1898, it was by the Amalgamated Society of Railway Servants.

Apart from this crucial coal sector, there was a motley collection of occupations on the waterfront. In the early 1890s the B.D.C. itself employed 1,480 as dock gatesmen, dredgers, cranemen, and labourers, as well as the tippers. Outside Bute employ were the riggers, boatmen, and casual labourers engaged in moving ships in the docks, and workers in the timber, corn, iron, and other trades. The Dockers Union was left with these ephemeral groups. It had declined from a peak of about 4,000 members to 50 by 1894, and did not make a serious recovery until 1911 when it benefited from unofficial strikes in sympathy with the seamen.

After 1911 the Dockers Union won recognition, and in some cases a closed shop, from the motley collection of non-coal trades, but the dock company withheld recognition and refused to negotiate a port wage rate in respect to the workers it directly employed. Despite this failure, it is true that after 1911, for the first time, the Dockers Union had a stable base and some measure of recognition. Apart from the trimmers since 1888 and the tippers since 1898, it was only then that union organization became a permanent rather than a spasmodic feature of the Cardiff waterfront. The union pattern at the docks in 1914 was not simple: Amalgamated Society of Railway Servants tippers (who as railwaymen had been granted a conciliation board by the settlement of 1910) tipped coal to be trimmed by members of the local trimmers' organization (which was fully recognized by the joint employers). The Dockers Union had surrendered control of these two key employment groups on the waterfront, and this considerably weakened its position, in view of the dominance of the coal trade. It was impossible for the groups remaining in the Dockers Union even to halt the docks, let alone the railways and the coal industry. The most important employer – the dock company – continued to deny recognition, but some dockside employers did after 1911 move towards acceptance of the union. Particularism had remained the keynote of the waterfront.

On first sight, the railways present a different picture, a few large railway companies facing the A.S.R.S.,[12] monolith against monolith. But in fact this impression of concentration is misleading, for the men (3·9 per cent of the male workforce in 1891) were split by companies, by grades, and also geographically along the line. While the employers were concentrated, the men very often were not, and the fact that they were often disunited was a major failing of the A.S.R.S. The Cardiff branch was formed in 1872 and continued to exist thereafter, but it frequently lost control of the disputes, which became unofficial. Often there was tension between the local railwaymen, split by companies and grades, and the official union leadership whose failures at vital times encouraged this fragmentation. The local leaders drawn from the companies' employees would clash with the directors, but, because their action was unofficial, they had to stop short of strike action, back down and follow the more conciliatory line of the official leadership. But when the agitation was official, as in 1890 and 1899, the tactics of the general secretaries might be and often were severely criticized by the local railwaymen. An official leadership which appeared to be too conciliatory gave way to the companies when more might have been achieved, and this led to more spontaneous unofficial movements.

The Taff Vale strike of 1900 illustrates these weaknesses. In 1899 the official leadership drew together the various sectional agitations within each company and brought matters to a head. But having reached the strategic moment for striking by a slow and patient process, the general secretary gave the companies another chance, the moment passed, the issue was clouded, and the official movement petered out in confusion and fragmentation. In mid-1900 agitation resurfaced on the T.V.R., with the men deciding to act independently of the official leadership. The situation became very confused, the organization being split both by grades and geographically: the signalmen had a committee run from Pontypridd; the guards, brakesmen, and shunters had a committee run from Cardiff, but control of these grades in the valleys was lost to the secretary of the signalmen; the firemen had their own committee; the local A.S.R.S. organizer, working outside official channels, was trying to hold the disparate elements together. The outcome was that the men played into the hands of the company, for notices of the various sections were permitted to expire at different times, leading to breach of contract. In this weak position, the union's general secretary took control and made a settlement which seemed to promise concessions by the employer, but which was a blatant trick. By 1901 the men again felt that they had been sold by the central leadership, and a movement towards spontaneous unofficial action again developed, but was aborted by the legal decision of 1901 arising from the strike.

The central feature of labour relations on the railway was tension between local and national leadership with the unity of the railwaymen fractured by the divisions between company, grade and area. Labour relations could not have been worse, but the agitation of the men could scarcely have been less effective.

Transport was the crucial employment sector in the town. Each sub-section was characterized by extreme hostility between employers and workmen. Amon Beasley of the T.V.R., W. T. Lewis of the B.D.C., and the shipowners generally, were notorious for their uncompromising anti-unionism. Beasley and Lewis in particular were clever and unscrupulous in their dealing with labour disputes, weaving a web of such complexity and confusion that the unions were usually trapped and reduced to frantic but useless writhings. They specialized in a remarkable technique of dealing with deputations and finding loopholes and ambiguities in agreements in a manner which still astounds. Class war would appear to be characteristic and was at times more than a metaphor, for example, in the battles between pickets and 'free labour' during the seamen's strikes, in the railway strike of 1900, and with the use of the police and army in 1911.

Sometimes, union leaders urged that the workers should take control of the political machinery. J. H. Thomas of the A.S.R.S. was actively pressing for independent labour politics after 1907, and in 1911 Ernest Bevin, leader of the Dockers Union in the area, urged that

> in order to secure their emancipation it was important they that should use their political and industrial weapons – the vote and the strike – for the political machine which had been so useful to the master class could be captured and modelled and used to restore that which had been stolen. He blamed the working classes for giving the authorities the power to send soldiers and police amongst them.[13]

But the practical effect was small. Indeed, the only worker in transport to have political success was a coal trimmer, and it was the trimmers who repeatedly provided officials for the Trades Council. The union secretary Samuel Fisher, summed up the C.C.T.U. view of labour relations:

> the relationships of masters and men at the docks had been cordial because of the reasonableness which actuated their discussions. The merchants, shipbrokers, shipowners, dock authorities and railway companies of the port had almost invariably received him with great courtesy and shown him the utmost consideration, and a good understanding had been established between employers and workmen without any loss of dignity and power on the one side or the forfeiture of manly independence on the other.[14]

Fisher was a leading Liberal as well as an official of the Trades Council. It was this moderation, rather than the hostilities found elsewhere in the transport sector, which continued to dominate in local politics, up to 1908 on the Trades Council and up to 1914 in the community at large.

It might have been expected that the manufacturing sector could have provided the organizational backing for a policy of political militancy which the transport sector could not. Such was not the case. While 23·6 per cent of the male workforce was engaged in manufacturing in 1891, only a small part was within large-scale factories. Most was in small-scale trades, especially of clothing and food preparation, and was not organized. The proportion engaged in what could be called 'heavy' industry – engineering, ship repair, and iron and steel – was 10·3 per cent in 1891. This did not form, as it did at Sheffield, a sector pushing the labour movement towards an independent political position. The steel works was not even unionized, in any meaningful sense, and played no role in moving the Trades Council towards the left. Attempts to organize in 1897 and 1911 failed, and wages continued to be fixed by a sliding scale agreement, the men being represented by the Amalgamated Association of Iron and Steel Workers of Monmouthshire and South Wales, which was in no way a genuine union.[15] Neither were the flour mills unionized until 1911 when the Workers Union moved in.

The ship repair yards, it has been seen, were becoming more capital-intensive in the 1880s. They were large-scale concerns, dominated by directors who as shipowners were rampantly anti-unionist. Could this not provide the basis for a more militant attitude, carrying into effect what the transport workers could not?[16] The answer is, it could not. Despite the presence of shipowning directors, there was considerable justice in the claims of the employers' association that 'the association was not meant to combat trades unionism but to protect the individual and collective interest of its members. Trades unionism was a necessity of the age.'[17] The craft unions – the Amalgamated Society of Engineers, the Boiler-makers, the Shipwrights – had a closed shop, with strict rules on the number of men employed on various jobs, the number of apprentices, and how they worked. This survived the change in the early 1880s from wood to iron, and the reorganization of the industry. Generally speaking, disputes were settled between the union secretaries and the secretary of the Shipbuilders and Repairers Employers Association. This approach to labour relations was extended to the labourers. They had been organized by the National Amalgamated Labourers Union in 1889, and in 1891 the union was granted secure recognition and an agreed code of working rules. The labourers remained unionized after the collapse of waterfront unions in the early 1890s. The N.A.L.U. was, it is true, broken in 1905, but the Dockers Union stepped in, securing recognition and working rules by 1907. Whatever the reasons for the strike and lock-out of 1905, the employers had not been opposing labourers' unions in principle. There is no reason to disbelieve the statement of the technical adviser of the employers' association (who was, indeed, ex-area organizer of the

Boilermakers Society) that its 'policy was protective and not aggressive: its methods were fair and conciliatory, and it was in no way averse to trades unionism'.[18]

The same sort of attitude was found in the building industry.[19] In 1891, 9·6 per cent of the male workforce was employed as building operatives. Unlike ship repair, there was a large number of small employers. The workforce was fragmented into a number of craft and labouring unions working mainly in small groups. But the potential for conflict and confusion inherent in the employment structure was largely avoided and relations were systematized. From the 1870s the unions – at first the crafts, but ultimately in 1912 also the labourers – made agreements with the Cardiff Master Builders Association establishing union recognition, collective bargaining, clearly defined codes to regulate wages, hours and working methods, alteration of terms only at six months' notice expiring on 1 May, and machinery to settle disputes. As Clegg, Fox, and Thompson state, 'the organized employers showed a persistent attachment to the methods of collective bargaining',[20] which is not, of course, to say that the employers did not wish to reduce wages or to break down craft restrictions, as in the lengthy strike of 1892–3. But the C.M.B.A., like the ship repair employers and unlike the railway companies, the dock company and the Shipowners Association, did not insist upon the figment of the individual bargain and refuse to recognize unions. The C.M.B.A. insisted upon the strict organization of industrial relations. It attempted to remove the initiative of individual employers, making all subordinate to the Association's policy. Where the Cardiff Shipowners' Association insisted that it had no control over wages which were a matter for individual owners, the C.M.B.A. insisted upon joint responsibility for wages.

The Association, however, excluded speculative builders who supplied the bulk of Cardiff housing. Only in 1910 did they form an organization which affiliated with the C.M.B.A. Although there were signs that the associated and non-associated employers could take separate lines, on the whole the very definite bargain and rules the unions made with the associated employers dictated industrial relations. The battle was always to alter these terms, and attempts to raise wages were always within the framework established by the C.M.B.A. There was never an attempt to raise wages for the non-associated employers in the hope that associated employers would fall into line. Such a policy would have been nonsensical. The non-associated employers were small-scale, unstable 'firms' liable to bankruptcy, with a small, casual workforce. Workers there were difficult to organize compared with the more permanent workforce of the larger, more stable, associated firms. In organizational terms it made sense to concentrate on the latter. More than this, it seems unlikely that the larger firms with a stable workforce and an established bargaining procedure would fall into line with the casual, shifting, speculative part of the trade. But if the unions could establish a definite agreement with the large associated firms it was likely that they could impose the agreement also upon the speculative builders. Such certainly seems to have been union policy. In a way, the main strength of the building unions was the existence of a strong organization of the larger builders. With a large part of the workforce engaged upon a casual basis and moving from site to site, and with a rapid turnover of employers, it was in the interests of the unions to have an employers association and joint regulation.

Table 50   Branches affiliated to Cardiff Trades Council

1887	1889	1891	1897
Boilermakers (2)	—	—	Boilermakers (2)
Engineers (3)	Engineers (3)	Engineers (4)	Engineers (3)
Iron moulders	Iron founders	Iron founders	Moulders
Shipwrights	Shipwrights	Shipwrights	Shipwrights
Steam Engine Makers	Steam Engine Makers	Steam Engine Makers	—
	Smiths	Smiths	Smiths
	Hammersmen	Hammersmen	Hammersmen
		Iron dressers	Iron dressers
Carpenters, Amalgamated (6)	Carpenters, Amalgamated (5)	Carpenters, Amalgamated (4)	
	Carpenters, General		Carpenters (4)
Masons (2)	Masons (2)	Masons (2)	Masons (2)
Plasterers	—	Plasterers	Plasterers
Plumbers	Plumbers	Plumbers	—
	Painters and Decorators	Painters	Painters
		Bricklayers	
			Lathrenders
Printers	Typographical	Typographical	Typographical
Steam Sawyers	Steam Sawyers	Steam Sawyers	Steam Sawyers
Tailors	Tailors	Tailors	Tailors
	Coachbuilders	Coachbuilders	Coachbuilders
	A.S.L.E.F.	A.S.L.E.F.	—
	A.S.R.S.	A.S.R.S.	A.S.R.S. (4)
	Wagon Builders	Carriage Builders	Wagon Builders

1887	1889	1891	1897
		Bookbinders	Bookbinders
		Wheelwrights	Wheelwrights
		Sailmakers	Sailmakers
		Shop Assistants	Shop Assistants
		Marine Engineers	—
		Bakers	—
			Musicians
			Upholsterers
			Cabinet Makers
			Chefs and Waiters
			Customs Assoc.
	N.A.L.U. (5)	N.A.L.U. (7)	Labourers (3)
	Dockers (6)	Dockers (9)	—
	Millers	Millers	—
	Riggers, Boatmen and Hobblers	Riggers, Boatmen and Hobblers	—
	Seamen	Seamen	Seamen
	Trade & Provident	Trade & Provident	Trade & Provident (6)
		Tinplate	Tinplate Workers
		Tramwaymen	Tramwaymen
			Coal Trimmers
			Gasworkers
			Labourers (District Committee)
			British Steel Smelters
			Labourers (Enginemen & Stokers)

Source: Annual Reports of Cardiff Trades Council.

Thus labour relations in Cardiff fall into two main categories. On the one hand were the sectors characterized by bad labour relations and militancy. Continued organization was extremely difficult, and after a brief spell of activity came collapse into quiescence or complete disarray. The experience of industrial conflict had no base from which to influence political activity or the policy of the Trades Council. On the other hand,

Table 51   Trades unionism in Cardiff c. 1894

	Unionists	Non-unionists
Carpenters, Amalgamated	750	50
General	50	—
Bricklayers	140	30
Masons	750	60
Painters	140	300
Plumbers	90	20
Plasterers	150	10
N.A.L.U.[a]	2,000	—
A.S.E.	980	nil
Steam Engine Makers[b]	120	nil
Pattern Makers[b]	20	nil
Boilermakers	800	nil
Ironfounders	100	20
Iron Dressers	35	5
Smiths Hammersmen[c]	130	30
Tinplate workers[d]	20	20
Wheelwrights	40	} 40
Coachbuilders[e]	20	
Railway wagon builders[f]	140	20
Bakers[g]	120	300 (say)
Millers[h]	50	100
Bookbinders	25	nil
Compositors	300	5
A.S.R.S.	900	—
Loco. Enginemen	100	—
Steamsawyers	4	10
Sailmakers	40	nil
Tailors	120	200–300
E.T.U.	40	—
Trade and Provident	1,500	—
Shop Assistants	500	—
C.C.T.U.	1,100	300
Sailors and Firemen[i]	200	—
Shipwrights	500	nil

Notes

a.   Predominantly ship repair.

b.   Declining as members join A.S.E.

c.   Local society, non-unionists in the town and not in ship repair.

d.   Established 1889. All work in shops and factories, none in ship repair. At one time all unionists.

e. Local society. At one time 50 members, but most left for Wheel-
   wrights Society.
f. Local society, railway shops well organized.
g. Local society, formed 1890, 1891 joined national body.
h. At one time 100 members, but defeated and dying.
i. Doubtful if really any members.
— indicates number of non-unionists not known.

Source: Webb Trade Union Collection E, Section A, vol. iv.

those who could maintain continuity of organization achieved recognition, worked with the employers and were characterized by moderation.
So, despite very strained labour relations and militancy in some sectors,
the organized labour movement was a congerie of diverse occupations
characterized by stable labour relations, recognition, and moderation.

The composition of the Trades Council and union membership after
the defeat of the early 1890s are shown in tables 50 and 51. There was of
course a third category – complete disorganization – which applies in the
diverse manufacturing trades, in dealing (10 per cent of the male workforce in 1891) and in general labouring (11·8 per cent). But taking the two
categories which did have some organization (temporary or permanent),
a very strong contrast emerges between the ship repair trades, building
and coal trimming on the one hand, and the railways and the rest of the
waterfront on the other hand. There was little contact between the strident
anti-unionism of Sir W. T. Lewis of the Bute docks, Amon Beasley of
the T.V.R. and the shipowners on the one hand, and the building and ship
repair employers' emphasis upon collective bargaining and systematiz-
ation on the other. There was a major divergence – and it was the organized, recognized, and moderate sector which dominated the labour
movement. The councillors elected as Lib-Labs were from these occupations – Crossman, a mason, Chappell, a trimmer, Jenkins, a shipwright,
Fox, a boilermaker. It is this which led to the ambiguity of the labour
movement in Cardiff. The considerable militancy of the transport sector
did not enter permanently into the outlook of the working class in the
town. It was something spasmodic. After a short period of activity, the
organizations collapsed into ineffectiveness. Recognition was not achieved
and adequate organization was not maintained to institute a move to
political militancy. Those who *did* maintain organization had no reason
to renounce moderation – they had recognition and collective bargaining
and were generally content.

What Cardiff lacked was another possibility, an important sector which
was experiencing bad labour relations but which maintained some organization to act politically. No one fulfilled this role; there was no work

group which was both well-organized and *militant*, and which might have united the fractured consciousness. In the case of Bradford, E. P. Thompson considers that the failure of new unionism impelled a move to an independent labour political stance, compared with Leeds where new unionism was a success and such a move did not seem necessary.[21] At Cardiff 'new unionism' virtually collapsed after initial successes, so the pattern was akin to Bradford. But lack of industrial success did not turn a union from industrial action to political action; rather, lack of success had been associated with complete collapse so that no organizational basis for political action remained in these occupations.

Further, the working class lacked a united experience. On an organizational level, the Trades Council was not dominated by one large occupational grouping, which could provide a hard core for the organization. This appears clearly from the two tables, as does the numerical dominance of the recognized, moderate groups. Going further, the industrial experience of any one group of workers did not usually coincide with that of another group. One of Thompson's requirements for success, the close-knit community, was missing. Exactly the same point has emerged in respect of the absence of building clubs and the difficulties faced by the co-operative movement. The essential heterogeneity of the workforce in Cardiff was a prime barrier to independent working-class politics. However, some historians play down the extent to which even the homogenous mining communities moved away from Lib-Labism. Perhaps they did not need to. Miners and cotton workers were concentrated heavily in certain areas, and could obtain representation of their interests through the Liberal and Conservative organizations without having to opt for independence. In Cardiff, the moderate recognized unions might feel close sympathy with the Liberal party, which was prepared to recognize their loyal support in its rhetoric, but they were too few and fragmented to ensure that their interests were in practice given much weight by the local caucus. These unions were not able to get much in real terms out of the Liberals, but their experience of industrial relations did not give them a great inducement to political revolt in order to achieve their ends – instead, resentment would gradually build up at the failure to reward their political services, until a fracture occurred. The key was the internal dynamic of the political process rather than a *deus ex machina* of industrial turmoil. Meanwhile, those whose industrial experiences did give them reasons for political revolt were organizationally too weak to do anything effective. The structure of the working class – the nature of the labour market and industrial relations – meant that there was no good base either for obtaining representation from within the existing parties, or for moving to a position of independence. It was a situation which led to political impotence.

II

The other side of the relationship was the structure of the bourgeoisie of the town, and the social distance between it and the working class. There could be two extremes. At one pole, the bourgeoisie could be small, closed, unified and cut off by a wide gulf from the working class. This would apply in factory towns with a concentrated and capital-intensive industrial structure. At Oldham, for example, there were 12,000 worker families selling their labour to 70 capitalist families in cotton, coal, and engineering, all of which were concentrated and with no chance of a man working his way into the employing class. Taking an example nearer Cardiff, the bulk of working-class families in Merthyr Tydfil had to sell their labour to just four families controlling the iron works. In such towns the bourgeoisie was a closed group, separated from the rest of society with few intermediate groups between it and the workforce, an immense distance below. At the other pole were towns in which the bourgeoisie was larger, open, and plural. This would apply in towns based upon workshop production with a fragmented industrial structure requiring only small amounts of capital. For example, in the cutlery trades in Sheffield small workshops with low capital requirements meant that 'the ascent from wage labour to manufacturer was gradual and fairly easy'. Growth was by addition to the number of producing units and not by an increase in the scale of existing enterprises. The employing class was more open and less cut off from the rest of the town. Social barriers were not so rigid, prospects of social mobility were greater, and this was given political reflection in mutuality and moderation.

The position of a town on the continuum between a closed bourgeoisie cut off from lower groups and an open employing class more integrated into the community, had great significance for the nature of social relationships. For the early nineteenth century, John Foster has shown how the closed bourgeoisie at Oldham resulted in the working class defining itself in opposition as a distinct group, whilst in South Shields the small-time threadbare élite of small shipowners closely integrated into the community was associated with common attitudes by masters and men. The same sort of contrast was found within Sheffield in the late nineteenth century as the heavy steel industry developed alongside the cutlery trades. The cutlery workers remained loyal to Liberal politics whilst the different economic and social position of the steel workers was reflected in a move to socialism. So where does Cardiff stand on the continuum, and how does its position help explain local politics?[22]

At the top of the social scale in Cardiff was the marquis of Bute. His position changed considerably during the nineteenth century. The second marquis had been, in a manner of speaking, the ruling monarch of the town. He was also the entrepreneur who had raised Cardiff to become the leading port in south Wales. He had dominated the corporation and parliamentary representation, both unreformed and reformed. But with his death in 1848, the subsequent 20-year minority of his heir, and the continued economic growth he had fostered, social and political control was lost. Parliamentary representation went in 1852, and an attempt to reimpose a Bute nominee in 1868, when the third marquis came of age, was a failure. In 1910 the third marquis's younger son did become Conservative M.P., but this was in no way a 'Bute' victory, the link with the Castle being almost incidental. At the municipal level the Bute agents did continue to intervene in some elections up to the early 1880s, and clearly such a large interest wanted some representation. But it is fair to say that 'election of the third marquis in 1890 marked the end of any effective Bute power over Cardiff's political affairs, for only when aristocratic influence had become a spent force would the prestige of peerage be exploited to further civic dignity'. It reflected the end of any really effective influence by the mid-1870s. Subsequent participation in the early 1880s was simply that of any economic interest needing to protect its investment, and was far removed from the earlier proprietorial politics.

The political stance of the third marquis was Disraelian Toryism. He believed in the hierarchical system with himself practising the patrician virtues of the great chieftain. This did not involve him in political action personally, for his main occupations were those of the leading private patron of building in the nineteenth century, and a dedicated student of medievalism, liturgy, and ritual. Any political action connected with the Bute estate was left to men like the estate solicitor, L. V. Shirley. In the early days of the local Conservative Association there was a very close connexion with the estate office, but this faded. 'Castle' and 'Conservative' ceased to be synonyms, even if Liberals did continue to be anti-aristocratic and hostile to Bute on the land question. The Conservatives were anxious to achieve independence, and there was indeed a split between a Shirley-inspired association and the 'official' Conservatives. The estate remained a Conservative concern, but by the late 1870s it did not comprise the whole of Conservatism – it was only one of many interests in the local party and did not function as an active element of the party machinery.

Neither did the third marquis take the active economic role of his father. This was left to Sir W. T. Lewis, first baron Merthyr (1837–1914), who joined the Bute estate in 1855, becoming mineral agent in 1864, agent for the Welsh estates in 1881, and in 1887 managing director of the B.D.C. Meanwhile, he built up his own interests, became a very large coalowner in his own right, and dominated the Monmouthshire and South Wales Coalowners Association. He was the architect of the sliding scale agreement for miners' wages, and was chairman of the sliding scale committee for 18 years. His general anti-unionism, not least at the Cardiff docks, made the Webbs describe him as 'the best-hated man in the Principality'. He was one of the most important figures in Cardiff, both as the manager of the Bute estate and as a coalowner. For all purposes, however, he follows the general pattern of the other members of the mercantile élite which is analysed below.[23]

The third marquis, then, was not directly involved in Cardiff to any extent. He had become a constitutional monarch, a mere figurehead who was generally an absentee. It might even be said that he had abdicated. And as had appeared in 1882, the coalowners and merchants were no longer dependent upon him for provision of docks as had once been the case.

It has already been shown that the mercantile élite was divided between coal and shipping, with one more open than the other. But the more open – the shipping industry – was not at all analogous to either the cutlery trades in Sheffield or to shipowning in early-nineteenth-century South Shields. An ordinary workman or sailor could not expect, as an integral aspect of the economy, to achieve economic independence or part-ownership of a small ship. In Cardiff, the leaders of the shipping industry did change, but only once and not as a continuous process, and only a handful of men were involved. Despite this relative difference within the élite, membership was absolutely closed and an immense social gulf was fixed between the élite and the working class, a gulf never likely to be crossed. But this was not how it appeared in terms of social consciousness. Objectively, the position of the working class *vis à vis* the élite might have been akin to Oldham or Merthyr, where aspiration to élite membership was virtually impossible, but subjectively, the perceptions of the working class were more akin to such towns as Sheffield or South Shields where there was a possibility at least to become master of a small workshop or part-owner in a small ship.

The working class was fragmented, as we have seen. But while the élite might be a closed group, it was not a major direct employer of labour within the town, and was not perceived as such by the workers. The mercantile élite called the trade of the town into existence, but the labour required to handle that trade was employed by a variety of agencies in a wide range of situations. At the one extreme were the casual waterfront workers engaged to move ships around the docks, or to load and unload non-coal cargoes: they were engaged on an *ad hoc* basis by the individual merchant or broker. At the other extreme were those employed by the railway and dock companies. The élite were nebulous; the companies which handled their trade were concrete and present factors to the workers. Labour relations were very bad between these companies and their employees, but the fragmentation of the work force and organizational difficulties meant that militancy in such a context had very little repercussion on other sectors. The loose articulation of the employment structure of the town isolated and emasculated the militancy of any group which did come into confrontation at least with its immediate employer – the managers of the dock and railway companies – if not with the ultimate arbiters of the local economy. The only group actually employed by the élite on the waterfront were the trimmers, and this was in a very complex way which kept the trimmers firmly wedded to moderation.

Such a complex and indirect relationship between the workmen and the ultimate employer helps to explain the paradox that although the élite was structurally of the Oldham type, the attitudes of the working class were not. The indirect employment of the work force by the élite removed the possibility of a simple conflict between capitalist and employee. There was no easy perception of a small group of capitalists employing the bulk of the workforce. The Cardiff élite was somewhat nebulous, its relations with the workforce complex and ambiguous, mediated by a variety of agencies and a range of employment situations: those who did experience militancy were ineffective. Ultimately, all engaged in the transport sector were catering for the trade of the élite, but the élite did not own large establishments in which the workers spent their days. Directly, they employed clerks in offices at the docks and in a very complex way the trimmers. Largely, they were indirect employers and were, to use Foster's phrase, 'over the horizon'. D. A. Thomas might appear as a powerful capitalist to miners in the Rhondda where he controlled over half the output, and to some extent this increase in concentration explains the Cambrian Combine strike of 1910. But in Cardiff he had only an office with a few clerks, and he could appear as an ally of the working class against the T.V.R. approach to labour relations and the attitude of the Liberal caucus to labour representation.[24] Again, Richard Cory's statue in Cardiff has the epithet 'Coalowner and Philanthropist'. The apparent contradiction was resolved by a geographical separation of roles. To Keir Hardie, the Cory philanthropy seemed mere hypocrisy when the miners were on strike for a living wage.[25] But in Cardiff he did not act as a major employer and his philanthropy was unsullied. As for the ship-owners, the men they employed were cut off from the rest of the town, an enclave of rapidly changing membership. The important point is not so much that the élite was open or closed, plural or unified, compared with other towns, but rather that it was a shadowy body, responsible for the trade passing through the port but without any major investment in or commitment to Cardiff.

A further complicating factor in class relations was an extension of this pattern. Whilst the commercial élite of the docks had the economic power, the local tradesmen had the political power. The élite's lack of a communal function, the fact that they were 'over the horizon', gave them a certain anonymity so far as the bulk of the population was concerned. The local tradesmen, with their investment in the town and their communal function, were more immediate. They employed shop assistants, service workers and a large number of miscellaneous workers providing for the needs of the town. Apart from a few department stores, this was not a concentrated or capital-intensive sector, being largely composed of small family firms and workshops. The existence of a small, closed élite was obscured.

Structurally, the Cardiff élite was inaccessible as it was at Oldham or Merthyr, but attitudes were closer to those in South Shields or Sheffield where the élite *was* accessible. The seeming paradox is to be explained by the fact that the structure of the élite – the fact that membership was strictly limited – was largely irrelevant to the working class. The relationship was not a simple one of employer-employee but was much more complex and ambiguous. And if this were true of the strategic transport sector, none of the secondary sectors could provide the foundation for a different outlook on social relationships.

There were two possible locations where a more class-conscious attitude might develop – the ship repair yards and the steel works. The ship repair industry was becoming capital-intensive, organized in larger units. This was not, however, associated with any great class consciousness by the workers. The craftsmen engaged in the ship repair yards might be cut off from the employers by an unbridgeable gulf, but their unions had a large and defined role in the employment structure. They were labour aristocrats who did not see themselves as members of an industrial proletariat all with the same class position. They were indeed frequently themselves employing men, paying part of the wages of the labourers working under them, and accordingly they did not assist in the organization of the unskilled workers. It is more surprising that the steel workers did not fulfil the same role as in Sheffield of sponsoring a militant and class-conscious outlook. In Cardiff, these workers were not even on the Trades Council, and despite one or two putative revolts, were tied to sliding scale agreements which did not permit effective trade union organization. The ambiguity of class relations in the strategic sectors was not contradicted by other work groups in any effective manner.

The nature of the two interacting social groups has been analysed, and various reasons have been suggested why moderation should in fact have prevailed. The next stage is to outline the actual course of the relationship between Liberalism and labour. A breach did after all occur, even if it was a long time coming and was not of great electoral significance before 1914.

III

The reasons for the ultimate break between Liberalism and labour must be sought largely within the dynamics of their relationship. The attitude of the Liberals themselves was what finally impelled the fracture between the Liberal Association and the Trades Council. The moderates who dominated the labour movement were loyal to Liberalism, but the Liberal caucus could afford to ignore them because they were relatively few and split between a number of different unions. Predominantly they were craftsmen (with the exception of the trimmers) who were unlike miners or cotton workers in that they did not have enough men in any one constituency to control the local party. It was not industrial experiences, therefore, but a growing feeling of resentment at their inferior role in the alliance with the Liberal party which was the key to the shift in political attitudes in the labour movement in Cardiff. The process was very protracted, with a number of false starts, and the labour movement was indeed remarkably patient in the face of neglect of its interests and disregard of its opinions. Ramsay MacDonald's comment on the stubborn attitudes of local caucuses is a fair analysis of relationships between the Liberal Association and the Trades Council in the selection of parliamentary candidates: 'we didn't leave the Liberals. They kicked us out and slammed the door in our face'.[26]

Some Liberals did see what was happening, and did try to reform the alliance with the Trades Council on a new basis of greater equality. It has been argued that this was achieved in Lancashire, where the Liberal party made a successful attempt to win the working-class vote and undermine the Conservatives. Class politics emerged, but this did not also entail a change to the Labour party. Rather, 'it looked as though both Labour and Liberalism would be subsumed in progressivism'. In arguing thus, P. F. Clarke contradicts K. O. Morgan's analysis of Wales. Morgan posits a conflict between religious politics (derived from the social structure of the countryside) and the economic issues of industrial communities (including Cardiff) which is to be seen as a direct analogue for the change from Liberalism to Labour. Lancashire shows that it was possible to have class politics based on economic interests within Liberalism. But there is a good deal of truth in Morgan's analysis for Wales. Liberalism even in Cardiff largely remained defined in terms of 'religious politics', as will be seen in the next chapter, and old Liberalism remained dominant. Although there was a move towards progressivism in the 1890s, it did not capture the local Liberalism as Clarke argues occurred in Lancashire.[27]

Perhaps the success of progressivism in Lancashire compared with its failure in Cardiff was the outcome of the fact that Liberalism in Lancashire had to overcome an established Conservatism and had nothing to lose; it did not have the established coalition of interests to maintain which introduced inflexibility into such an old-established Liberal area as Cardiff. Liberalism in Cardiff was a 'bizarre coalition' of interests – Welsh patriots, Nonconformist businessmen, industrial magnates, Irish nationalists, and trade unions. A lurch towards progressivism would weaken this coalition, and so primacy was given instead to the needs of Cardiff as a commercial centre – which required that the Liberal candidate be a man of commercial weight, who was also sound on the issues of religious politics. Working-class interests and a claim to participation in the choice of candidate received little attention, and this eventually impelled even the moderate Lib-Labs who were staunch adherents of the religious and moral ethic of Liberalism towards the idea of a Labour parliamentary candidate. The Trades Council was not of such predominant importance within the coalition that its interests had to be given high priority, and so, for understandable reasons, progressivism did not fulfil its promise of the 1890s and subsume labour and Liberalism.[28]

The changing relations between labour and Liberalism within this context must now be analysed, and the first stage is to show how the labour movement was brought within Liberalism. The formation of the Cardiff Liberal Association in 1869 had not, as at Birmingham in 1868, institutionalized an already existing alliance between the working class and Liberals. Only in 1878 was the Cardiff body remodelled with ward committees and a central General Committee – the 'Two Hundred', or from 1879 the 'Three Hundred' – and it did not extend its role from parliamentary to local elections until 1880.[29] But it made no approach at all to the working class. If any single date is important, it is 1882. During the opposition to the proposed Bute monopoly of labour at the docks which was contained in the Bute Docks Bill of that year, an *ad hoc*, informal alliance was formed between prominent Liberals and leaders of the working-class opposition. The issue of the 1880s was whether or not this could be institutionalized and made permanent.

The crisis of 1882 over the docks issue had placed the Liberals in a delicate position. If they opposed the Bute Dock Bill, they would alienate those with interests confined to Cardiff who wanted a dock in the town on any terms, and who were also turning from the Liberals on the economy question. But the working class was overwhelmingly opposed to the clauses creating a Bute monopoly of labour and decasualizing the work force at the docks. The Liberals did on the whole come out in opposition to the labour clauses and during the agitation on the issue in 1882 Lib-Labism in Cardiff took on reality, as a rather paternalistic and protective relationship in which the middle-class Liberals appeared to themselves and to the dockers as benevolent custodians of the best interests of the workers.[30]

The Liberal Association before 1882 had made no particular attempt to reach the working class. The problem after 1882 was going to be whether the Liberal 300 would be able to forge the alliance between Liberalism and the working class, in the face of the alienation of a section of the middle class. How, if at all, were the relationships informally established between the leading Liberals and an *ad hoc* working men's committee to be institutionalized? Would middle-class leadership be so readily accepted, or would the working class move to a more independent role within Liberalism? The possibility was not as yet a rejection of Liberal ideology, but a rejection of middle-class leadership and a claim for a share of political power within Liberalism. In the 1880s, there were a number of tensions in this direction, aided by Liberal splinter groups, in the face of official Liberal indifference.

The Liberal Association was loath to act. Its concession to reform in 1886 was to transform the Liberal 300 into the Liberal 500, in order to 'democratize' the Association, a manifest failure.[31] The 1882 alliance was *not* institutionalized and the working class was becoming impatient. The Cardiff Working Men's Radical Association was formed in 1886, and at the end of the year it broke the existing pact between the Conservatives and Liberals for an uncontested School Board election, asserting its liberty 'to take whatever action the members deemed advisable in the interests of radical working men'. It strongly criticized the Liberal 500 for neglecting the claims of workers to representation. The C.W.M.R.A. candidate was in fact withdrawn before polling day, but it was urged that 'working men must not be the mere retainers, the mere rank and file of the party'. The Trades Council, formed by skilled artisans in 1883, was also by 1886 showing impatience with Liberal neglect of the working class, and this built up to a peak in 1889 when Lascelles Carr, the Conservative newspaper editor, agreed to stand as Trade Union candidate. This led to revolt by many trade unionists and Liberals and the crisis finally brought about an agreement between Liberalism and labour, admitting the claims of labour to direct representation within the Liberal party and to a larger role than that of 'mere retainers'. Ideological convergence, it had been seen, would not necessarily entail unquestioning acceptance of middle-class leadership – an independent share of political power within Liberalism had been claimed.[32]

Pressure had been building up for change from middle-class groups outside the Liberal 300 or 500 as well as from working-class bodies. The Cardiff Junior Liberal Association was formed in 1886, pressing for a much more radical programme of social reform, 'a bold and aggressive policy which shall appeal powerfully to the masses'.[33] Also in 1886 the Liberal Reform Association was set up to present 'a clear and definite exposition and full and free representation of advanced Liberal principles and measures of reform'. A number of L.R.A. supporters were returned to the council. These in 1887 called a meeting of workingmen in one ward to select a candidate 'with a view to securing more direct labour representation in the Cardiff Town Council'. They selected E. F. Kennard, an ex-labourer but now an auctioneer, as 'a fit and proper person to represent the labour interest'. He was simply recommended to the Liberal ward committee, and support was made conditional upon his selection by that committee. He was in fact both selected and elected. It was a movement led and inspired by middle-class Liberals, it was not a specifically working-class body, and it was firmly within 'official' Liberalism. What is more, it was firmly within *old* Liberalism. The leading L.R.A. members, and the candidate, were prominent advocates of temperance, sabbatarianism and the Nonconformist conscience, and were, indeed, to be hostile to the later progressive new Liberals and main supporters of 'economy'. They were not appealing to specifically working-class interests as the new Liberals were to do, by advocating social reform; they sought to institutionalize the working class within old Liberalism, combining the middle class and working class to secure temperance and disestablishment. Ideological convergence between sections of the middle and working classes on Nonconformist issues was the key to their position, distinct from that of the later critics of official Liberalism who wanted to show concern for specifically working-class interests. This was a position which the Junior Liberals had already started to adopt, and their Association was indeed to become the main centre of progressivism. The L.R.A. meanwhile was trying to bring the working class within traditional Liberalism.[34]

By 1888 the new Liberal agent, R. N. Hall, was strongly urging reform, to involve the working class in formulating the programme and selecting municipal candidates, to discover their requirements and incorporate them in the objects of the party. But while the general committee now became the Liberal 1,000, there was still no change in attitudes, and indifference persisted. The policy recommended by Hall was instead implemented by a group of Liberal councillors who in 1888 were urging that workers should not just select candidates – they should become candidates. The result of their efforts was the Cardiff Workingmen's Liberal Institute, and it was here that the move towards direct representation of labour from within Liberalism took on practical form. In 1889 a new Labour Association was formed at the Institute to secure direct representation of labour, working with the Liberal agent.[35]

The final breakthrough came in 1889 when the Trades Council, annoyed by the failure of the Liberals to sanction any working-class representation, backed Carr. The alliance of 1882 was then finally accepted, so that labour had some positive role within Liberalism rather than simply being treated as the servants of the party. For the first time a union official stood – unsuccessfully – as an official Liberal candidate. The claim of trade unionism to representation on the council was recognized. As Hall said, 'trades unionism and Liberalism were synonymous'. The bulk of unionists and the Trades Council agreed, and the new *modus vivendi* was celebrated at a meeting in the Workingmen's Liberal Institute.[36] This was a moment of equipoise in Liberal-labour relations, but the dynamics of union growth made it of short duration. The events of 1889 marked the fulfilment of attempts since 1882 to alter the basis of Liberal organization. But the agreement of 1889 was very much between a chastened Liberalism and a Trades Council of skilled artisans. The transformation of the Trades Council by new unionism, and the need to select candidates and raise funds to exploit the chance of representation now offered, created an embryo separate political party which would again alter the basis of the relationship between labour and Liberalism. By 1889, then, the Trades Council had won from Liberalism recognition of claims to *direct* labour representation *within* Liberalism. This was a distinct advance upon the earlier paternalistic protection of the working class in their just rights, but without granting the working class a share of political power.

In the 1890s the vital question was whether a strengthened Trades Council would go beyond the 1889 position to direct labour representation *apart from* Liberalism by a separate institutionalization of working-class political ambitions, or if it would remain content with representation *at the convenience* of Liberalism. It was implausible to expect a break with Liberal ideology, but there was a possible change in the character of the Trades Council's challenge for a measure of political power. The next 15 years were marked by two unsuccessful attempts to move towards an independent institutionalization of working-class politics, the failure of which left the Trades Council still dependent upon working through the Liberal Association.

Liberals had now admitted the desirability of direct labour represent-ation, and this required a methodical plan to select candidates and raise funds. In turn this meant there was a potential centre of independence from Liberalism (organizationally if not ideologically) developing from the very need now created for a rudimentary political organization. In the early 1890s it appeared as if this potential would be exploited; but in the later 1890s, while the Trades Council was not the unquestioning political servant of Liberalism and there were tensions, they were tensions to secure a more adequate representation within Liberalism; the potential of the early 1890s was not realized until the years before 1908 when the decisive break between the Trades Council and the Liberal Association occurred, on the level of both political organization and ideology.

Between 1890 and 1897 four Lib-Labs were returned to the council. The two victories of 1897 were the last by labour in any form before the war. As these councillors retired, they were not replaced, so from a peak of four in 1897, labour representation was non-existent by 1912. Each was a union official. John Jenkins (elected 1890) was local organizer of the Shipwrights Society; W. S. Crossman (elected 1892) was treasurer of the Masons Society; John Chappell (elected 1897) was president of the Trimmers Union; Frank Fox (elected 1897) was district secretary of the Boilermakers Society. All were leading Liberals. Although Chappell in 1897 was not an official Liberal candidate, and indeed defeated the sitting Liberal, this was not a breakthrough. He had been chairman of the ward Liberals, and within a few months had healed the split, remaining a thorough Liberal. This was the only occasion that the Trades Council won an election against the official Liberal. In every other election, success depended upon Liberal backing. An independent political base was not constructed despite two attempts.[37]

The first attempt was made in the early 1890s, when the employers' attack on 'new' unionism was encouraging thoughts of independent representation, but before that attack succeeded and removed the basis of support for independent labour politics. Jenkins in 1890 had been put up as Trades Council candidate, but shortly before the election the Liberal candidate withdrew because Jenkins was 'a pronounced Liberal and a member of the Liberal 1,000 and its executive'. The Trades Council in return gave full support to Liberals in other wards and hailed Jenkins on his election as the first 'bona-fide Labour representative on the Cardiff County Council'. But in 1891 it announced that it wanted direct representation, and that capitalists would not simply 'divest themselves of their selfish interests'. In consequence, next year it formed the Cardiff Progressive Labour League, which was to be 'non-political' and open to all who 'give Labour a primary position'. It attracted 500 members and had a Fabian-inspired programme. But of the six candidates it ran, only one – Crossman – succeeded, and that because he was adopted by the Liberals. The C.P.L.L. had failed to emerge as an independent force in Cardiff politics, and in 1893 it was wound up.[38]

The Trades Council retreated into quiescence until the late 1890s. The second move to independence came when a Labour Representation Committee was formed in 1899. Although this was associated with the emergence of a socialist group on the Trades Council, it was in no sense a watershed. T. J. Hart, a member of the Cardiff Socialist Party, was president of the Trades Council in 1900 and 1901, and secretary of the L.R.C. in 1901. He had great hopes for the L.R.C., but he was very much alone. He had to go along with the Trades Council in supporting Liberals, and the other positions continued to be held by Lib-Labs – Chappell, Fisher, Crossman, and Jenkins. All continued to be very active in Liberal politics. Only when Hart's term of office ended could he stand as an I.L.P. candidate, and significantly he had no support from the Trades Council when he did. Neither did the L.R.C. become a financially strong base for labour representation. The most it did was to pay part of the salary of one councillor, and when even this proved impossible it was abandoned in 1907. Hart's presidency and the formation of the L.R.C. did not constitute a watershed in Cardiff labour politics. Nevertheless, the ground was being prepared for the watershed which *did* occur in 1907-8.[39]

Local Liberalism had become distressingly inflexible, and eventually justified annoyance with the local caucus led to a split. But at the time of the formation of the C.P.L.L. in 1892, it seemed some alliance with the Liberals on a progressive policy was indeed possible. The movement of 1892 was not a reaction against Liberal principles but against the old-fashioned Liberalism which still dominated the Liberal Association. There was an identical reaction from a group of middle-class Liberals. The C.P.L.L. programme was essentially that of the London progressives, and some Liberals attempted to make the Liberal 1,000 adopt a similar programme. Some members of the Trades Council were also trying to get this adopted within the Liberal 1,000, and it was their failure which led to the formation of the C.P.L.L.

In 1893 the C.P.L.L. was paralleled by the formation of the Cardiff Radical Democratic Union, to work for 'advanced and progressive Liberalism . . . to extend and consolidate the Liberal party, so that it shall embrace every phase of progress and every true interest and aim of labour'. The C.R.D.U. was the Junior Liberal Association transformed. The policies of the C.P.L.L. and C.R.D.U. were indistinguishable, and they were both calling for 'progressivism' against the old clique of the Liberal 1,000 which was 'wholly selfish and one sided. The claims of the labourer were entirely disregarded'. According to the Liberal agent, the Liberal 1,000 was exhausted and old-fashioned, and there was an emerging conflict between a group of young progressives and the dominant 'old gang' or 'happy family' or 'village party': 'the corporation is full of men who have grown up with village ideas and cannot exchange them for metropolitan ideas. The Village Party . . . tremble at the prospect of the New Cardiff. They are frightened at their responsibilities. The Metropolitan Party must take the reins into their own hands.' Two issues had come together. The old Liberals were 'economists' as well as neglecting the interests of labour. To them Liberalism was temperance and sabbatarianism and disestablishment – and economy. To the progressives it was social reform directed to the working class – and an expansive municipal policy. Although some progressives did get on the council, the victory lay with their opponents. When the president of the 1,000 resigned in 1893 in opposition to the new ideas, his successor, Robert Bird, was in exactly the same tradition: his main political activity was leading the passive resisters, and he was a national figure in the Methodist Free Church. There were some concessions to reform in 1895 when the parliamentary seat was lost for the first time since 1852. The old policy of extending the general committee was taken to its conclusion: the 1,000 was removed, and all members were now to form the general committee; similarly, ward committees were to have no restriction. Since there were not 1000 members in all until 1904 this was rather pedantic, and did not alter the fact that a small group took decisions and treated the Association as a rubber stamp. Also, in 1896–7 a municipal programme was framed for the first time. But it was only *suggested* to candidates, and did not form a permanent change – it was revived only twice after 1897. The success of the progressives was very limited and short-lived.[40]

There might have been some change at the municipal level, but on the constituency level there was a complete failure to consult the Trades Council on the choice of parliamentary candidates. There was increasing resentment about this, and opposition to the caucus developed on the parliamentary level, while the alliance continued at the local level. Gradually, however, and especially between 1904 and 1908, the attitude formed on the one level was transferred to the other.

The sitting Liberal M.P., E. J. Reed, was defeated in 1895. Before the next election, the Liberals decided to select a new candidate. There was no attempt at consultation, and in 1900 the choice fell on Robert Bird who was accepted by 50 to 1 by the executive, although they were warned he could not carry the working-class vote. In the event he withdrew and Reed was invited to stand again. At his adoption meeting various unions protested – they had not been consulted and Reed had alienated himself from the union movement. The Liberal Association countered that it was completely unnecessary to consult any other body; the Trades Council responded by inviting W. M. Thompson of the *Reynolds News* to stand as Labour candidate. As it happened, he could not stand because the Trades Council had no money and expected him to pay his own expenses. In the election of 1900 Reed did eventually get full union support. But it is clear that there was a developing hostility at the parliamentary level to the attitudes of the Liberal caucus, and its failure to consult labour. The change which occurred around 1900 was not a movement away from Liberalism, which continued to receive support at the municipal level, but rather the growth of justifiable grievance against the failure of the Liberal Association to consider labour interests in selecting parliamentary candidates. The quarrel was not with Liberalism but with the local caucus.[41] On the municipal level the same had happened ten years earlier, and the Liberal Association had reluctantly given trade unionists a role within Liberalism. The pressure had now moved to the parliamentary level.

The Trades Council had a low opinion of Reed despite its eventual support for him. As one delegate put it in 1902, he was 'one of those blockhouses between Liberalism and Toryism who long since should have taken an excursion ticket to Toryism which was his proper station'. In 1903 the Trades Council resolved that 'the time has come when a Labour man should contest the united boroughs of Cardiff, Cowbridge and Llantrisant, and pledges itself individually and collectively to do all in its power to return a Labour man to parliament at the next general election'. This resolution was proposed and backed by leading Lib-Labs – the proposer was next month adopted as a Liberal municipal candidate. Some radical Liberals were sympathetic, but the local caucus did not take the Trades Council threat seriously, and blatantly ignored them. The Lib-Labs had been content to accept some voice in municipal elections whilst simply endorsing the parliamentary candidate; now they also wanted to be heard in the selection of the parliamentary candidate, and it remained to be seen if, when this was refused, there would be a feed-back to municipal politics.

In 1904 Reed 'took his excursion ticket to Toryism' and resigned on the tariff question. When the Liberals looked for a new candidate they had two criteria: adherence to free trade, and a position of commercial influence. Within days the candidate was found – Ivor Guest of Guest, Keen and Nettlefold, a sitting Conservative M.P. who had just taken an excursion ticket in the opposite direction on the tariff reform question. A section of the Liberals, led by D. A. Thomas, was appalled at the speed and at the failure to consult labour. An irrevocable split was feared. Opposition was unavailing, and Guest's selection was confirmed. The Trades Council was hostile to Guest, but was prepared to support an advanced Liberal favourable to labour and to drop the proposal to run an independent candidate. D. A. Thomas was sure the Liberals had misjudged the situation and promised 'uncompromising opposition to . . . a farcical candidature', pledging support to a Trades Council candidate if he was a sound Liberal. Thomas and some sympathizers united with the leading members of the Trades Council to set up a separate progressive organization, the Cardiff Progressive Council. The Liberal Association had denied the Liberal-labour alliance, or at least the right of labour to be consulted over which Liberal was to be supported. The C.P.C. was an attempt to heal the breach. As Thomas said, 'such action as that of the Cardiff Liberal Association . . . was justifying everything the I.L.P. said about the Liberal party'. However, the C.P.C. petered out without achieving anything.[42]

The Trades Council had to act alone, without the progressives, and in consequence it called a conference of unions and the I.L.P. to consider putting up a candidate. At this conference, two distinct views emerged. On the one hand were the Lib-Labs, still loyal to Liberalism but incensed by the 'clique of an Association' which had ignored them. They wanted a more sympathetic candidate than Guest, but not one who was tied to the

L.R.C. or independent of Liberalism. On the other hand was the I.L.P. which wanted to act under the auspices of the L.R.C. and establish a distinct Labour party. The voting at the conference was divided. On the parliamentary level, the I.L.P. won – a candidate was to stand under the auspices of the L.R.C. But the Lib-Labs won on the local level where there was still no pledge to 'independent' labour representation without Liberal support. Later in 1904, both Crossman and Chappell worked closely with the Liberals in the municipal elections. The I.L.P. group objected to this continued Lib-Labism and called a special meeting of the Trades Council to censure them on the grounds that the town council was divided only into capital and labour, and the 'time had come when they should take the purely labour view of matters in local affairs'. The Trades Council disagreed and gave the culprits a vote of confidence. Although the Trades Council had moved decisively towards parliamentary labour representation, there had not yet been a feed-back to local politics where the break with Liberalism which the I.L.P. wanted had not occurred.[43]

The momentum of 1904 was not maintained. By mid-1905 Keir Hardie was attacking the Trades Council for being 'lukewarm and indifferent'. The leadership was still predominantly Lib-Lab, and support for action had never been overwhelming. By the end of 1905 the idea of running a candidate at the forthcoming election was dropped amidst general indifference. The fracture in Lib-Labism should certainly not be exaggerated. In the municipal election of 1905 it was as firm as ever, and Guest was making a largely successful effort to win the union vote. Indeed, early in 1906 Crossman and Chappell came out in support of Guest. The I.L.P. was, it is true, stepping up its activity in late 1905. The Cardiff branch of the I.L.P. had in 1899 amalgamated with the Social Democratic Federation to form the Cardiff Socialist Party, bringing around 25 and 50 members respectively to the new organization. In 1902 this was reconstituted as the Cardiff branch of the I.L.P. By 1908 the I.L.P. had won control of the Trades Council. But in 1906 it was promise for the future. In that year it put up a candidate in the municipal election: 'the Liberal and Tory parties were divided by a tissue paper wall. The new Labour party was going to pull down that tissue paper wall.' But the I.L.P. candidate came bottom of the poll by a long way, and the tissue paper wall persisted with the Trades Council back on the Liberal side. The Trades Council had refused to sanction the I.L.P. candidate, but did support Chappell, complete with his letter of commendation from the Liberals. Crossman stated the still dominant belief: 'I would not be doing justice to myself in declaring myself a Labour man only . . . I cannot be what a section of my fellow workmen are trying to drive me into – an Independent Labour man. I am going to die a Liberal, although I am a Labour man.' In 1907 the I.L.P. on the Trades Council had to acquiesce in the abandonment of the L.R.C. rules and the formation of a separate wage fund to pay Crossman. There appeared to be a complete retreat from the move to independence since 1900.[44]

It was in fact the turning point. The I.L.P. was building up support; it had about 500 members in mid-1907, and held 340 meetings during the year. The Trades Council was being pushed to the left. At the end of the year an I.L.P./Trades Council committee was formed to select a parliamentary candidate. This it had done by early 1908, although the person selected subsequently withdrew. Also, the rejection of Lib-Labism was carried to the municipal level. At the end of 1907 the Trades Council again nominated Crossman and refused to support an I.L.P. candidate. But in 1908 it was proving impossible to raise money to pay him, and the Trades Council reported that opinion had so changed that branches would support only independent representation. Crossman was therefore invited to sign the L.R.C. constitution. He refused and instead became vice-president of the Liberal Association. The Trades Council Committee which had considered the issue

> felt that Labour was not independent at Cardiff at present, that Labour was subordinate to the Liberal party, and that the time had come, if Labour was to be adequately supported, that it should cut itself adrift from either of the two political parties and stand as a party itself.

This was soon achieved.[45]

The decision to fight the parliamentary election led the I.L.P. and unions in 1908 to resolve that 'the formation of a distinct Labour party is absolutely necessary'. By the end of 1908 the constitution of the Cardiff and District Labour Party was complete. It was a joint I.L.P./Trades Council body affiliated to the L.R.C. The party was officially inaugurated in 1909, and was immediately given control of municipal elections. The crucial event was the Splott election of 1908. For the first time the Trades Council nominated an I.L.P. candidate – J. H. Thomas, who was at this time local agent for the A.S.R.S. Crossman and Chappell refused to support him, and by 37 to 10 the Trades Council resolved 'that this meeting condemns Alderman Sir William Crossman and Councillor John Chappell for their failure to support the candidature of Mr. J. H. Thomas in the recent Splott ward election, and herewith expresses its lack of confidence in them'. Unlike 1904, their excuses were not accepted. Since then, the I.L.P. had taken control. As one delegate put it, 'the contest in Splott had brought into being in Cardiff a pure Labour party for the first time – a party which would not seek the support of any other organization. They had come to the parting of the ways.' So ended – it was hoped – the political subordination of labour.[46]

The Cardiff and District Labour Party was the third attempt at separate working-class political organization, and unlike the C.P.L.L. and L.R.C. did mark a decisive ideological and organizational severance between the Trades Council and Liberalism. However, it was not an electoral success. While the Trades Council never again supported Liberalism, perhaps the majority even of organized workers remained loyal to Liberalism before 1914. The key contest was in 1909 when new faced old in Splott. Chappell was up for re-election, and the Labour party put up J. H. Thomas against him. Thomas might argue that 'the day of Liberal-Labour representation was gone. . . . They would never again in Cardiff have a system of Labour representation "by the indulgence of the Liberal party".' But Chappell was elected. Indeed, before 1914 no candidate of the Cardiff Labour Party was successful. Lib-Labism was remarkably persistent. A good example is James Taylor, secretary of a branch of the A.S.R.S. but who was working as an insurance agent since being sacked by the company for his union activities. He was an official Liberal candidate, supported by his branch. No one, he claimed, could be 'more of a Labour man than himself':

> he was seeking their suffrages under the flag of Liberalism but he also claimed to be a true Labour candidate. It was true he was not fighting under the Labour banner but that was because Liberalism was broad and wide enough for him, and although he had worked for many years on behalf of Labour he refused to be shackled by the L.R.C.

He was elected with over twice as many votes as the Labour candidate.[47]

It was not that Cardiff Liberalism had become more responsive. If anything, it was more static and conservative. The progressives had been contained. Labour claims were persistently ignored in choosing the Liberal candidate in 1910 – he was 'introduced into Cardiff and recommended principally because of the soundness which he had displayed in diverse capitalist enterprises from China to Peru'. He lost, and in the aftermath of defeat there was much criticism of the Liberal executive as a self-perpetuating clique of 'older Liberals [who] spoke of politics of 25 years ago rather than the present time'. This was true, but the defeat did not lead to any reform. The 'official' explanation of defeat was merely that the register was stale, and that there was no fault within Liberalism. When a new candidate was chosen in 1911, the same old attitudes prevailed.[48]

The stagnation of Liberalism and the upsurge of unionism in 1911 did not lead to the growth of the Cardiff Labour Party which might have been expected. Ernest Bevin was urging that 'to secure their emancipation it was important that they should use their political and industrial weapons – the vote and the strike – for the political machine which had been so useful to the master class could be captured and remodelled and used to restore that which had been stolen'. But nothing happened. No

parliamentary candidate was selected by 1914 and there are signs that
the Cardiff Labour Party was faltering like the C.P.L.L. and L.R.C.
By 1914 it had to fuse with the Trades Council to survive.[49]

The Trades Council had decisively rejected Liberalism organizationally
and ideologically; the Liberal Association was static; but it does not seem
that Cardiff Liberalism had been decisively undermined before 1914.
Those who were politically active might be annoyed by the attitude of
the Liberal caucus, but this essentially political resentment did not filter
through to the electorate since the socio-economic structure was in
many ways unfavourable. Political impotence persisted for structural
reasons, even if it was now resented rather than accepted by the leaders
of the working class. Their attitudes had changed, but there was still no
real basis for a successful independent political movement. The movement away from Liberalism had come about not as the result of an industrial experience affecting a large part of the working class, but for reasons
internal to the relationship between the Liberal caucus and the Trades
Council. Consequently, only the most politically conscious were affected.
The moderate organized workers did not have enough weight to achieve
their ends within Liberalism, and ultimately their leaders moved to
independence as a result of political rather than industrial dynamics.
But the ordinary mason or trimmer had little motivation to change his
voting behaviour based upon his everyday experience at work: his
union was recognized and collective bargaining accepted. The work
experience of those who were still unrecognized was frustrated by the
fragmented structure of the working class. And the ambiguity of relationships with the élite provided a generally unfavourable context for political
militancy based upon any well-defined class consciousness. The significance of the revolt of the politically conscious against Liberalism in
1908 must therefore not be exaggerated. Lib-Labism still had a lot of life.
Liberalism might be based upon religious politics rather than class
politics, but to many in Cardiff class was not a meaningful concept in
their definition of their social position. Liberalism in Cardiff did not, as
it did in Lancashire, adopt a class basis, but before 1914 it still was
stronger than the Labour party, which did. The structural basis of moderation outlined in the first two sections of this chapter could before 1914
withstand without too much difficulty the blow to which it was subjected
by the break between the Trades Council and the Liberal Association.
It was the undermining of the structural foundations after the First
World War which was to give the political revolt of 1908 its real significance.

Attitudes to municipal expenditure, to the labour movement, and to urban culture were three inter-related traits. The old Liberals wanted retrenchment and reform, were hostile to a separate political labour movement, and wished to purify urban culture, banning traditional recreations in a negative manner. The new Liberals wanted expansion of municipal functions, a progressive alliance with the labour movement, and a positive approach to urban culture based less upon moral outrage than upon an attempt to raise standards. The Conservatives straddled the two. They sided with the old Liberals on municipal policy, whilst relationships with the labour movement were generally outside their competence. On attitudes to urban culture, however, they were closer to the new Liberal position. Many had a direct economic interest in the forms of recreation under attack from the old Liberals and were accordingly prepared to erect more of a positive defence than the new Liberals. However, both were agreed upon opposing the old Liberal definition of the new moral order which was sought for the town. This chapter will consider how problems of urban life and their solution were perceived by the different groups in society.

The pattern in Cardiff was in many ways unique for a town of its size, largely because of its links with Welsh society. To appreciate this point, the usual English pattern must first be outlined. The definition of what constituted the problem differed in Cardiff, as well as the solutions put forward for restructuring urban society.

In London, the key problem as perceived by the middle class was based upon the casual labourer and housing. The issue was not seen as one of poverty and irregular work defined in economic terms, but as pauperism and the demoralization of the working class as personal failings. The London middle class had no real conception of the casual labourer problem as such – for them the problem was that the working class had been demoralized by indiscriminate alms-giving which made work unattractive, so that the workers turned from thrift and self-help to idleness and dissipation. The work of the Charity Organization Society and the settlement movement was directed to a problem so interpreted, by 'moralizing' the casual poor, leading them back to thrift and hard work.[1] Another approach of considerable importance was what W. S. Jevons called 'the providing of good moral public amusements', which had important links with religion and with the temperance movement. Jevons stated the issue clearly:

> among the means towards a higher civilization, I unhesitatingly assert that the deliberate cultivation of public amusements is a principal one. . . . The old idea of keeping people moral by keeping their noses to the grindstone must be abandoned. As things are going, people will, and what is more, they ought to have all possible means of healthy recreation. The question is, the Free Library and the Newsroom versus the Public House.

This, of course, is back to the question of moralizing the poor. Their 'dissipated' pastimes – which were so 'clumsy and vulgar . . . as to disgust one with the very name of amusement' – must be replaced with 'rational' amusements.[2] The old amusements were based to a very large extent upon the public house, and the aim of the temperance movement had to be to provide alternative facilities.[3] Linked to this was the activity of the churches.

If the temperance movement was obliged to consider not merely drink but also recreation, neither could the churches be solely concerned with religion. Dr Yeo in his study of Reading points out that while religious services were basic, as much time and commitment were put into huge arrays of sub-organizations. In the late nineteenth century, churches of all denominations aimed for comprehensiveness in an effort to relate to and control in a total way man's life in the urban society. In this they failed, for the working class remained predominantly outside the churches. But the outcome of the aim to encompass the entire life of those who were church members was a confusion between institutional and spiritual success. Groups were started and took on their own logic, the aim being to keep them functioning rather than to consider the purpose for which they had originally been established, to increase church attendance. As Yeo puts it,

> an elision did take place between means and ends: a confusion was apparent between agency and church resolved very often by the replacement of the latter by the former. The church became an agency. Its agencies became the whole work, delivering the most elevated goods themselves, not enabling them to be delivered.

Methodism is a good example of the change which was occurring. It began as a search for a 'method' to bring men to 'perfection', resulting in an uncompromising world-rejecting ethic. But by the late nineteenth century a new ideology of 'friendly' religion had emerged. The 'perfectionist' ban on dancing, cricket, football, and novels ended, and chapel life came to rely on secular culture and entertainment – it was, indeed, 'entertainment orientated'. The search for perfection had created the chapel community, and this had become increasingly dominant as the original ethic and doctrine were eroded, to be replaced by respectability and moderation. But while the change was coming over Methodism, recreation and leisure were also changing. Churches sought to provide means of utilizing leisure hours, tried to concentrate all types of sound human activity within the church. The development of commercial activity in leisure changed the situation, and agencies formed by the churches to maintain their congregations in the central activity of worship were forced in turn to adapt to maintain their appeal. All the time the distance from the central purpose of the church became greater. Agencies formed to make churches attractive had themselves to adapt to maintain attractiveness in the face of the commercialization of leisure.[4]

Charity, religion and temperance appear as major attempts to order the new urban society, but it must also be noted that they divided that society at a number of points. As Brian Harrison has suggested, the result was a culture conflict rather than a class conflict, with groups from each social class being opposed on questions such as temperance and sabbatarianism.[5] This chapter will be concerned both with attempts to order, 'moralize' or 'civilize' the new urban society, and with the conflicts set up by such attempts.

The obvious starting point in Cardiff is, in fact, a division, between Welsh Nonconformists and the rest of society. This was in many ways a major break within the town, being associated with the difference in attitudes on temperance, sabbatarianism, recreation and other elements of the religious ethic. Unfortunately, there are no adequate figures on membership of the various churches. In 1906, the Anglicans had 19,000 attendances and the Roman Catholics 8,000. The Nonconformists claimed to have 18,281 communicants, 28,799 adherents and 28,516 Sunday scholars. It is impossible to make the two sets of figures comparable. Presumably, Cardiff stood somewhere between the situation in the south Wales mining communities and in the large English towns. Attendance in the mining areas was high – for example, 80·3 per cent in Bedwellty and Ebbw Vale, 76·8 per cent in Blaenavon. The level of religious attendance in Cardiff was certainly not so high, but was probably above the large English towns.[6]

However, Cardiff stands apart from other large towns less in the matter of church attendance than in the type of religion which dominated. An entertainment-oriented religion, moving from a world-rejecting ethic of 'perfection' to a 'friendly' religion of moderation, is far less applicable to the Nonconformity of Wales. The new movements in English theology had little effect in Wales.[7] Dr Lambert, in his study of the temperance movement in Wales, shows how Nonconformity continued to be based upon a barrier of prohibitions and customs between the withdrawn religious groups and society. To quote a Baptist circular of 1875,

> The Gospel rule for the regulation of the practical conduct of believers is clearly defined and rigid, demanding a stern nonconformity to the principles, practices and aims of the worldlings and godless. A Christian is one who has been *'called out of the world'*. He is to *live in* the world ... but he is no longer OF IT. There is to be a sacred visible separateness or distinction between him and those who are *of it*.[8]

Unlike the situation at Reading, Welsh Nonconformity tended to maintain this attitude up to the war, although Cardiff in being only partly Welsh stood at an uneasy point of tension between the two approaches to religion. On the one hand, there was a tension between the old Nonconformist world-rejecting ethic which persisted in rural Wales and the mining valleys and which was boosted by the religious revival of 1904–5, and the newer, out-going ethic designed to meet the needs of urban communities. On the other hand there was the tension between religion and those who were entirely of the world. The problem was whether the churches would maintain their world-rejecting ethic and attempt to impose abstinence and sabbatarianism upon all, or whether they would rather adopt a policy breaking down the barriers with the world to reach those who were outside their sphere. The dangers of the latter course are clear from Reading, an elision between means and ends. However, in Wales as a whole, and in Cardiff to the extent that it was Welsh, the latter course was *not* followed. Cardiff is interesting in that the division between the world-rejecting ethic of the early nineteenth century and the friendly religion of the later nineteenth century was not, as it was in England, a chronological division. Both attitudes co-existed, so that the division was not merely between the worldly and the unworldly, but also within the middle-class church and chapel goers on how to tackle problems of urban society. On the side was the Anglican, drink, Conservative grouping; on the other side, the Nonconformist, temperance, Liberal grouping. But this second grouping had a splinter party, in broad terms the same that opposed 'economy' and supported progressivism, which renounced the world-rejecting ethic and to this extent sided with the Conservatives and Anglicans (although not, of course, on attitudes to social reform). This may best be illustrated by two issues, temperance and sabbatarianism, which united in the Welsh Sunday Closing Act of 1881.

Support of temperance and sabbatarianism was defined as 'Welsh pharisaism' by its opponents.[9] This exactly brings out the nature of the dominant religious ethic in Cardiff. By pharisaism was meant the denial that Israel – or Wales – was one organic community of good and evil. The relationship with God was narrowed down from humanity to the respectable. As Lambert has said,

> for the evangelical and dissenting Welshman, the idea that God, by the Incarnation, had entered into a covenant with humanity . . . was abhorrent. It became rank blasphemy to teach that God loved the non-religious, non-teetotal Welshman. . . . In nineteenth century Wales nonconformity was the basis of the social and cultural pattern of life, and the general picture was of a strict form of puritanism which insisted on piety and the observance of certain sacraments. Sunday observance became a formal religious practice.[10]

The Welsh Sunday Closing Act of 1881 seemed to impose this upon all. The public houses were closed, so that only the churches were open. The outcome was a three-fold division in society, between those who wished to maintain a rigid sabbatarianism as a religious sacrament, those who wished to provide something positive for the working class on Sundays, in the nature of 'rational' amusements, and those who, in the absence of 'rational' amusements, did not attend chapel or church, but did provide themselves with 'vulgar' amusements.

The last of these concentrated upon opening drinking clubs and she-beens. As soon as the Sunday Closing Act was passed, clubs with nominal membership fees were formed to circumvent the law. From one before 1881, the number rose to 13 by 1883, and at one point in 1886 to 141. These were, said the temperance reformers with some justice, 'simply boozing clubs of the very worst and most demoralizing kind'. When the clubs were suppressed, shebeens sprang up, of which there were a thousand in 1889. Shebeens, unlike clubs, did not make even a pretence at being within the law. The clubs had led to an increase in drunkenness, and with the shebeens it was feared that men 'were attracted to the loathsome dens [and] in due course inoculated with the poisonous virus which is ruining their morals . . . which is more fatal to the well-being of a community than the most general drinking when subject to control and regulation'.[11]

The Sunday Closing Act split the working class of Cardiff more than was the case elsewhere in Wales. The majority of Welsh working men supported the Act, but Cardiff was an exception. The Cardiff Licensed Victuallers Association in 1881 obtained 16,800 signatures against the Act, and in 1889 a meeting of workingmen resolved that the Act was 'inconsistent with the customs and liberty of a large and respectable section of the community'. But there was certainly not a simple division of working class against middle class, for the measure did have a large working-class backing. This was given articulation in the Blue Ribbon movement which was important from 1881. This was a 'gospel temperance' organization, and its weekly meetings combined temperance propaganda, evangelical religion, and musical entertainment. Enthusiastic meetings of about 3,000 working men and women pressed for Sunday closing. While the Blue Ribbon choir of total abstainers – which was good enough to win the chief choral prize at Crystal Palace – provided a major attraction, it would be wrong to under-estimate attachment to the ideas of temperance and Sunday closing among a section of the working class. The movement does illustrate Harrison's point of a culture conflict cross-cutting a class conflict. The prominent middle-class leaders of the Blue Ribbon movement and the working-class rank and file did have a common ethic against another section of the two classes. It was this convergence which was expressed in 1882 over the labour clause issue; the Liberals supporting the men were the Blue Ribbon leaders, the men's spokesmen were members, and the organization was closely involved in celebrations of victory. At this time the aim was to bring the working class within old Liberalism, and this was being accepted. Indeed, many of the working-class leaders were staunch supporters of the Nonconformist religious ethic. This could place them in a dilemma later as they remained loyal to the old Liberal ethic but wanted separate parliamentary representation. Tensions and contradictions were set up as the irrefragable ideology collapsed.[12]

The result of the Act of 1881 was, then, to make Cardiff 'the chosen battle ground of the two opposing factions – those who would enforce and those who do evade the measure',[13] and this battle was not entirely on class lines. But neither was the conflict dual. There was also the division between the rigid adherents of sabbatarianism and those who wished to provide 'rational' amusements to fill the void. However, this latter group was probably the least important for the greater part of the period, although the situation was changing by 1914.

The temperance, Nonconformist ethic dominated the council and the School Board, which interpreted their duty as being to press for Sunday closing as a responsibility to the inhabitants, and to teach temperance as a necessary part of morality. At least up to the 1880s the Good Templars had done battle with the Licensed Victuallers Association in elections to ensure that this control was secured. But it was quite clear that the attempt to impose the ethic had led in practice to disorder and increased drunkenness. This went absolutely counter to the attempt to make general the observance of the sabbath as a sacrament. The outcome was a struggle on the council (and within Cardiff) between the rigid sabbatarians and a group of moderates urging rational amusements. The Conservatives and Anglicans were opposed to the sabbatarians – and so were the progressive Liberals who in other respects were hostile to the Conservatives. The sabbatarians were the old Liberals with their religious politics, 'economy', and refusal to reconcile the Labour movement – and up to 1914 they generally won.[14]

Supporters of the 1881 Act treated the sabbath as a sacrament, so to provide some facilities for recreation on Sunday was no less a sin than to consume beer on the Sabbath. It was ideologically impossible to admit that closing of licensed premises was not a 'great boon . . . carrying richer blessings every week of its existence', for both alcohol and a breach of the sabbath were sins. But to James and Herbert Thompson, the 'Puritanical Sabbatarian organizations' had made Sunday a day of laziness and drunkenness. Their policy was 'instead of closing everything and turning our cities into prisons, let us *open* everything and breathe freely'. Here was a very important ethical division. To the world-rejecting Non-conformists, recreation appeared sinful. To the Thompsons it was 'religious work of the highest and best kind to teach and to coax our working population to place themselves, or allow themselves to be brought within reach of anything that tends to elevate men's thoughts or touch their hearts'. The Thompsons and the Cardiff Sunday Society tried to implement this philosophy by opening art galleries in 1888 and 1894 respectively. But it was only very slowly that the hold of the Welsh Nonconformist ethic on the council slackened. The new Liberals might condemn 'puritanical intolerance and bigotry', but the old Liberals such as Richard Cory who 'rejoiced to be a Puritan' still held sway. The cultural conflict ran alongside the conflict between different approaches to municipal policy and labour politics, and there was a first sign of a breach in 'puritanism' around 1900, paralleling the change in municipal policy. But the break was slight and called forth a swift reaction. Only in 1913 were the supporters on the council of 'the old Mosaic law' defeated by the Conservatives/Anglicans and progressives, when the council decided to provide refreshments and concerts in the parks on Sundays. Although there was Nonconformist outrage against this 'selfish indulgence', for the first time the Welsh Nonconformist ethic had lost its dominance. It might be asserted that 'it was for the corporation to set a high and noble standard of living and action instead of taking the lead in setting this torrent of Sunday desecration'. To the old Liberals it was a denial of 'the commandments of God Almighty'. But to the new Liberals and the Conservatives 'this was purely a matter of expediency and there was not a single principle involved. . . . Were they going to govern Cardiff by antiquated and narrow dogmatic ideas, or was that great community to be governed with regard to expediency and balance of convenience.'[15]

While the comparative roles of 'expediency' and the world-rejecting Welsh Nonconformist ethic were being reversed by 1914, the hold of strict puritanism, of 'Welsh pharisaism' upon the government of Cardiff had been slow to slacken. When signs of weakening control *did* become apparent, the puritan ethic was institutionalized in bodies such as the Free Church Council of 1896, the Welsh Protestant League of 1898, the Citizens League of 1903 and the Citizens Union of 1908. These organizations institutionalized the ethic of Welsh Nonconformity and attempted to impose it upon the urban society. Individual chapels had of course institutionalized the ethic before, but there were now central agencies to act upon Cardiff as a unit. Their concern was with political power and the desire to enforce a morality upon the town, 'to fight sin and the devil', not, it was said, by praying while the devil made the laws, but by acting as pressure groups. A world-rejecting ethic of the exclusive religious élite was to be imposed upon the whole urban society, which was to be purified and elevated. The intention was to take active political steps to control Cardiff's ethical and moral framework, to bring about a reformation of urban society. It would be completely mistaken to play down such issues. In 1913, for example, the Citizens Union's defence of sabbatarianism was a far more important election issue than housing, and very important tensions were set up, between two religious ethics, between the chapel-going and non-attending working class, and between two segments of the middle class. The aim of these organizations was not merely to impose sabbath observation, which was simply the most obvious way in which conflicts were set up. There was a general 'purity crusade'. The nature of this movement to 'purify' the town connects with the nature of charity, with the slowness of response to housing problems, and with the general perception of the social problems of the city.[16]

What dominated middle-class responses to the city were prostitution and temperance, which required a 'purification' of the city; housing and the problem of the casual poor were neglected. If housing was scarcely mentioned before 1910, from the activities of the charities it would be difficult to know that there was a casual labourer in Cardiff at all. In London, charity was concerned above all with the problem of the casual labourer. Indiscriminate charity had, it was said, demoralized the labourer, and social control had to be re-established by organizing charity and making it a reward for correct social behaviour. Hence the Charity Organization Society. The settlement movement worked parallel to this. It would provide an 'urban squirearchy' to establish bonds between rich and poor. Both of these features *were* found in Cardiff. The Cardiff C.O.S. was formed in 1886, the university settlement at Splott in 1901. But such organizations were not central to the middle-class perception of the problems of urban society in Cardiff as they were in London – and of course there was no reason why they should be, for the London middle class was very different from that of Cardiff, even if (as is not necessarily true) the problems of the casual poor were similar. The dominant response to urban society was not to restructure social relationships, to re-establish social control through the C.O.S. and settlements. It was to save society and purify it. While it is possible to find examples of a concern for the gap between classes, such a concern was not to be central for the churches and the middle class in Cardiff. Rather it was to deal with what the Rev. J. Waite called vice in its two worst forms, drink and prostitution.[17]

Concern about prostitution was apparent from the late 1850s, with the notorious brothel prosecutions of the late 1850s and early 1860s when the question agitated the town. In 1860 there were calculated to be 229 brothels, and prosecutions continued at a high level up to the early 1880s. The issue then died down somewhat, until it revived with full force after 1907. Concern about drink was more constant, but with the problem of clubs and shebeens dominating the 1880s and 1890s. The two concerns were essentially part of the same problem, of vice leading to the 'fall' of urban man.

The response to this problem had both a preventive and a curative aspect, and there was to be a link with the provision of 'rational' and 'moral' entertainment. Women who had 'fallen' had to be saved, and women arriving in the town had to be supported to prevent them from falling. Meanwhile, men had to be kept out of bad company. This was a large part of the motive behind providing facilities for recreation, for if 'sound recreation' was not provided, men might go to public houses, dancing saloons, and music halls, where they might be led astray. The intention of the Y.M.C.A., a branch of which was formed in Cardiff in 1852, 'was to supply a place of resort for young men after business hours, and surround them with everything likely to please and interest them and keep them from the attraction of the public house and the influence of bad companions'. The general aim was 'to draw young men away from associations of a hurtful and demoralizing nature', and it was found in a variety of other bodies whose dominant motive was to keep the young in particular, and the working class in general, away from the 'contaminating' influences of urban society.[18]

In this aim there was a paradox. The chapels generally accepted that Cardiff should be purified; their dominating ethic was world-rejecting and this caused unease about the provision of entertainments. A conference of the local Welsh Ministers Union in 1895 stressed the mission of the churches in relation to the immorality of the town. The young, it was said, came to Cardiff 'sober and pure' but were then 'lost'. However, it was felt that churches ought not to provide amusements, for their mission was spiritual. This sort of attitude led to criticisms:

Our temperance and moral reformers have been busying themselves for years in destroying the means for amusement formerly favoured by the people . . . but what have they done towards replacing the banned pleasures by something more elevated and refined? They have shown absolutely no constructive policy whatever. . . . Cardiff is singularly deficient in places of innocent recreative resort, though it is full of moral reformers.

Some attempt was made, it is true, to provide alternative amusements within the chapels and by the Pleasant Sunday Afternoon movement and the temperance organizations. But it was fundamentally impossible to cater for a *mass* demand, particularly with the underlying doubt about whether it was any part of the functions of the chapels. Insofar as chapels did provide entertainment, it was usually for members only and not the whole populace of the area. They catered for those who were already saved and respectable, and did not aim for mass appeal. Within each chapel, willingness to attend week-night classes declined, so an attempt was made at least to keep the social life of the members in the chapel, if they were not prepared to give up so much leisure for purely religious meetings. But the provision was for members and adherents rather than the mass outside. There is little sign, as there was at Reading, of an aim to include all the community, and the more popular recreations – especially sport – seem to have been shunned.

There were few organizations of the nature of the Cardiff Social Society which had a brief existence in 1876. As its founder pointed out, 'there was almost nothing between the religious services at the churches and chapels, and the singing saloons of the lower parts of the town'. The intention was to fill the gap by 'a series of pleasing and instructive entertainments' which would keep the workers out of public houses. But this line was not congenial to many moral reformers, for there was a fundamental opposition to mass entertainment arising out of 'Welsh pharisaism'. As a commentator in the 1880s saw, amusements attracted all, good and bad – pleasure was not moral but appealed generally. However, all institutions were condemned because they were used by the questionable as well as by the moral. The commentator urged that the moral élite should recognize that amusement was attractive to both good and bad and should openly patronize the institutions of popular entertainment. But such a policy was completely alien to 'Welsh pharisaism' which refused to accept good and bad as part of one nation. This belief went counter to the excluding ethic, and mass entertainment was seen to be inherently dangerous, the very fact that it did attract good and bad being its main drawback. The 'good' had to be segregated and provided for within the chapels, not to be tainted by the 'bad'.

Of course, the gap between the chapels and the singing saloons was eventually filled, by the municipal parks after 1881 and by the development of commercial entertainment outside the sphere of the public house during the 1880s–90s. To the Welsh pharisees this was only slightly less welcome than 'singing saloons' – the theatre and football were in fact scarcely distinguishable from sin and drink, a point of view which was strongly asserted (perhaps as a last recrudescence) in the religious revival of 1904–5. Unlike the entertainment-oriented religion of England, the chapels in Wales remained suspicious of, if not downright hostile towards, new facilities for recreation.[19]

The 'puritan' approach to urban society was of greater importance than bodies such as the C.O.S. and university settlement. Those who supported the C.O.S. and settlement were drawn from amongst those who proposed a 'rational' Sunday. The Thompson family were the leading advocates of the alleviation of sabbatarianism, and also of the C.O.S., the university settlement, the Cardiff Recreative Evening Classes. These organizations were also concerned to elevate the working class, but their target was chiefly deprivation; they wished to realize potentiality, rather than 'save' the working class from besetting sin. If the Thompsons exemplify the one attitude, the Corys exemplify the attitude of those who 'rejoiced to be a Puritan', supporting the Y.M.C.A., the Blue Ribbon movement, the Cardiff Temperance and Prohibition Association. There were two largely separate groups of men, agencies, and attitudes, a difference between encouraging the full use of potentiality, and purifying the working class and urban society. The latter attitude dominated up to 1914. Drink, prostitution, and sin were the key to the middle-class response to urbanism. This philosophy was given expression by the Rev. Rhys Jenkins. He castigated those who concentrated on facilities for physical cleanliness, on drains, water and paving, for 'the real danger is rather in the ever-increasing facilities for drinking and in the enormous growth of vice and intemperance consequent thereupon. Let us cleanse our town of its too many allurements to sin and vice.' This is very different from the Nonconformist response in Birmingham, that men could not be temperate unless they were given decent conditions in which to live.

It is necessary to consider the problems of the city – the whole process of creating a new urban social order – not only objectively, but also as it appears through the distorting medium of the dominant ideology of each town. The problems differ, and so does the ideology, which dictated the manner in which the problem was perceived, and the nature of the solutions proposed. In Birmingham, the Nonconformist conscience and temperance were main bastions of an expansive municipal policy; in Leeds, on the contrary, they were the basis for 'economy'. In Cardiff, the problem and its solutions as seen by the dominant ideology was never better put than by Rhys Jenkins – to 'cleanse our town of its too many allurements to sin and vice'.[20]

12 Epilogue

The society and economy described in the previous pages were destroyed by the First World War. The coal export trade received a blow from which it never recovered. It is true that even before 1914 costs in the south Wales coal industry were rising and productivity declining;[1] that production was increasing abroad which would reduce the need for imports; and that alternative fuels would be used in place of coal, in particular oil for navigation. But as G. C. Allen has put it, 'the war of 1914–18 crowded into a few years the changes of decades and strengthened influences which might otherwise have long lain dormant'.[2]

The demand for coal stagnated. Before 1914, world coal consumption had been rising at 4 per cent per annum, but in 1924–6 consumption was below the pre-war level, and by 1929 it was only up by 9 per cent. Coal was being used more economically as the result of improvements in boiler and furnace techniques; alternatives were being developed such as lignite in Germany and hydro-electric power in Italy; the internal combustion engine was revolutionizing internal transport with serious consequences for the railways; and perhaps most importantly for south Wales oil was replacing coal in steam-ships, and motor ships replacing steam-ships. At the same time, world capacity in the coal industry increased. During the war, exports had been restricted and markets closed. Resulting shortages and high prices had led to the replacement of imports by home production. The outcome was a large surplus of capacity in the world's coal industry after the war.

In such a situation, exports of coal might be expected to suffer. But the British coal export trade suffered more than proportionately, for the British *share* of total coal exports fell. In 1913, Britain was responsible for 55 per cent of world coal exports. By 1929 the figure was 47 per cent, by 1937, 40 per cent. In part, this was because of restrictions on imports which discriminated against British coal, but it was also because of the low productivity and high costs of the British industry.[3]

The coal trade of the Bute docks was severely affected. In 1914, coal shipments had been 10·3 million tons. The post-war peak was 8·8m. tons in 1923, and in the 1930s coal exports were running at just under 5m. tons or half the pre-war level. By the mid-1950s Barry and Cardiff were together shipping only half a million tons of coal where 40 years earlier they had handled over 20m. tons. Imports held up much better, running at 1·1m. to 1·7m. tons in the 1930s compared with 1.9m. tons in 1914. Imports formed a rising proportion of total trade, but did not offset the fall in coal exports. The decline in coal exports did not, by creating a surplus capacity at the docks, permit a restructuring of trade towards imports and general exports. Total trade of the docks remained export dominated, and exports were still dominated by coal. In this, the inter-war period was basically similar to the pre-1914 period. The hopes which had been expressed that a surplus capacity at the docks would lead to a more diversified trade had not been fulfilled. Non-coal trade merely retained its pre-war level better than coal with little sign of any positive sectoral readjustment.[4]

With the decline in the coal industry, there was a decline also in local shipping and in the ship repair industry. The shipowners never recovered from the experience of the post-war boom and slump. Ships were bought during 1919–20 at inflated prices, and when the boom broke in 1921 they were worth only a fraction of their book value. It was calculated that the Cardiff fleet was worth £41½m. at the average selling price of 1920 but only £8¼m. at the average selling price of 1921. Some companies were forced into liquidation by their inability to pay for ships bought during the boom, often through bank loans. Those companies which survived were often unable to pay a dividend, being dominated by the necessity to reduce the book value of their fleets to a figure nearer the market value. It was, indeed, difficult even to keep the ships operating, and in 1932 60 per cent of the Cardiff tonnage was laid up. The industry declined until at present (1976) only one Cardiff shipping company survives. And with owners unable to afford large repair bills, coal providing a less attractive outward cargo, and a larger proportion of ships visiting Cardiff being foreign-owned, the local ship repair industry suffered. By 1939 it was working at half capacity. The basis of the pre-1914 economy had been thoroughly undermined.[5]

As it declined, so the coal trade moved further towards combination, the virtual exclusion of middlemen, and the adoption of pricing and marketing schemes. By 1936 the Powell Duffryn Associated Collieries controlled 11m. tons of a total output of 29m. tons. South Wales had the most highly concentrated industrial structure of any of the coalfields. Production and marketing became ever more closely linked, so that not only the speculative but also the legitimate middlemen were squeezed out. With the introduction of minimum prices in 1928 and output restrictions in 1929 the whole mode of operation of the Cardiff coal market was fundamentally changed.[6]

The outcome was a transformation of the social structure. The mercantile élite ceased to exist, at the very latest when coal was nationalized in 1947. The old distinction between the dockmen and the townsmen disappeared, a fact which was given expression by the fusion of the Chamber of Trade and the Chamber of Commerce. The Exchange was until recently derelict, but has now found a new role, as a concert hall. Around it in Mountstuart Square the offices of the coal companies and shipowners are under-used if not positively decaying. Most of the ship repair yards are closed; not one coal tip remains; the dock of 1839 has been filled in to become the site of a museum; not one tipper or trimmer is at work; the Taff Vale Railway has become a single-track line which no longer reaches the docks. All in all, coal in particular and transport in general has ceased to be the key to the local economy and society.

Other changes took place alongside the economic and social transformation following upon the collapse of the coal trade. The Bute estate completely withdrew from the city: the docks were transferred to the Great Western Railway in 1922 as part of the grouping scheme; the building estate was sold; and finally in 1948 the castle and park were given to the corporation. In housing, there was large-scale building by the corporation, a decline in rented accommodation, and a large rise in owner-occupation. Politics were in flux. In 1919 Labour won four seats, the first gains by the party. Liberals and Conservatives drew together as anti-socialists, and the Ratepayers Association emerged as a political force. All in all, society as it existed before 1914 has virtually disappeared.

After the First World War a process of adaptation had to take place which was as far-reaching as the transformation a century earlier. Once again, the basis of the economy had to be altered. During the inter-war period, the economy as it existed at 1914 was in decline whilst still being dominant; since 1945 it has been peripheral. The problems of adjustment were great, and have not been solved in a completely satisfactory manner. The fact that coal made Cardiff the biggest town in Wales with a regional function has provided a continuing administrative role when the originating factor has disappeared. Cardiff's great failure has been its inability to develop a manufacturing sector. During the period when this book was being researched and written, there was indeed a crisis in the local economy. The steel works were threatened with closure which would remove the only major industrial employer in the city. The council mounted a campaign to prevent this, but the outcome is still uncertain. Also, an attempt was made to bring in alternative industry: the Rover car company established a components plant; overtures were made to British Leyland; and in 1975 a plan was drawn up to turn the coastal land to the east of the city into an industrial area. It remains to be seen if such an ambition will be realized now when it was not in the years before 1914.

The process of transformation up to 1870 and the process of transformation after 1914 still await their historian. This study has concentrated on the period in the middle when Cardiff was without any doubt the 'coal metropolis of the world'. It was a period of great assurance and confidence. 'It is no great arrogance on the part of this great town', it was said in 1905, 'to be ambitious, to exert itself to serve the interests of the Welsh people to such an extent as to deserve the title of the Metropolis of Wales.'[7] There was, in the eyes of its 'boosters',

> an impression of modernity and progressiveness, of spacious streets and buildings, of docks and ships, and of great commercial activity which well merit the epithet 'the Chicago of Wales' . . . It is both ancient and modern; Celtic and Cosmopolitan; progressive; wealthy; enterprising, and a centre of learning. There is a Metropolitan ring about its large ideas and 'go' which makes all other Welsh towns seem parochial in comparison.[8]

Events showed that this was the pride which comes before a fall.

Abbreviations

C.C.L.	Cardiff Central Library
C.J.C.	*Cardiff Journal of Commerce*
D.N.B.	*Dictionary of National Biography*
E.H.R.	*Economic History Review*
G.R.O.	Glamorgan Record Office
H.L.R.O.	House of Lords Record Office
J.R.S.S.	*Journal of the Royal Statistical Society*
N.L.W.	National Library of Wales
N.L.W.J.	*National Library of Wales Journal*
P.R.O.	Public Record Office
S.W.D.N.	*South Wales Daily News*

Notes

Note places of publication are given only for works published outside the U.K.

Chapter 1

1. M. I. Williams, 'Cardiff—its people and its trade 1660–1720', *Morgannwg*, VII (1963); 'Cardiff and its history: the town's claim to the title metropolis', *Western Mail*, 11 May 1905; *Cardiff Journal of Commerce*, 15 September 1908.
2. W. Smyth, *Nautical Observations on the Port and Maritime Vicinity of Cardiff* (1840); Williams, *op. cit.*; T. M. Hodges, 'The peopling of the hinterland and port of Cardiff 1801–1914', *E.H.R.*, XVII (1947), 62–72; W. E. Minchinton, 'Bristol – metropolis of the west in the eighteenth century', *Trans. Roy. Hist. Soc.*, 5th ser., IV (1954).
3. Hodges, *op. cit.*; Smyth, *op. cit.*; C. H. Hadfield, *The Canals of South Wales and the Border* (1960), ch. 6; A. H. John, *The Industrial Development of South Wales 1750–1850* (1950).
4. Smyth, *op. cit.*; T. M. Hodges, 'The history of the port of Cardiff in relation to its hinterland with special reference to the years 1830–1914' (M.Sc. (Econ.) thesis, University of London, 1946).
5. J. H. Morris and L. J. Williams, *The South Wales Coal Industry 1841–75* (1958), 7, 48; A. Birch, *The Economic History of the British Iron and Steel Industry 1784–1879* (1967), 128; J. P. Addis, 'The heavy iron and steel industry in south Wales 1870–1950' (Ph.D. thesis, University of Wales, 1957).
6. Morris and Williams, *op. cit.*, 76; Morris and Williams, 'R. J. Nevill and the early Welsh coal trade', *N.L.W.J.*, x (1957–8); R. Craig, 'R. Nevill and the early Welsh coal trade – a comment', *N.L.W.J.*, x (1957–8).
7. Hodges, *op. cit.*, thesis and article; Morris and Williams, *South Wales Coal Industry*, 104–8.
8. Hodges, *op. cit.*, thesis and article; E. D. Lewis, *The Rhondda Valleys* (1959); Census for 1911.
9. Hodges, thesis and article; B. Thomas, 'The migration of labour into the Glamorganshire coalfield 1861–1911', *Economica*, x (1930), 275–94.
10. D. A. Thomas, 'The growth and direction of our foreign trade in coal during the last half-century', *J.R.S.S.*, LXVI (1903), 498.
11. *Ibid.*, 469; Morris and Williams, *South Wales Coal Industry*, 33–41.
12. H. Carter, *The Study of Urban Geography* (1972), 211–21.
13. B. Thomas, *op. cit.*; B. R. Mitchell and P. Deane, *Abstract of British Historical Statistics* (1962), 240–7.

14. Williams, *op. cit.*; I. Humphreys, 'Cardiff politics, 1850–74', in S. Williams (ed.), *Glamorgan Historian Volume 8*; T. W. Rammell, *Report to the General Board of Health on . . . the Town of Cardiff* (1850).

Chapter 2

1. C. H. Hadfield, *The Canals of South Wales and the Border* (1960), 90–117, deals with the Glamorganshire Canal.
2. *Ibid.*, 107, and W. H. Smyth, *Nautical Observations on the Port and Maritime Vicinity of Cardiff* (1840), 10–11.
3. C.C.L. Bute XI 4.
4. Hadfield, *op. cit.*, 99 *et seq.*
5. *Ibid.*, 112.
6. Earl of Bessborough (ed.), *Lady Charlotte Guest. Extracts from her Journal 1833–52* (1950), *passim*; see comments of Bute in N.L.W. Bute Box 70, letterbook 7, Agents in Wales 1840–4; G.R.O. D/DG W. Crawshay to J. J. Guest, 6 March 1836, 1836 (1) f. 590.
7. N.L.W. Bute Box 70, letterbook 2 (Coutts and Co., Farrar and Co., Roy and Co., 1827–44), Bute to Roy, 10 February 1837; C.C.L. Bute V 5, 6, 8, 10, 15, 17, 19, 25; H.L.R.O., Minutes of Evidence, H.C., Bute Docks, 1866, Q35.
8. H.L.R.O. Minutes of evidence, H.C., 1866, Bute Docks, Q.45,296 *et seq.*, 2315–2531; C.C.L. Bute XII 28; J. Davies, 'The Rhymney Railway and the Bute estate', *Gelligaer,* VIII (1971), 7–10.
9. C.C.L. Bute XI 4.
10. N.L.W. Bute Box 70, letterbook Roy 1840–3, 13 February 1840.
11. N.L.W. Bute Box 70, letterbook 2, Bute to Roy, 14 February 1832.
12. N.L.W. Bute Box 70, letterbook 7, Bute to Smyth, 25 and 31 July, 20 August 1840, 9 January 1841; J. H. Morris and L. J. Williams, *The South Wales Coal Industry 1841–1875* (1958), 113–15.
13. Smyth, *op. cit.*, 21, and H.L.R.O., Minutes of evidence, H.C., 1866, Bute Docks, Q.103.
14. C.C.L. Bute XI 4, XII 20; N.L.W. Bute Box 70, letterbook Roy 1840–3, Roy to Bute 13 February 1840.
15. C.C.L. Bute V 9, XI 4; N.L.W. Bute Box 70, letterbook 7, 23 April 1840, 11 March 1841; G.R.O. D/DG W. Crawshay to J. J. Guest, 6 March 1836, 1836 (1) f. 590; T. M. Hodges, 'The history of the port of Cardiff in relation to its hinterland' (M.Sc.(Econ.) thesis, University of London, 1946); J. Davies, 'Glamorgan and the Bute estate, 1776–1947', (Ph.D. thesis, University of Wales, 1969), chapter VII (1).
16. C.C.L. MS. 329.51, Crawshay to Bute, 15 September 1847, quoted by Davies, thesis.
17. C.C.L. Bute XII 42; N.L.W Bute Box 70, letterbook 6, Bute to Richards, 29 June 1839.
18. Morris and Williams, *op. cit.*, 20–6; R. Craig, 'R. Nevill and the early Welsh coal trade – a comment', *N.L.W.J.* X (1957–8), 59–64.
19. C.C.L. Bute XI 4, XII 42.
20. *Welsh Coal and Shipping Handbook for 1919.*

21. C.C.L. Bute V 9, XI 4. The proposals for alterations in the canal are in Hadfield, *op. cit.*, 100–1.
22. J. E. Vincent, *John Nixon, Pioneer of the Steam Coal Trade in South Wales. A Memoir* (1900), 27.
23. A. W. Kirkaldy, *British Shipping. Its History, Organisation and Importance* (1914), 554–5.
24. *S.W.D.N.*, 29 September 1906.
25. C.C.L. Bute XI 29.
26. H.L.R.O. Minutes of evidence, H.L., 1882, Bute Docks, speech of counsel for Bute; H.C., 1882, Bute Docks, Q.22, 219.
27. H.L.R.O. Minutes of evidence, H.C., 1866, Bute Docks, Q.104 and 1882, Bute Docks, Q.20–1.
28. H.L.R.O. Minutes of evidence, H.L., 1913, Cardiff Railway, statement showing the capital expenditure, ordinary expenditure and profits of the Bute Docks, and the amounts paid for rates and wages (exclusive of new railways).
29. *Ibid.*, Q.106, 120 and statement on result of expenditure on new dock (excluding railway capital).
30. *Ibid.*, statement showing the capital expenditure...; C.C.L. Bute XII 32.
31. H.L.R.O. Minutes of evidence, H.L., 1913, Cardiff Railway, Q.107.
32. *Ibid.*, Q.8 *et seq.*, dividend of B.D.C. and C.R.C., statement on C.R.C.; Annual Reports of C.R.C.; Davies, thesis, VII(II).
33. C.C.L. Bute XI 20.
34. C.C.L. Bute IV 4; H.L.R.O. Minutes of evidence, H.L., 1913, Cardiff Railway, Q. 441–456, Table of shipping at Bute docks, Tables showing proportion of tons net register to tons shipped on steamers.
35. H.L.R.O. Minutes of evidence, H.C., 1882, Bute Docks, Q.224, 5096.
36. C.C.L. Bute IV 1, 4; H.L.R.O. Minutes of evidence, H.L., 1882, Bute Docks, speech by counsel for Bute; H.C., 1882, Bute Docks, Q. 3427–518; H.L., 1894, Bute Docks Q.3335–747; H.L., 1909, T.V.R. (Cardiff Railway) Vesting, evidence of A. Beasley and speech of counsel for promoters; H.L., 1913, Cardiff Railway, Cost incurred by dock owners in shipping coal.
37. C.C.L. Bute XII 31.
38. C.C.L. Bute XI 20; the quotation is cited by Davies from British Transport Historical Records, B.D.C. 1(2), Report of G. A. Jamieson, 31 October 1894.
39. Davies, thesis, 531.
40. H.L.R.O. Minutes of evidence, H.C., 1882, Bute Docks, Q.5267.
41. H.L.R.O. Minutes of evidence, H.L., 1909, T.V.R. (Cardiff Railway) Vesting, evidence of Lord Edmund Talbot; Davies, thesis, VII(II).
42. Cited by Davies from G.R.O., papers of E. P. Richards (O. T. Bruce to Richards, 22 January 1853).
43. H.L.R.O. Minutes of evidence, H.C., 1882, Bute Docks, Q.19.
44. C.C.L. Bute XI 17.
45. Dock bills were rejected in 1864 and 1865; in 1866 powers were granted to build the Roath Basin, but not the dock.
46. *D.N.B.* and J. Mordaunt Crook, 'Patron extraordinary: John, third marquis

of Bute 1847–1900', in *Victorian South Wales – Architecture, Industry and Society,* seventh conference report of the Victorian Society (1971), 3–22.

47. See *D.N.B.*
48. *S.W.D.N.,* 16 November 1876.
49. Speech by R. Cory in J. C. Parkinson (ed.), *Newport and Cardiff as Shipping Ports* (1878), 31.
50. *S.W.D.N.,* 18 November 1880; C.C.L. Bute IX 29; Minutes of Cardiff Town Council, 29 November 1880, 10 October 1881.
51. Council Minutes, *loc. cit.*
52. H.L.R.O. Minutes of evidence, H.L., 1882, Bute Docks, speech by counsel for Bute, Q.290, 924–6, and petition of colliery proprietors and freighters. Eventually, the 1*d.* was not charged –instead the railway companies provided the gratuitous services. Neither did the Bute estate proceed with the monopoly of labour at the docks.
53. H.L.R.O. Minutes of evidence, H.L., 1882, Bute Docks, Q.1044–5, 1065.
54. H.L.R.O. Minutes of evidence, H.L., 1883, Barry Docks and Railway Q.6031–2, 6055–7; H.C., 1883, Barry Docks and Railway, Q.5375 *et seq.,* H.C., 1884, Barry Docks and Railway, Q.5958–67, 6079, 6084.
55. R. J. Rimmell, *History of the Barry Railway Company 1884–1921* (1923), 77–8, 80–1; H.L.R.O. Minutes of evidence, H.L., 1882, Bute Docks, Q.1034, 1036–40; H.C., 1883, Barry Docks and Railway, p. 552 of printed volume.
56. C.C.L. Bute V 49, IV 13.
57. C.C.L. Bute V 49, XII 32.
58. C.C.L. Bute IV 28, V 33, 36, 42, IX 30, 32, 33, XI 5; H.L.R.O. Minutes of evidence, H.L., 1884, Barry Docks and Railway, pp. 136–42 of printed volume. For the T.V.R. side see *Taff Vale Railway 104th Half Yearly Meeting. The Proposed Amalgamation with the Bute Docks: Statement by J. Inskip, 7 February 1888; Taff Vale Railway and Bute Docks: Proposed Amalgamation Circular, James Inskip, 5 January 1888; Circular of Directors to the Shareholders of the T.V.R., 10 February 1888; Bute-Taff Amalgamation: Letter by H. J. Paine and others* (1888).
59. H.L.R.O. Minutes of evidence, H.C., and H.L., 1897, Bute Docks, speech by counsel for B.D.C.
60. H.L.R.O. Minutes of evidence, H.L., 1909, T.V.R. (Cardiff Railway) Vesting, evidence of A. Beasley and speech by counsel for promoters. For examples of pressure, see *S.W.D.N.,* 1 February, 3 and 4 December 1912; G.R.O. D/D Com/C Cardiff Chamber of Commerce, General Minute Book 1913–17, 31 March, 29 April and 27 May 1914.
61. Morris and Williams, *op. cit.* 94, 100.
62. *S.W.D.N.,* 18 February 1880.

Chapter 3
1. *C.J.C.,* 18 March 1907.
2. *C.J.C.,* 16 September 1908.
3. Centre Nationale de la Recherche Scientifique, *L'Industrialisation en Europe au XIX Siècle* (1972), 522.

4. S. W. Allen, 'Engineering and shipbuilding', in J. Ballinger (ed.) *Cardiff. An Illustrated Handbook* (1896), 114.

5. J. Morgan, *Address to the Cardiff Chamber of Commerce on the Present Aspect of Commercial Affairs* (1869).

6. A. H. John, *The Industrial Development of South Wales 1750–1850* (1950), 98.

7. *Ibid.*

8. *Ibid.*, 165.

9. John in Centre Nationale de la Recherche Scientifique, *op. cit.*, 524.

10. See, for example, C. Wilkins, *The History of the Iron, Steel, Tinplate and Other Trades of Wales* (1903), 298–301. The ambition became a commonplace in local publications.

11. E. L. Chappell, *History of the Port of Cardiff* (1939), 120.

12. S. G. Sturmey, *British Shipping and World Competition* (1962), 34–5, 73–4, 78; B. R. Mitchell and P. Deane, *Abstract of British Historical Statistics* (1962), 219.

13. D. A. Thomas, 'The growth and direction of our foreign trade in coal during the last half century', *J.R.S.S.,* xvi (1903) 454–5.

14. *C.J.C.,* 15 September 1908; H.L.R.O. Minutes of evidence, H.C., 1866 Bute Docks, Q.973, 1047; H.L., 1883, Barry Dock and Railway, Q.645, 1206–1212, 2729; H.C., 1883, Barry Dock and Railway, Q.2099–2100, 5023; H.L., 1894, Bute Docks, Q.1041.

15. *C.J.C.,* 11 May 1904 and 31 March 1905; Thomas, *op. cit.,* 456.

16. 'To a large extent the one and a half millions of people in south Wales and Monmouthshire depend upon imported provisions, and yet the quantity brought by sea via Cardiff is comparatively small. Most of the food supplies are brought from London, Liverpool, Bristol, Glasgow and Belfast.' Ballinger, *op. cit.,* 217.

17. H.L.R.O. Minutes of evidence, H.L., 1874, Bute Docks, Q.150; H.C., 1883, Barry Dock and Railway, Q.4875, 4879, 4934; H.L., 1883, Barry Dock and Railway, evidence of J. Watson, S. Aitken and W. Riley.

18. H.L.R.O. Minutes of evidence, H.L. 1883, Barry Dock and Railway, Q.2726.

19. H.L.R.O. Minutes of evidence, H.C., 1883, Barry Dock and Railway, evidence of J. Guthrie; H.L., 1883, Barry Dock and Railway, Q.646.

20. *S.W.D.N.,* 21 February 1872; J. Davies, 'Glamorgan and the Bute estate' (Ph.D. thesis, University of Wales, 1969), 643 *et seq.*

21. Davies, *op. cit.,* chapter VII (II); statement by J. Boyle, Cardiff Chamber of Commerce, Annual Report, 1877.

22. H.L.R.O. Minutes of evidence, H.C., 1883, Barry Dock and Railway, Q.4881.

23. G.R.O. D/D Com/C Chamber of Commerce General Minutes 1884–92, 30 June 1891.

24. These schemes are mentioned in chapter 8.

25. *S.W.D.N.,* 21 February 1894, 8 January 1908; Chamber of Commerce Annual Report, 1897.

26. H.L.R.O. Minutes of evidence, H.L., 1909, Taff Vale Railway (Cardiff Railway), questions unnumbered.

27. The general industries are discussed in Ballinger, *op. cit.,* and the *Cardiff Tide Tables and Almanac* from 1882.

28. J. P. Addis, 'The heavy iron and steel industry in south Wales, 1870–1950' (Ph.D. thesis, University of Wales, 1957); M. Elsas (ed.) *Iron in the Making. Dowlais Iron Co. Letters 1782–1860* (1960), 90, 93, 98, 103; G.R.O. D/DG Section C Box 3, Orconera Iron Ore Co., contract 1873, Section E Box 2, Notes on D.I.C., 19 March 1890, Cardiff Agency Letters 1875–6, S.S. Howard to Houlson, 7 June 1877.

29. Addis, *op. cit.*; *Engineer,* XLVI (1878), 104; G.R.O. D/DG Cardiff Works Letters 1902–15; D. McCloskey, *Economic Maturity and Entrepreneurial Decline. British Iron and Steel 1870–1913* (1973).

30. Addis, *op. cit. S.W.D.N.,* 15 March 1872, 9 June 1873, 8 October 1883, 19 September 1888; *C.J.C.* 18 March 1907; Annual Statement of the Navigation and Shipping of U.K., in Accounts and Papers annually.

31. Allen, *loc. cit.*; *Cardiff Tide Tables and Almanac; S.W.D.N.,* 23 December 1879, 2 March 1881, 30 September 1881, 22 December 1881, 20 February 1882, 7 June 1882, 26 March 1883, 26 November 1883, 27 February 1884, 5 May 1905, 9 March 1906, 28 September 1910; *C.J.C.* 15 and 28 April 1905, 15 July 1907, 24 January 1910.

32. *Royal Visit to Cardiff 1912. Programme of Events and Souvenir.*

33. N.L.W. Jevons IV 40; M. J. Daunton, 'Suburban development in Cardiff: Grangetown and the Windsor estate, 1857–75', *Morgannwg,* XVI (1972), 58; *Engineer* XLIX (1880), 186, XXXI (1881), 568, LV, (1883), 370, XXXVII (1874), 426.

34. *C.J.C.,* 16 September 1908; W. Turner, *The Port of Cardiff* (1882), 70.

35. A. Pred, *The Spatial Dynamics of U.S. Urban-Industrial Growth, 1800–1914* (1966); W. R. Thompson, *A Preface to Urban Economics* (1965).

36. R. A. Church, *Economic and Social Change in a Midland Town. Victorian Nottingham 1815–1900* (1966).

37. H. W. Richardson, *Urban Economics* (1971), 93.

38. J. Prest, *Industrial Revolution in Coventry* (1960); K. Richardson, *Twentieth Century Coventry* (1972); S. B. Saul, 'The motor industry in Britain to 1914', *Business History,* V (1962).

39. John in Centre Nationale de la Recherche Scientifique, *op. cit.,* 520–1, 523–4.

40. Daunton, *loc. cit.*; Statement by J. Boyle in annual report of Chamber of Commerce, 1877; *S.W.D.N.,* 21 February 1877, 23 March 1877.

41. *C.J.C.,* 5 October 1906, 24 January 1910; *Maritime Review,* 5 October 1904, 5 October 1912; *S.W.D.N.,* 31 July 1878, 6 September 1897.

42. Turner, *op. cit.,* 57.

43. *Maritime Review,* 29 March 1907.

44. L. Jones, *Shipbuilding in Britain* (1957), 26.

45. E. Lloyd Dobbins, *Inception of a Great Business 1865–1925* (?1925); *Cardiff's Most Progressive Store. Amazing Development of the Great Department Business of David Morgan Ltd., the Hayes and St. Mary Street* (?1929).

46. *Cardiff Tide Tables and Almanac; S.W.D.N.,* 13 February 1885, 13 April 1886, 1 September 1886, 1 November 1886; G. Hawkins, *C.W.S. Ltd. and its Relations to the Co-operative Societies in South Wales. . .* (1893).

47. H. Carter, *The Towns of Wales* (1966), 111–16; R. Jones, 'The functions of Cardiff as a regional capital' (M.A. thesis, University of Wales, 1953).

Chapter 4

1. E. D. Lewis, *The Rhondda Valleys* (1959), 46, 117.
2. *Ibid.*, 83–4, 88, 170–218; *S.W.D.N.*, 6 May 1882, 22 June 1906, 28 January 1910, 24 March 1910, 4 April 1910; M. H. Green, 'A world wide organisation. The origin and activities of Cory Bros., and Co. Ltd.,' *Syren and Shipping*, 3 July 1946, 43–59, *C.J.C.*, xv, Sept. 1908.
3. J. H. Morris and L. J. Williams, *The South Wales Coal Industry 1841–75* (1958), 85–9; G.R.O. D/DG Section E Box 2, Report on Dowlais entering the coal trade, 7 November 1861, and Notes on D.I.C., 19 March 1890, Cardiff Agency Letters 1861–2, 1879–81, 1885–7, 1891–3, G.K.N. Letters Cardiff Docks – P. C. Cooke 1903.
4. H. S. Jevons, *The British Coal Trade* (1915), 293–4, Morris and Williams, *op. cit.*, 167–8.
5. *Ibid.*, 125–8, 135–43; Lewis, *op. cit.*, 88, 100; D. J. Williams, *Capitalist Combination in the Coal Industry* (1924), 90 *et seq.*
6. Williams, *op. cit.*, 111–12 and 76, 81, 96, 97; Lewis, *op. cit.*, 89–91, 253; D. A. Thomas, *Viscount Rhondda by his Daughter* (1921); 'A great Welsh coal combine', *Syren and Shipping*, 30 March 1910.
7. *R.C. on the Coal Industry* 1919, PP. 1919 XI–XIII, vol. 2., 143–52, 793–9, Q.3657; Jevons, *op. cit.*, 304–5; W. Phillips, *South Wales Coal Buyers Handbook* (1924); Green, *op. cit.*; *C.J.C.*, 15 September 1908; *S.W.D.N.*, 20 November 1899, 9 November 1908, 1 April 1911, 30 June 1913, 1 April 1914.
8. Jevons, *op. cit.*, 306.
9. D. A. Thomas, *Some Notes on the Present State of the Coal Trade in the U.K. with Special Reference to that of South Wales and Monmouthshire together with a Proposal for the Prevention of Undue Competition and for Maintaining Prices at a Renumerative Level* (1896); G.R.O. D/DG Cardiff Agency Letters.
10. E. S. Gregg, 'The decline of tramp shipping', *Quarterly Journal of Economics*, xl (1926); S. G. Sturmey, *British Shipping and World Competition* (1962), 34–5, 73–4, 78; *C.J.C.*, 15 July 1907.
11. *Annual Statement of the Navigation and Shipping of the U.K.*, in Accounts and Papers annually.
12. *S.W.D.N.*, 23 March 1892, 18 March 1893; *C.J.C.*, 11 February 1905, 23 August 1905, 20 May 1908, 18 July 1908, 21 July 1908, 25 March 1909; *Maritime Review, passim.*
13. *S.W.D.N.*, 8 October 1903, 24 February 1908; *C.J.C.*, 25 February 1908; 'Our Shipping Headlights', reprinted from *Syren and Shipping*, 1900.
14. R. Cory, *A Century of Family Shipowning. John Cory and Sons 1854–1954* (1954).
15. T. C. Wignall, *The Life of Sir Edward Nicholl R.N.R., M.P.* (1921).
16. *C.J.C.* 27 July 1906, 23 August 1909.
17. D. H. Aldcroft, 'Port congestion and the shipping boom of 1919–20', *Business History* III (1961); *South Wales Journal of Commerce Industrial Reviews*,

1919, 1920, 1921; *Syren and Shipping: Cardiff 1921*; Williams, *op. cit.*, 82–9; A. M. Neuman, *Economic Organisation of the British Coal Industry* (1934).

18. Morris and Williams, *op. cit.*, 138; John in Centre Nationale de la Recherche Scientifique, *op. cit.*, 520–1.

19. Wignall, *op. cit.*; *C.J.C.* 27 July 1906; Cory, *op. cit.*; *South Wales Journal of Commerce*, 2 January 1930, 6 June 1925; R. S. Craig, 'The emergence of a shipowning community at Llanelli, 1800–50', *Carmarthen Antiquary*, III (1959); J. Foster, 'Nineteenth Century Towns – a class dimension', in H. J. Dyos (ed.), *The Study of Urban History* (1968), 292; F. E. Hyde, *Liverpool and the Mersey. The Development of a Port 1700–1970* (1971), 103–14.

Chapter 5

1. J. R. Kellett. *The Impact of Railways on Victorian Cities* (1969), 421.
2. H. J. Dyos, *Victorian Suburb. A study of the growth of Camberwell* (1961), 87 *et seq.*
3. D. Olsen, *Town Planning in London: the Eighteenth and Nineteenth Centuries* (1964), 9–10.
4. N.L.W. Jevons IV 40 and 126; J. Davies 'Glamorgan and the Bute estate 1776–1947' (Ph.D. thesis, University of Wales, 1969), quoting C.C.L. MS. 4. 713, E. P. Richards to Bute, 14 February 1835.
5. T. W. Rammell, *Report to the General Board of Health on the Town of Cardiff* (1850).
6. C.C.L. Bute IX 2; N.L.W. Bute Box 142; W. J. Trounce, *Cardiff in the Fifties* (1918).
7. C.C.L. Bute XI 20; Davies, *op. cit.*, chapter V (II), 431–55, which contains a detailed analysis of 'Urbanisation and the Bute Estate'.
8. N.L.W. Jevons IV 126.
9. This section is based upon the estate papers held by the G.R.O., which have been analysed in detail in M. J. Daunton, 'Suburban development in Cardiff: Grangetown and the Windsor estate 1857–75', *Morgannwg*, XVI (1972).
10. A. A. Pettigrew, *The Public Parks and Recreation Grounds of Cardiff*, (unpublished manuscript in C.C.L., 1926); Return of Endowed Charities, 1897.
11. Pettigrew, *op. cit.*
12. *Western Mail*, 8 June 1891.
13. *Particulars of Valuable Freehold Estates belonging to the Messrs. Romilly. . .* (1852).
14. *Cardiff and Merthyr Guardian*, 30 October 1852, 27 November 1852; C.C.L. Strawson Plans of N.F.L.S. at Canton, 1852 and 1856; *Christopher Crayon's Recollections: the Life and Times of the Late James Ewing Ritchie as told by Himself* (1898).
15. N.L.W. Jevons IV 40; C. F. Sanders, *The Growth of a City* (paper read at the annual meeting of the Building Societies Association at Cardiff, 31 May 1912).
16. D. A. Reeder, 'The politics of urban leaseholds in late Victorian England', *International Review of Social History*, VI (1961); K. O. Morgan, 'D. A.

Thomas. The industrialist as politician', in S. Williams (ed.), *Glamorgan Historian, volume 3, 33.*

17. C.C.L. MS. 4.488 (1/3); *S.W.D.N.*, 24 July 1896, 30 March 1897, 29 October 1897, 3 November 1897, 15 April 1902, 6 October 1906, 5 February 1909, 23 October 1912, 5 December 1912, 13 December 1912; United Committee for the Taxation of Land Values, *Taxation of Land Values from the Townsman's Point of View. Cardiff To Whit* (1909).

18. *S.W.D.N.*, 11 June 1897.

19. *S.W.D.N.*, 25 August 1882, 19 March 1903, 17 December 1904, 4 February 1907, 5 February 1909, 20 June 1910, 19 January 1912, 1 January 1913, 4 May 1914; Select Committee on Town Holdings, P.P. 1887, XIII.

20. N.L.W. Jevons IV 41, 126 N.L.W. Bute Box 142; C.C.L. Strawson Plans.

21. *Western Mail Record of Property Sales* (1907–14).

22. M.O.H. Annual Reports for 1873, 1876, 1884; *S.W.D.N.*, 12 February 1914.

23. N.L.W. Jevons IV 40, 126; Chappell, *op. cit.*, 15; *S.W.D.N.*, 14 February 1913, 5 June 1913, 25 June 1913, 18 July 1913, 10 December 1913, 14 March 1914.

24. N.L.W. Jevons IV 40; Chappell, *op. cit.*, 12.

Chapter 6

1. Dyos, 'The speculative builders and developers of Victorian London', *Victorian Studies,* XI (1967), 677.

2. B. Thomas, *Migration and Economic Growth. A Study of Great Britain and the Atlantic Economy* (1954).

3. B. Thomas, *Migration and Urban Development. A Reappraisal of British and American Long Cycles* (1972), 170–8, and 'Wales and the Atlantic economy', *Scottish Journal of Political Economy,* 1959, 169–92.

4. J. Hamish Richards, 'Fluctuations in house building in the south Wales coalfield, 1851–1954' (M.A. thesis, University of Wales, 1956), 134.

5. See J. H. Richards and J. Parry Lewis, 'House building in the south Wales coalfield 1851–1913', *Manchester School,* XXIV (1956), 297.

6. D. A. Thomas, *J.R.S.S.*, LXVI (1903), 499–500. France and the Mediterranean took 71 per cent of Welsh coal in 1900.

7. D. A. Thomas, *Some Notes on the Present State of the Coal Trade* ... (1896), 9.

8. S. B. Saul, 'House building in England 1890–1914', *E.H.R.*, 2nd ser., xv (1962); Dyos, *op. cit.*, 663; H. J. Habakkuk, 'Fluctuations in house-building in Britain and the United States in the nineteenth century', *Journal of Economic History,* XXII (1962).

9. *Borough of Cardiff; Reports of Council and Sub-Committees,* 1879/80–1883/4, 1889/90–93/4, 1899/1900–1903/4, 1909/10–13/4.

10. The information on Barry was made available to me from the *Barry Dock News*; see also *S.W D.N.*, 20 December 1912; Minutes of Public Works Committee; Rate Books for 1884 and 1914; *Cardiff Tide Table and Almanacs,* 1882 onwards; G.R.O. D/D Pl. 202; *R.C. on Housing of the Working Classes, 1884,* P.P. 1884–5, XXX, QQ. 11, 241–11, 333; *Annual Report of M.O.H. for 1905; S.W.D.N.*, 23 August 1872, 14 March 1876, 15 February 1884, 26 July 1884, 7 September 1885.

11. P. N. Jones, *Colliery Settlement in the South Wales Coalfield 1850–1926* (University of Hull Occasional Paper in Geography 14), 46–7; Rate Books for 1884 and 1914; G.R.O. D/DG Section H Box 8, Cardiff Cottages.

12. N.L.W. Jevons IV 126; *S.W.D.N.*, 25 August 1882.

13. T. Glyde, *Growth of Cardiff from 1875 to 1880* (1880), 7; *S.W.D.N.*, 12 April 1879, 25 August 1882.

14. N.L.W. Jevons, IV 126.

15. Dyos, *op. cit.*, 664–9.

16. D. Olsen, 'House upon House. Estate development in London and Sheffield' in H. J. Dyos and M. Wolff (eds.), *The Victorian City. Images and Realities* (1973), vol. 1, 334–5.

17. H. J. Dyos, 'The slums of Victorian London', *Victorian Studies,* XI (1967), 27–34; H. J. Dyos and D. A. Reeder, 'Slums and Suburbs', in Dyos and Wolff, *op. cit.,* 359–86.

18. *Annual Reports of M.O.H.,* 1873–1914; B.O.T. *Enquiry into Working Class Rents, Housing and Retail Prices, 1908* P.P. 1908, CVII; *S.W.D.N.,* 28 December 1912.

19. *S.W.D.N.,* 5 June 1913.

20. *Ibid.,* 18 July 1913.

21. *Ibid.,* 15 and 16 May 1894, 5 June 1913.

22. B.O.T. *Enquiry* 1908, pp. 134–5; *Annual Report of M.O.H. for 1914;* Chappell, *op. cit.*

23. *S.W.D.N.,* 5 June 1913; N.L.W. Jevons IV 126.

24. On London, G. Stedman Jones, *Outcast London: A Study in the Relationship between Classes in Victorian Society* (1971); on Cardiff, chapter 11 below.

25. *Annual Reports of the M.O.H.*; Council Minutes 1899/1900 *et seq.*

26. *Annual Report of M.O.H. for 1905*; Welsh Housing and Development Association, *Building for the Future – How Wales is Tackling her Social Problems* (1917); *S.W.D.N.,* 1 November 1910, 6 and 10 January 1911, 31 May 1911.

27. W. Ashworth, *The Genesis of Modern British Town Planning* (1954), chapter 7; T. C. Horsfall, *The Relation of Town Planning to the National Life* (1908); E. R. Dewsnup, *The Housing Problem in England: its Statistics, Legislation and Policy* (1907); J. S. Nettlefold, *Practical Housing* (1908); P. Geddes, *City Development* (1904); *Annual Reports of M.O.H.*

28. *Housing Reformer,* 1911 and 1912; N.L.W. Jevons IV 172; E. L. Chappell, *Report on Welsh Housing Schemes* (1915); *Prospectus of Cardiff Workers Co-operative Garden Village Society; Welsh Housing and Development Year Book, 1916.*

29. Council Minutes for 1912 and 1913; *S.W.D.N.,* 18 January 1911, 14 February 1911, 7 April 1911, 18 October 1911, 4 January 1912, 3 May 1912, and generally for references to the housing question.

30. E. L. Chappell, *Gwalia's Homes* (1911) and *Cardiff's Housing Problem; Housing Reformer,* January and February 1912; *S.W.D.N.,* 1 August 1912, 8 October 1912, 28 December 1912, 14 February 1913, 9 May 1913, 11 June 1913, 18 July 1913, 10 December 1913.

31. *S.W.D.N.,* and Council Minutes for 1913 and 1914 refer continually to this issue.

Chapter 7

1. S. B. Saul, 'House building in England 1890–1914', *E.H.R.*, 2nd ser., xv (1962), 136.
2. The Rate Books are held at City Hall, Cardiff. The methodology has been outlined in M. J. Daunton, 'House-ownership from rate books', *Urban History Yearbook 1976*, 21–7.
3. M. Bowley, *Housing and the State* (1945), 8; J. Blackman and E. M. Sigsworth, 'The home boom of the 1890s', *Yorkshire Bulletin*, xvii (1965), 81.
4. S. D. Chapman (ed.), *The History of Working-Class Housing* (1971), 238; *R.C. on Friendly Societies*, P.P. 1872, xxvi, 16–17; *R.C. on Housing of the Working Classes*, P.P. 1884–5, xxx, Q. 10791–980; *The Land. The Report of the Land Enquiry Committee, Vol. II Urban* (1914), 90–3; G. Stedman Jones, *Outcast London; A Study in the Relationship between Classes in Victorian Society* (1971), 226.
5. *R.C. on the Coal Industry* 1919, P.P. 1919 xi–xiii, Q.25,498, and appendix 72; N.L.W. Jevons IV 126.
6. N. G. Butlin, *Investment in Australian Economic Development 1861–1900* (1964), 275–8.
7. P. N. Jones, *Colliery Settlement in the South Wales Coalfield 1850–1926* (University of Hull Occasional Paper in Geography 14), 43–5; H. S. Jevons, *British Coal Trade* (1915), 646–8; *S.W.D.N.*, 17 June 1907.
8. S. J. Price, *The Building Societies. Their Origins and History* (1958), 151–5; *S.C. on Building Societies*, P.P. 1893–4, ix, Q.2081–2, 3237; *S.W.D.N.*, 18, March 1886, 14 April 1886, 16 September 1897, 23 February 1899.
9. *Rules of the Cambrian Terminating Mutual Benefit Building Society* (1874); *Principality Building Society. 1860 to 1910, a Jubilee Souvenir of the Principality Permanent Investment Building Society*; A. Noakes, *Principality Building Society, 1860–1960* (1960); *Cardiff Times*, 31 December 1859, 10 March 1860; *S.W.D.N.*, 25 August 1882.
10. I. G. Jones, 'The south Wales collier in the mid-nineteenth century', in The Victorian Society, *Victorian South Wales–Architecture, Industry and Society* (1969), 43; A.S., 'Co-operation in Cardiff', in *Souvenir of Co-operative Congress, Cardiff 1900* (1900); see chapter 11 below.
11. N.L.W. Jevons IV 126; P. N. Jones, *op. cit.*, 45–7.
12. *Report to the Minister of Health by the Departmental Committee on Valuation for Rates, 1939* (1944); *Daily Telegraph Building Society Supplement*, 29 May 1933; M. Abrams, *The Condition of the British People 1911–45* (1946), 54.
13. Bowley, *op. cit.*, 88–9; *The Land, op. cit.*, 89–92.
14. *S.W.D.N.*, 10 November 1908, 4 May 1909; I. and A. C. Vachell, *A Short History of the Family of Vachell* (1900).
15. C.C.L. John Jenkins Accounts.
16. *Housing Reformer*, October/November 1912.
17. *Ibid.*, January 1912; *The Land, op. cit.*, 81–2, 89.

Chapter 8

1. H. J. Perkin, *The Origins of Modern English Society 1780–1880* (1969), 118; R. E. Pahl, *Patterns of Urban Life* (1970), 53.

2. Perkin, *op. cit.*, 172–5; C. F. G. Masterman (ed.), *The Heart of the Empire* (1901), 8, 13.

3. G. Stedman Jones, *Outcast London: A Study in the Relationship between Classes in Victorian Society* (1971), 251, 257, 261; C. F. G. Masterman, *The Condition of England* (1909, new ed. 1960), 59.

4. P. Mann, *An Approach to Urban Sociology* (1965), 173–182; H. Orlans, *A Sociological Study of a New Town* (1952), 82.

5. B. T. Robson, *Urban Growth* (1973), 13–14; S. B. Warner, *The Urban Wilderness. A History of the American City* (1972), 62, 81–3, 101–9, and *The Private City. Philadelphia in Three Periods of its Growth* (1968), 21, 61–2, 169–71; J. E. Vance, 'Land assignment in the precapitalist, capitalist and postcapitalist city', *Economic Geography*, XLVII (1971).

6. Warner, *loc. cit.*

7. W. G. Hoskins, *Industry, Trade and People in Exeter 1688–1800* (1935), 113; London Record Society, *London Inhabitants within the Walls 1695* (1966), xxiii; M. D. George, *London Life in the Eighteenth Century* (1925), 67–8, 85–8; Vance, *op. cit.*, 106; F. Engels, *The Condition of the Working Class in England in 1844* (Panther edn 1969), 60–2, 78–81; J. Langton, 'Residential patterns in pre-industrial cities: some case studies from seventeenth century Britain', *Institute of British Geographers Transactions*, LXV (1975).

8. J. R. Kellett, *The Impact of Railways on Victorian Cities* (1969); G. W. Hilton, 'Transport technology and the urban pattern', *Journal of Contemporary History*, IV (1969); G. R. Taylor, 'The beginnings of mass transport in urban America, I and II', *Smithsonian Journal of History*, 1 (1966); D. Ward, 'A comparative historical geography of street car suburbs in Boston, Mass. and Leeds, England, 1850–1920', *Annals of the Association of American Geographers*, LIV (1964); H. J. Dyos, *Victorian Suburb: a study of the growth of Camberwell* (1961), 60–80, and 'The slums of Victorian London', *Victorian Studies*, XI (1967), 34; Stedman Jones, *op. cit.*, 169, 173; W. A. Robson, 'The public utility services', in H. J. Laski, W. I. Jennings, and W. A. Robson (eds.), *Century of Municipal Progress* (1935), 320–4; T. C. Barker and M. Robbins, *A History of London Transport Vol. II* (1974), chapter 2.

9. Ward, *op. cit*; R. Fogelson, *The Fragmented Metropolis. Los Angeles 1850–1930* (1967), 89,104; S. B. Warner, *Streetcar Suburbs. The Process of Growth in Boston 1870–1900* (1962), 60, 63.

10. Warner, *Streetcar Suburbs*, 52–64; Stedman Jones, *op. cit.*, 170–3, 227, 284; E. J. Hobsbawm, 'The nineteenth century London labour market', in Centre for Urban Studies, *London. Aspects of Change* (1964); R. Q. Gray, 'Styles of life, the "labour aristocracy" and class relations in later nineteenth century Edinburgh', *International Review of Social History*, XVIII (1973).

11. Dyos, 'Slums. . .', 27–34.

12. D. W. G. Timms, *The Urban Mosaic. Towards a Theory of Residential Differentiation* (1971), 7; R. E. Park, *Human Communities* (1952), 17; M. Young and P. Willmott, *Family and Kinship in East London* (1962 edn), 114–16; P. Willmott, *The Evolution of a Community. A Study of Dagenham after Forty Years* (1963), vii–ix, 111.

13. R. Roberts, *The Classic Slum* (1971); R. Hoggart, *The Uses of Literacy* (1957),

58–63; R.C. *on Local Taxation,* P.P. 1898, XLI, Q.1164; Charles Booth, *Life and Labour of the People of London First Series: Poverty, Vol. 1* (1902 edn), 26–7.

14. S. Thernstrom, 'Working class mobility in industrial America', *Bulletin of the Society for the Study of Labour History,* XVII (1968), 24–5; S. Thernstrom and P. Knights, 'Men in Motion. Some data and speculations about urban population mobility in nineteenth century America', *Journal of Interdisciplinary History,* I (1970), 11, 32.

15. J. Foster, *Class Struggle and the Industrial Revolution. Early Industrial Capitalism in Three English Towns* (1974), 125–6.

16. K. E. and A. F. Taueber, *Negroes in Cities* (1965), Appendix A, p. 195 *et seq.*; S. Lieberson, *Ethnic Patterns in American Cities* (1963), 30.

17. W. A. Armstrong, 'The use of information about occupation', in E. A. Wrigley (ed.), *The Study of Nineteenth Century Society* (1972); P.R.O., R.G. 10 5356–68.

18. Warner, *Private City,* 170.

19. *South Wales Investment Circular* 11 and 14 (1 June 1888 and 1 September 1888); *Electrical Engineer,* 16 May 1902; detailed references to *S.W.D.N.* on pp. 397–400 of my thesis.

20. Slaters', Wrights', and Owens' directories for 1884 to 1894.

21. H. P. Chudacoff, *Mobile Americans. Residential and Social Mobility in Omaha 1880–1920* (1972), 40.

22. N. Birnbaum, 'Afterword', in S. Thernstrom and R. Sennett (eds), *Nineteenth Century Cities. Essays in the New Urban History* (1969), 429.

23. *S.W.D.N.,* 4 November 1885.

24. K. L. Little, *Negroes in Britain. A study of Racial Relations in English Society* (1947); S. Hugill, *Sailortown* (1967).

25. H. Carter and G. Rowley, 'The morphology of the central business district of Cardiff', *Institute of British Geographers Transactions,* XXXVIII (1966), 119–34.

26. H. McLeod, *Class and Religion in the Late Victorian City* (1974), 6–13.

27. J. Hickey, 'The origins and growth of the Irish community in Cardiff' (M.A. thesis, University of Wales, 1959); *S.W.D.N.,* 18 December 1877, and generally for commentary on Irish voting.

28. K. Lynch, *The Image of the City* (1960); D. Lowenthal (ed.) *Environmental Perception and Behaviour* (1967).

29. R. Sennett, *Families Against the City. Middle Class Homes of Industrial Chicago* (1970), 10–11, 24, 42–3, 50–4, 96–7, 147–9, and *The Uses of Disorder. Personal Identity and City Life* (1970), 51–73.

Chapter 9

1. M. H. Frisch, 'The community elite and the emergence of urban politics: Springfield, Mass. 1840–80', in S. Thernstrom and R. Sennett (eds), *Nineteenth Century Cities. Essays in the New Urban History* (1969), 277.

2. E. P. Hennock, 'Finance and politics in urban local government in England 1835–1900', *Historical Journal,* VI (1963); and *Fit and Proper Persons. Ideal and Reality in Nineteenth Century Urban Government* (1973).

3. Quoted in S. Finer, *The Life and Times of Sir Edwin Chadwick* (1952), 434.

4. More detail is provided on membership of these categories in table 2, p. 311 of volume II of M. J. Daunton, 'Aspects of the social and economic structure of Cardiff 1870–1914' (Ph.D. thesis, University of Kent, 1974).

5. C.C.L. Bute MSS. XI 5, statement by Lascelles Carr.

6. H.L.R.O., Minutes of evidence, H.L. 1882, Bute Docks, evidence of Mayor; Minutes of Cardiff Town Council 1880–1; *S.W.D.N.,* 14 and 23 February 1882, 22 and 27 June 1882, 3 July 1882, 17 and 23 August 1882.

7. C.C.L. Bute MSS. XI 20; *S.W.D.N.,* 17 July 1891, November 1893 to November 1894 *passim,* September to October 1906.

8. *Ibid.,* 28 October 1902.

9. *Ibid.,* 30 March 1908, *C.J.C.,* 30 March and 5 May 1908.

10. *S.W.D.N.,* 9 November 1908, *C.J.C.,* 9 November and 19 December 1908, *S.W.D.N.,* 2 May 1910, *South Wales Journal of Commerce,* 15 April 1919.

11. The regional and wider concerns are apparent in the Annual Reports of the Cardiff Chamber of Commerce and the minute books in G.R.O. D/D Com/C.

12. *S.W.D.N.,* 29 September 1906.

13. *Ibid.,* 11 April 1876, 29 October 1879, 15 October 1906.

14. *S.W.D.N., passim*; T. Glyde, *Growth of Cardiff from 1875 to 1880 with some particulars of Cardiff in the last century* (1880); *Cardiff Corporation Bill – Statement as to the principal objects of the proposed bill for the information of owners and ratepayers* (1898); *Reports of the Department Committee,* 12 April 1906.

15. Borough (City) of Cardiff, Borough Treasurer's Accounts; Bute docks trade data.

16. *S.W.D.N., passim*; *Cardiff Ratepayer and Trader,* 1912; Cardiff Property Owners and Ratepayers Association, *Facts for Ratepayers* (1906).

17. *S.W.D.N.,* 3 November 1876; *Cardiff Times,* 25 September 1869.

18. K. O. Morgan, *Wales in British Politics 1868–1922* (1963), 22–7; I. Humphreys, 'Cardiff Politics 1850–1874', in S. Williams (ed.) *Glamorgan Historian Volume* 8, 105–120; J. Davies, 'The second marquess of Bute. A landowner and the community in the nineteenth century', in Williams (ed.), *op. cit.,* 13–28 and 'Glamorgan and the Bute estate, 1776–1947' (Ph.D. thesis, University of Wales, 1969), v–viii, chapters III and IV; *Cardiff Times,* 14 October 1864, 7 November 1868, 25 September, 27 November and 25 December 1869, 17 September 1870; *S.W.D.N.* 18 June 1878, 1 December 1880.

19. *S.W.D.N.,* 24 and 25 October 1872.

20. *Ibid.,* October to November 1874.

21. *Ibid.,* 11 September, 28 October and 13 November 1876.

22. *Ibid.,* 1 June 1877, 30 May 1883, 27 October 1874, 1 October 1883, *Cardiff Times,* 18 November 1871; I. and A. C. Vachell, *A Short History of the Family of Vachell* (1900).

23. *S.W.D.N.,* 13 October, 3 November 1880, 22, 25, 28 October, 1 November 1881, 27 February, 6, 13 June 1882, 13 March, 2 November 1883, 26 February 1884, 4 November 1885.

24. The political composition of the council is broken down on p. 381 of Daunton, thesis, vol. II.

25. Rate books for 1884.
26. *S.W.D.N.,* 29 January 1898, 19 February, 13 November 1902; 20 January, 20 February, 15 July 1903; 14 March 1904; 31 January, 1 February 1905; 10, 22, 23 February, 17 March, 22 November 1906; 19 September 1907; 6 May 1913.
27. *S.W.D.N.,* 19 October 1874, 21 October 1882, 17, 19, 22 May 1883; Report of the Departments Committee.
28. *S.W.D.N.,* October 1904 and October 1905, *passim.*
29. E. W. Edwards, 'Cardiff becomes a city', *Morgannwg,* IX (1965).
30. C.C.L. MSS. 4.488 (1/3), eight Progressive Leaflets; *S.W.D.N.,* 3 November 1894; *South Wales Radical,* 1892–3; *South Wales Labour Times,* 1893.
31. A. Pettigrew, *The Public Parks and Recreation Grounds of Cardiff* (1926), vol. 2; *S.W.D.N.,* 28 July, 25 September, 18 December 1900, 5, 12 March, 18 June 1901, 11 February, 15 July, 24 September 1902, 20 February, 22 September 1903, 21 April 1904, 6 January 1905, 19 September 1911, 12 June 1913; *Cardiff Ratepayer and Trader,* 1 (February 1912).
32. *S.W.D.N.,* 21 October 1905; see the election campaigns in *S.W.D.N.* for October 1904–7; on the defeat of 1910, *S.W.D.N.,* 9, 14, 15, 21 December 1910; reports on the Departments Committee were regular in *S.W.D.N.* during the first part of 1905; for outcome see 13 December 1905, 8 February, 13 March 1906.
33. E. J. Hobsbawm, 'The Fabians reconsidered' in *Labouring Men. Studies in the History of Labour* (1964), 257. K. O. Morgan, 'D. A. Thomas: the industrialist as politician', in Williams (ed.), *Glamorgan Historian volume 3*; on attitudes of Chamber of Commerce see, for example, *S.W.D.N.,* 23 July 1903, 21 February 1907; on Renwick, *ibid.,* 12 October 1903; for Clifford Cory's involvement with the Welsh Protestant League, see *ibid.,* 21 December 1898 *et seq.* and for role in selecting a candidate, *ibid.* 27 November 1911. Information on the progressives can be found in *South Wales Labour Times* and *South Wales Radical,* and in many references in *S W.D.N.* in the 1890s.

Chapter 10

1. This chapter is the most condensed from my original thesis. The analysis of labour relations was a substantial part of the thesis in its own right, and the chapter on labour politics was also lengthy. It is accordingly difficult to supply footnote references for a statement which was originally developed over a whole chapter. Interested readers seeking substantiation are therefore referred to the thesis.
2. H. Clegg, A. Fox, and A. F. Thompson, *A History of British Trade Unions since 1889, Vol. 1, 1889–1910* (1964), 286–91; S. Pollard, *A History of Labour in Sheffield* (1959), 198, 201, 266.
3. See H. J. Perkin, *The Origins of Modern English Society 1780–1880* (1969), chapter 9, and discussion by M. J. Daunton, 'La crescita della societa classista: prospettive Inglesi e Americane', *Quaderni Storici,* XXX (1975).
4. T. R. Tholfsen, 'The origins of the Birmingham caucus', *Historical Journal* II (1959), and 'The transition to democracy in Victorian England', *International Review of Social History,* VI (1961).

5. E. P. Thompson, *The Making of the English Working Class* (1963), 9.
6. The section on seamen is based upon *S.W.D.N.* for 1872 to 1914; Webb Trade Union Collection E Section A, vols. IV, XLII; evidence presented to Royal Commission on Labour 1892 Group B, P.P. 1892, xxxv–xxxvi; G.R.O. minutes of Chamber of Commerce and Shipowners Association; P.R.O. MT9; J. H. Wilson, *My Stormy Voyage Through Life* (1925); E. Tupper, *Seamen's Torch* (1938); W. Campbell Balfour, 'Captain Tupper and the seamen's strike at Cardiff in 1911', *Morgannwg*, XIV (1970).
7. E. Taplin, *Liverpool Dockers and Seamen 1870–90* (University of Hull Occasional Papers in Economic and Social History no. 6 1974), 84–5.
8. B. Mogridge, 'Militancy and inter-union rivalries in British shipping, 1911–29', *International Review of Social History*, VI (1961).
9. M. J. Daunton, 'The Cardiff Coal Trimmers Union 1888–1914', *Llafur*, forthcoming. The analysis of trimming is largely based upon the minutes of the C.C.T.U. at University College, Swansea and of the Cardiff Chamber of Commerce and Cardiff Shipowners Association at the Glamorgan Record Office.
10. For the Dockers Union, information was obtained from *S.W.D.N.* for 1872 to 1914; Webb Trade Union Collection E Section A, vols. IV, XLII; annual reports of the Dockers Union; Royal Commission on Labour 1892 Group B, P.P. 1892, xxxvi; G.R.O. Minutes of Chamber of Commerce. See also L. J. Williams, 'The new unionism in south Wales 1889–92', *Welsh History Review*, I (1960), and P. W. Donovan, 'Unskilled labour unions in south Wales 1889–1914' (M.Phil. thesis, University of London 1969).
11. *S.W.D.N.*, 13 May 1891.
12. See P. Bagwell, *The Railwaymen* (1963). This account is based upon *S.W.D.N* to give a view from the locality rather than from the centre.
13. *S.W.D.N.*, 28 August 1911.
14. *Ibid.*, 23 March 1903.
15. Pollard, *op. cit.*, 198; J. P. Addis, 'The heavy iron and steel industry in south Wales 1870–1950' (Ph.D. thesis, University of Wales, 1957).
16. This section is based upon *S.W.D.N.* for 1872 to 1914.
17. *S.W.D.N.*, 5 February 1906.
18. *Ibid.*
19. This section is based upon *S.W.D.N.* for 1872 to 1914.
20. Clegg, Fox, and Thompson, *op. cit.*, 354.
21. E. P. Thompson, 'Homage to Tom Maguire', in A. Briggs and J. Saville (eds), *Essays in Labour History* (1960).
22. These comments are based upon A. Briggs, *Victorian Cities* (1963), 186–7; Pollard, *op. cit.*, 3, 56; J. Foster, *Class Struggle and the Industrial Revolution. Early Industrial Capitalism in Three English Towns* (1974).
23. For all aspects of the Bute estate in Glamorgan, see J. Davies's thesis (Ph.D., University of Wales, 1969); on politics, I. Humphreys, 'Cardiff politics 1850–75', (M.A. thesis, University of Wales, 1970); on the interests of the third marquis, see J. Mordaunt Crook, 'Patron extraordinary: John, 3rd Marquis of Bute', in Victorian Society, *Victorian South Wales – Architecture, Industry and Society* (1969). For Sir W. T. Lewis, see *D.N.B.*

24. K. O. Morgan, 'D. A. Thomas: the industrialist as politician', in Williams (ed.), *Glamorgan Historian volume 3*; *S.W.D.N.*, 19 January 1904, 30 April 1904, 2 May 1904, 16 May 1904, on his opposition to the neglect of labour interests, 22 January 1900 on attitude to railway unions.
25. R. Page Arnot, *South Wales Miners. A History of the South Wales Miners Federation 1898–1914* (1967), 48–9.
26. Quoted by H. Pelling, *The Origins of the Labour Party* (2nd edn, 1965), 224.
27. K. O. Morgan, *Wales in British Politics 1868–1922* (1963), and P. F. Clarke, *Lancashire and the New Liberalism* (1971). See also M. Petter, 'The Progressive alliance', *History*, LVIII (1973), which criticizes that interpretation.
28. Morgan, *Wales in British Politics*, 168; *S.W.D.N.*, 24 September 1903, 6 January 1904.
29. *Cardiff Times*, 27 November 1869; *S.W.D.N.*, 18 June 1878, 24 September 1879, 1 December 1880.
30. *S.W.D.N.*, 23 May, 20 June 1882; H.L.R.O. Minutes of evidence, H.C., 1882, Bute Docks, *passim*.
31. *S.W.D.N.*, 7 May, 4 November 1886.
32. *S.W.D.N.*, 29 December 1883, 9 February 1884, 9 January, 27 October, 24, 27 and 29 December 1886, 27, 29 and 30 April, 3, 7, 8 and 30 May 1889; Trades Council Reports for 1888 and 1889.
33. *S.W.D.N.*, 4 February 1886; C.C.L. MSS. 4.616, Minutes of Cardiff Junior Liberal Association, 14 November 1889.
34. E. F. Kennard, *The Remarkable Career of a Well-Known Athlete* (1913); *S.W.D.N.*, 25 November 1886, 14 February, 18 May and 15 December 1887.
35. R. N. Hall, *Liberal Organisation and Work* (1888), 7–8; *S.W.D.N.*, 23 February, 26 May and 2 July 1888, 26 February and 11 March 1889.
36. *S.W.D.N.*, 9 May, 10 and 13 September, 14 and 18 November, and 2 December 1889, 6 January 1890.
37. Morgan, *Wales in British Politics*, 168; *S.W.D.N.*, October 1890 and October 1897, *passim*, 5, 6, 15, 19 October and 29 November 1897, 11 March 1898, 9 November 1903, 3 November 1906, 20 June 1908.
38. S. G. Hobson, *Pilgrim to the Left* (1938); Trades Council Report 1890, 1891 and 1892; *S.W.D.N.*, 1, 22, 29, 30 and 31 October, 1 November 1890, 25 September, 2, 16, 20, 23 October and 3 November 1891, 4 an 8 April, 4, 5, 6, 7, 10, 11, 12, 14, 21, 22, 26 October and 2 November 1892, 12 January, 24 August and 2 November 1893.
39. *Labour Pioneer*, April, October, November and December 1900, January, July, August and September 1901, February and August 1902; *S.W.D.N.*, 18, 30 October and 1 November 1900, 21, 27 September and 1 October 1901, 27 November, 2, 4, 5 and 12 December 1902, 7, 24, 27 and 29 October 1901, 27 November, 2, 4, 5 and 12 December 1902, 7, 8, 24, 27 and 29 Ocotber 1903, 17 September 1906, 5 April 1907.
    (4 March 1893) to 13 (27 May 1893); *S.W.D.N.*, 31 January, 1, 9 February, 9 June and 15 July 1893, 5 and 7 November 1894, 24 June, 24 July, 7, 11 and 12 August 1896, 29 October 1897, 28 January 1905, 6 October 1906, 4 January 1908, 11 September 1912.

41. Trades Council Report for 1895; *S.W.D.N.*, 2, 8, 21 and 23 February 1895, 7 and 14 March, 22 August, 14, 18, 19, 21 and 24 September, 2 October 1900, 2 January 1901.

42. *S.W.D.N.,* 6 October 1902, 9, 18 and 19 September 1903, 6 and 19 January, 25 February, 16 March, 8, 9, 15, 21, 22, 27 and 30 April, 2, 13, 16 and 20 May, 4 June 1904, 1 June 1905.

43. *S.W.D.N.,* 16 and 26 May, 17 June, 6, 27 and 28 July, 16 August, 18 October, 4 and 11 November, 5 December 1904.

44. K. O. Fox, 'The emergence of the political labour movement in the eastern sector of the south Wales coalfield 1894–1910' (M.A. thesis, University of Wales, 1965), 58–9; *Labour Pioneer*, August 1902; *S.W.D.N.*, 14 and 23 September 1897, 1 March 1899, 13 January, 1, 5, 6 and 15 June, 17 and 25 July, 15 August, 7, 28 and 29 September, 2, 7, 12, 16, 25, 28, 30 and 31 October, 1 November, 15 December 1905, 5, 9 and 29 January, 12 and 26 February, 5 and 30 March, 2 and 9 April, 19 June, 17 September, 5, 12, 13, 16, 29 and 31 October 1906, 5 April 1907.

45. *S.W.D.N.*, 4 February, 1, 8 April, 13 May, 23 and 25 July, 1, 17 and 19 August, 13 and 26 September, 11, 18 and 24 October, 9, 25 and 28 November, 30 December 1907, 6 March, 17 and 30 April, 15 May, 16 June, 13 and 14 July 1908.

46. *S.W.D.N.,* 27 August, 3, 5, 6, 12 and 13 October, 6 November, 4 December 1908.

47. *S.W.D.N.,* 1 April, 22 July, 28 and 30 August, 3, 15, 23 and 30 September, 14, 21 and 25 October, 1 November 1909, 3 September 1910, 5, 19 and 31 October 1911.

48. Cardiff Liberal Association, Report of Executive Committee for 1910; *S.W.D.N.,* 9, 14, 15 and 21 December 1910, 15 March, 27 November, 23 December 1911, 19 July 1912.

49. *Justice,* 28 January 1911; *S.W.D.N.,* 28 August 1911, 9 August 1912, 5 and 6 June, 22 August 1913, 8 May 1914.

Chapter 11

1. G. Stedman Jones, *Outcast London: A Study in the Relationships between Classes in Victorian Society* (1971), part III; C. L. Mowat, *The Charity Organisation Society 1869–1913* (1961), chapter 1.

2. W. S. Jevons, *Methods of Social Reform* (1883), 4, 7.

3. B. Harrison and B. Trinder, 'Drink and sobriety in an early Victorian country town: Banbury 1830–60', *English Historical Review Supplement,* 1969.

4. E. R. Wickham, *Church and People in an Industrial City* (1957); K. Inglis, *Churches and the Working Classes in Victorian England* (1963); A. Briggs, 'Mass entertainment: the origins of a modern industry', *29th Joseph Fisher Lecture in Commerce,* (1960); R. Currie, *Methodism Divided. A Study in the Sociology of Ecumenicalism* (1968); C. S. Yeo, 'Religion in society: a view from a provincial town in the late nineteenth and early twentieth centuries' (D.Phil. thesis, University of Sussex, 1971).

5. B. Harrison, 'Religion and recreation in nineteenth-century England', *Past and Present,* xxxviii (1967).

6. *S.W.D.N.*, 23 October 1906; *Royal Commission on the Church of England and other Religious Bodies in Wales*, P.P. 1910, XIV–XIX; E. T. Davies, *Religion in the Industrial Revolution in South Wales* (1965), appendix 1.

7. Davies, *op. cit.*, 61.

8. Quoted by W. R. Lambert, 'Drink and sobriety in Wales, 1835–95' (Ph.D. thesis, University of Wales, 1969).

9. *Western Mail*, 21 June 1889.

10. Lambert, *op. cit.*

11. *Club Life in Cardiff: The Fruits of the Welsh Sunday Closing Act* (1883); D. Davies, *The Welsh Sunday Closing Act. Lord Aberdare's Challenge to the Western Mail* (1889); *Royal Commission on the Sunday Closing (Wales) Act 1881*, P.P. 1890 XL.

12. *S.W.D.N.*, 24 October 1889 and *passim* from 1881 for Blue Ribbon movement; W. R. Lambert, 'The Welsh Sunday Closing Act, 1881', *Welsh History Review*, VI (1972), 188.

13. D. Davies, *op. cit.*

14. *R.C. on Sunday Closing (Wales) Act 1881*, report, vi; *S.W.D.N.*, October–November 1873, 26 June and 2 July 1879, 23 March 1881, 8 May 1883, 7 June, 5 and 20 July 1889.

15. E. Beavan, *The History of the Welsh Sunday Closing Act* (1885); H. M. Thompson, *Our English Sunday* (1887); J. P. Thompson, *Sunday Emancipation. A Paper Read before the Cardiff Society for the Impartial Discussion of Political and other Questions* (1887); *S.W.D.N.*, 27 June 1888, 25 May 1893, 16 May 1899, 11 February 1902, 15 April 1913.

16. *S.W.D.N.*, *passim*; Cardiff Citizens Union, *Third Annual Report and Balance Sheet for 1909–10;* T. W. Chance (ed.), *The Life of Principal William Edwards* (1934); J. A. Jenkins and R. E. James, *The History of Nonconformity in Cardiff* (1901).

17. *Cardiff Times*, 30 October 1869; *S.W.D.N.*, 26 January and 22 October 1886, 21 December 1898, 16 and 29 July 1903; *1st to 25th Annual Reports of Charity Organisation Society;* B. M. Bull, *The University Settlement in Cardiff* (1965).

18. *Cardiff Times* for 1860–3; *S.W.D.N.*, *passim*; Ladies Association for the Care of Friendless Girls, *Work Among our Girls – Free Registry and Training Home for Young Servants* (1885); *Cardiff Y.M.C.A. Diamond Jubilee Campaign Booklet 1912*.

19. *S.W.D.N.*, 26 October 1876, 24 April 1882, 7 August 1894, 20 November 1895; G.R.O. D/D Wes/Cr: C. R. Williams, 'The Welsh religious revival 1904–5', *British Journal of Sociology*, III (1952).

20. Bull, *op. cit.*; C.C.L. MS. 2.652; *S.W.D.N.*, 10 December 1902, 16 May 1899, 22 June 1906, 28 January 1910; E. P. Hennock, *Fit and Proper Persons. Ideal and Reality in Nineteenth Century Urban Government* (1973), 153.

Chapter 12

1. R. Walters, 'Labour productivity in the south Wales steam-coal industry, 1870–1914', *E.H.R.*, 2nd ser., XXVII (1975).

2. G. C. Allen, *British Industries and their Organisation* (4th edn 1959), 52.

3. Allen, *op. cit.*, 53–9; W. H. B. Court, 'Problems of the British coal industry

between the wars', *E.H.R.* xv (1945); A. M. Neuman, *Economic Organisation of the British Coal Industry* (1934).

4. Annual reports of the Cardiff Chamber of Commerce.

5. *South Wales Journal of Commerce Industrial Reviews*, Annual Reports of Cardiff Shipowners Association; E. L. Chappell, *History of the Port of Cardiff* (1939), 125.

6. P.E.P., *Report on the British Coal Industry* (1937); Neuman, *op. cit.*; H. H. Merrett, *I Fight for Coal* (1932).

7. J. Austin Jenkins, 'Cardiff and its history: the town's claims to the title metropolis', *Western Mail,* 11 May 1905.

8. *Cardiff Times,* 1 April 1905. I owe this and the previous reference to Mr Neil Evans.

Table of £ s. d./£p equivalents

£	s.	d.	£p		£	s.	d.	£p
		1d.	½p			6s.		30p
		2d.	1p			7s.		35p
		3d.	1p			8s.		40p
		4d.	1½p			9s.		45p
		5d.	2p			10s.		50p
		6d.	2½p			11s.		55p
		7d.	3p			12s.		60p
		8d.	3p			13s.		65p
		9d.	4p			14s.		70p
		10d.	4p			15s.		75p
		11d.	4½p			16s.		80p
		12d.(1s.)	5p			17s.		85p
	2s.		10p			18s.		90p
	3s.		15p			19s.		95p
	4s.		20p			20s. (£1)		100p
	5s.		25p					

Because all costs and prices in the book are taken from pre-1972 sources, they are quoted in £ s. d. currency; however, it was felt that it would be helpful to include this conversion table giving decimal currency equivalents.

Index